Data Structure and Algorithms in Java

From Basics to Expert Proficiency

Contents

Introduction

Data structures and algorithms are fundamental concepts in computer science and essential tools for software development. Proficiency in these areas enables developers to design, implement, and optimize efficient software that can handle complex tasks and large data sets. This book, "Data Structure and Algorithms in Java: From Basics to Expert Proficiency," is intended to provide a comprehensive guide to understanding and mastering these critical topics, all while using the Java programming language.

In the realm of computer science, data structures refer to the systematic way of organizing and storing data so that it can be accessed and modified efficiently. Familiarity with various data structures and their appropriate applications is crucial for crafting performance-efficient software solutions.

Algorithms, on the other hand, are definite procedures or formulas for solving problems. They describe a sequence of steps that need to be performed to reach a particular goal. The study of algorithms involves understanding their design, analysis of their efficiency, and the contexts in which they can be most effectively applied.

The importance of data structures and algorithms extends beyond academic study and is crucial in practical, day-to-day programming tasks. Whether you are designing software that needs to process large amounts of data in real-time, implementing complex features such as search and sort operations, or optimizing existing code, a solid understanding of these concepts is indispensable.

This book is structured into meticulously chosen chapters that build upon each other, ensuring a coherent and progressive learning experience. We begin by introducing the fundamental concepts of data structures and algorithms and move on to delve into specific types such as arrays, linked lists, stacks, queues, trees, heaps, and more. In the process, we will explore various algorithmic techniques including sorting, searching, and traversal, all illustrated with practical examples and Java code snippets.

Given the critical role of the Java programming language in this book, an early chapter is devoted to Java basics, ensuring that readers are comfortable with necessary Java syntax and features. This foundational knowledge is vital as we demonstrate the implementation of various data structures and algorithms in Java in the subsequent chapters.

Each chapter is designed to be self-contained, providing thorough explanations, code examples, and exercises to reinforce the concepts learned. Our goal is to ensure that by the end of this book, readers will have developed a deep understanding of data structures and algorithms, and the ability to apply this knowledge to solve real-world problems efficiently using Java.

This book is ideal for students, software developers, and anyone looking to deepen their understanding of data structures and algorithms. It serves as both a learning resource and a reference guide, suitable for individuals at different stages of their programming journey.

In conclusion, mastering data structures and algorithms is pivotal for anyone seeking to excel in computer science and software development. This book is crafted to equip you with the knowledge and skills necessary to understand, implement, and optimize these core components of programming, all through the lens of Java. We invite you to immerse yourself in this comprehensive study, confident that it will significantly enhance your problem-solving capabilities and programming proficiency.

Chapter 1

Introduction to Data Structures and Algorithms

Data structures and algorithms are the cornerstone of efficient programming in computer science. Understanding what they are, their types, and their importance lays the foundation for more advanced concepts. This chapter delves into the essential definitions, the critical role they play in software development, and offers an overview of different data structures and algorithms. It also introduces fundamental concepts such as time and space complexity and Big O notation, providing a clear understanding of how to analyze the efficiency of algorithms.

1.1 What are Data Structures?

Data structures are specialized formats for organizing, processing, retrieving, and storing data. They are fundamental to designing efficient algorithms and effective programs. The choice of a suitable data structure can make a substantial difference in the performance and scalability of the software.

Definition: A data structure is a systematic way to organize data in order to use it efficiently for various operations.

Classification: Data structures can generally be classified into two main categories:

- **Primitive Data Structures**: These include basic types and are directly operated upon by machine instructions. Examples include integers, floats, characters, and pointers.
- **Non-primitive Data Structures**: These are more complex structures that are derived from primitive data structures. They are further classified into linear and non-linear data structures.

Linear Data Structures: In a linear data structure, elements form a sequence or a linear list. Each element is connected to its previous and next element. They are easy to implement because of their organized structure. Examples include arrays, linked lists, stacks, and queues.

An array is a collection of elements identified by index or key. Arrays allow constant-time access to elements, given their index. However, inserting or deleting elements can be costly since it may require shifting elements.

```
// Java Implementation of an Array
int[] array = new int[10];
array[0] = 1;
array[1] = 2;
// Accessing elements
System.out.println(array[0]); // Output: 1
```

A linked list consists of nodes where each node contains a data field and a reference (or link) to the next node in the sequence. It is dynamic in nature, allowing for efficient insertions and deletions.

```
// Java Implementation of a Singly Linked List Node
class Node {
    int data;
    Node next;
    Node(int data) {
        this.data = data;
        this.next = null;
    }
}
```

Stacks follow the Last In First Out (LIFO) principle. Operations include push (insert), pop (delete), and peek (retrieve the top element).

```
// Java Implementation of a Stack using Array
class Stack {
    int top;
    int capacity;
    int[] stack;
```

```
    Stack(int size) {
        top = -1;
        capacity = size;
        stack = new int[capacity];
    }

    void push(int data) {
        if (top == capacity - 1) {
            System.out.println("Stack overflow");
            return;
        }
        stack[++top] = data;
    }

    int pop() {
        if (top == -1) {
            System.out.println("Stack underflow");
            return -1;
        }
        return stack[top--];
    }

    int peek() {
        if (top == -1) {
            System.out.println("Stack is empty");
            return -1;
        }
        return stack[top];
    }
}
```

Queues follow the First In First Out (FIFO) principle. Operations include enqueue (insert) and dequeue (delete).

```
// Java Implementation of a Queue using Linked List
class Queue {
    Node front, rear;

    Queue() {
        front = rear = null;
    }

    void enqueue(int data) {
        Node temp = new Node(data);
        if (rear == null) {
            front = rear = temp;
            return;
        }
        rear.next = temp;
        rear = temp;
    }

    int dequeue() {
        if (front == null) {
            return -1;
        }
        int data = front.data;
        front = front.next;
        if (front == null) {
            rear = null;
        }
```

```
        return data;
    }
}
```

Non-linear Data Structures: In these structures, data elements are not organized in a sequence. Examples include trees and graphs.

A tree is a hierarchical structure where each node contains a value and references to its children. One of the most common types of trees is the binary tree, where each node has at most two children.

```
// Java Implementation of a Binary Tree Node
class TreeNode {
    int data;
    TreeNode left, right;

    TreeNode(int item) {
        data = item;
        left = right = null;
    }
}
```

Graphs consist of nodes (vertices) and edges (connections between nodes). They are used to represent networks and relationships. Graphs can be directed or undirected, and can include cycles.

```
// Java Implementation of a Graph using Adjacency List
class Graph {
    private int V; // Number of vertices
    private LinkedList<Integer> adj[]; // Adjacency lists

    Graph(int v) {
        V = v;
        adj = new LinkedList[v];
        for (int i = 0; i < v; ++i)
            adj[i] = new LinkedList();
    }

    void addEdge(int v, int w) {
        adj[v].add(w); // Add w to v's list.
    }
}
```

Each type of data structure has specific usage scenarios, strengths, and weaknesses. For example, linked lists are suitable for applications where frequent insertions and deletions occur, but arrays are preferred when constant-time access to elements is required.

Choosing the appropriate data structure requires considering factors such as the operations to be performed, memory usage, and the complexity of each operation. Deciding the correct data structure for a given problem is a critical skill for software engineers and computer scientists, enabling the creation of efficient and maintainable code.

1.2 What are Algorithms?

An algorithm is a finite sequence of well-defined instructions typically used to solve a class of specific problems or to perform a computation. Algorithms are cornerstone elements of computer science and are implemented within programs to execute defined tasks. Their structured nature allows for reproducibility, reliability, and efficiency, which are crucial for developing robust software systems.

An algorithm transforms input data into a specified output through a series of computational steps. Each step must be unambiguously defined, executable, and lead the problem closer to a solution. The efficiency and effectiveness of an algorithm are gauged by analyzing its time and space complexity.

Consider a basic example, the algorithm for finding the maximum value in an array of integers. The algorithm iterates through each element, maintaining a record of the largest observed value:

```
public class MaxValueAlgorithm {
    public static int findMax(int[] numbers) {
        int max = Integer.MIN_VALUE; // Start with the smallest possible integer
        for (int number : numbers) {
            if (number > max) {
                max = number;
            }
        }
        return max;
    }
}
```

In this example, numbers is an array of integers, and the findMax method iterates through each integer in the array to determine the maximum value. This straightforward approach is foundational in understanding more complex algorithms.

Algorithms can be categorized based on various criteria such as their purpose, implementation strategy, and design paradigm. Below are some significant categories:

- **Sorting Algorithms:** Algorithms intended to reorder elements in a list into a particular order, such as ascending or descending. Examples include QuickSort, MergeSort, and BubbleSort.

```
public class BubbleSort {
    public static void bubbleSort(int[] arr) {
        int n = arr.length;
        for (int i = 0; i < n-1; i++) {
            for (int j = 0; j < n-i-1; j++) {
                if (arr[j] > arr[j+1]) {
```

```
                int temp = arr[j];
                arr[j] = arr[j+1];
                arr[j+1] = temp;
            }
        }
    }
  }
}
```

- **Search Algorithms:** Techniques to find specific elements within a data structure. Examples include Binary Search and Linear Search.

```
public class BinarySearch {
    public static int binarySearch(int[] arr, int key) {
        int low = 0;
        int high = arr.length - 1;
        while (low <= high) {
            int mid = (low + high) / 2;
            if (arr[mid] < key) {
                low = mid + 1;
            } else if (arr[mid] > key) {
                high = mid - 1;
            } else {
                return mid; // key found
            }
        }
        return -1; // key not found
    }
}
```

- **Graph Algorithms:** Methods used for tasks such as traversing or searching graph data structures. Examples include Breadth-First Search (BFS), Depth-First Search (DFS), and Dijkstra's Algorithm.

- **Dynamic Programming:** A methodology for solving complex problems by breaking them into simpler subproblems and storing the results of these subproblems to avoid redundant computations. Examples include Fibonacci sequence calculation and the Knapsack problem.

```
public class Fibonacci {
    public static int fibonacci(int n) {
        int[] fib = new int[n+1];
        fib[0] = 0;
        fib[1] = 1;
        for (int i = 2; i <= n; i++) {
            fib[i] = fib[i-1] + fib[i-2];
        }
        return fib[n];
    }
}
```

- **Greedy Algorithms:** Approaches that make locally optimal choices at each step, intending to find the global optimum. Examples include the activity selection problem and Prim's algorithm for finding the Minimum Spanning Tree.

Algorithms are not limited to these categories and can be hybrid, combining elements from different paradigms to optimize their performance based on the problem context.

To formalize an algorithm, pseudocode or formal programming languages are used. Pseudocode provides a high-level description of the algorithm that is clear and easy to understand but omits specific syntax details of a programming language. This makes it excellent for teaching and documenting as it conveys the logical flow and structure without syntactic distractions.

Here is an example of pseudocode for the insertion sort algorithm:

Algorithm 1: Insertion Sort Pseudocode

```
Input: An array A of n integers
Output: The array A sorted in ascending order
for i ← 1 to n − 1 do
    for j ← i to 1 downto 1 do
        if A[j] < A[j − 1] then
            swap( A[j], A[j − 1] );
        end
        else
            break;
        end
    end
end
```

Algorithm analysis considers both the time complexity, which measures the number of operations an algorithm performs relative to the input size, and the space complexity, which measures the amount of memory an algorithm requires during its execution. These metrics provide insights into the efficiency and scalability of algorithms.

Understanding algorithms involves not just knowing how they work but also when and why to use them in practice. This requires recognizing the nature of the problem, the properties of the data involved, and the performance requirements. Mastery of algorithms ultimately enables the design of efficient and effective computational solutions.

1.3 Importance of Data Structures and Algorithms in Computer Science

In computer science, data structures and algorithms are fundamental concepts that underlie the creation of effective and efficient software. The importance of these topics cannot be overstated, as they play a critical role in determining the performance and scalability of applications. To understand their significance, we must examine several key areas where they make a substantial impact.

One of the primary reasons data structures and algorithms are crucial is their influence on the efficiency of software operations. Suppose a program requires the frequent retrieval and update of data. In that case, the choice of the correct data structure, such as hash tables for constant-time data access or balanced binary search trees for logarithmic-time queries, will dramatically affect the execution speed. Efficient algorithms further complement this by reducing the number of computational steps required to achieve a task, producing efficient and high-performing code. This directly translates into faster applications with reduced resource consumption, which is vital in both small-scale and large-scale systems alike.

To illustrate the difference that a well-considered choice of data structure and algorithm can make, consider the example of sorting a list of integers. A naive approach using the bubble sort algorithm, which has a time complexity of $O(n^2)$, may be suitable for small lists. However, as the list grows, this approach becomes impractical. In contrast, an algorithm like quicksort, with an average time complexity of $O(n \log n)$, will perform significantly better on larger datasets. This reduction in time complexity leads to substantial performance gains, highlighting the importance of selecting the right algorithm for a given task.

Another vital aspect is the maintainability and scalability of code. By employing appropriate data structures and algorithms, developers can create code that is more modular and easier to understand, thereby simplifying debugging and maintenance tasks. For example, using a well-defined tree structure to represent hierarchical data can make traversal and manipulation operations straightforward. This clarity in code structure reduces complexities during updates or extensions to the software, leading to more scalable and adaptable systems.

Furthermore, understanding data structures and algorithms enhances problem-solving skills by providing systematic approaches to tackling computational problems. It involves recognizing patterns and leveraging existing structures and techniques to devise optimal solutions. A computer scientist equipped with this knowledge can abstract complex problems into simpler sub-problems, identify the most effective data structures and algorithms to address these sub-problems, and combine them into comprehensive solutions.

Additionally, the relevance of data structures and algorithms extends to resource optimization. Many modern applications run in resource-constrained environments, where efficient use of memory and processing power is crucial. For instance, embedded systems, mobile apps, and IoT devices all benefit from carefully chosen data structures and algorithms that minimize memory usage and processing cycles. This is pertinent in scenarios where hardware capabilities are limited, and optimizing software performance can mean the difference between functional and non-functional applications.

Beyond immediate technical benefits, mastery of data structures and algorithms is also highly valued in the industry. It is a core competency that many employers look for during technical interviews. The ability to reason about and implement efficient solutions to algorithmic and data structure problems is a skill set that is synonymous with computer science proficiency. This aptitude is essential not just for creating performant software but also for participating in cutting-edge research and development, contributing to advancements in fields such as artificial intelligence, machine learning, and data science.

In real-world applications, the importance of data structures and algorithms is evident in various domains. Search engines, databases, operating systems, networking components, and even simple web applications leverage these concepts to function efficiently. For example, databases use indexed data structures like B-trees to speed up query processing, while network routers use shortest-path algorithms to determine the most efficient routing of data packets. Each of these applications demonstrates how critical data structures and algorithms are to the efficient functioning of systems that we rely on daily.

Considering future trends, the importance of data structures and algorithms will only grow. As we encounter increasingly large datasets and more complex problems, the demand for optimized computational solutions will continue to rise. Innovations in quantum computing and parallel processing are poised to introduce new paradigms of problem solving, yet the foundational knowledge of data structures and algorithms will remain indispensable. Achieving breakthroughs in these advanced areas will still require a profound understanding of how information is organized and manipulated effectively.

Understanding the importance of data structures and algorithms is not only about recognizing their utility but also about appreciating their foundational principles in computer science. This insight enables the development of robust, efficient, and scalable software that meets the needs of diverse applications, both now and in the future.

1.4 Types of Data Structures

Data structures are essential constructs that enable efficient storage, retrieval, and modification of data. They can be broadly categorized into two main types: linear and non-linear data structures. Each type has various implementations and use cases. In this section, we explore both categories, along with specific examples and their applications.

Linear Data Structures: Linear data structures organize elements sequentially, where each element is linked to its previous and next element. Common linear data structures include arrays, linked lists, stacks, and queues.

- Arrays: Arrays are collections of elements, typically of the same data type, stored in contiguous memory locations. Arrays allow random access to elements using an index. For example:

```
int[] numbers = {10, 20, 30, 40, 50};
int number = numbers[2]; // Accesses the third element, which is 30
```

  Arrays are efficient for indexed access but have limitations in terms of dynamic resizing and insertion and deletion operations, which can be costly as it may require shifting elements.

- Linked Lists: A linked list is a collection of nodes where each node contains a data element and a reference (or link) to the next node in the sequence. There are various types of linked lists: singly linked lists, doubly linked lists, and circular linked lists. For example:

```
class Node {
    int data;
    Node next;

    Node(int d) {
        data = d;
        next = null;
```

```
    }
}

Node head = new Node(10);
head.next = new Node(20);
head.next.next = new Node(30);
```

Linked lists are advantageous for dynamic memory allocation and frequent insertion and deletion operations. However, they do not support random access, so traversal from the head node is required to access elements.

- Stacks: A stack is a linear data structure that follows the Last In, First Out (LIFO) principle. Elements can be added (pushed) or removed (popped) only from the top of the stack. For example:

```
Stack<Integer> stack = new Stack<>();
stack.push(10);
stack.push(20);
int topElement = stack.pop(); // Removes and returns the top element, 20
```

  Stacks are used for managing function calls, evaluating expressions, and backtracking algorithms like depth-first search.

- Queues: A queue is a linear data structure that follows the First In, First Out (FIFO) principle. Elements are added (enqueued) at the rear and removed (dequeued) from the front. For example:

```
Queue<Integer> queue = new LinkedList<>();
queue.add(10); // Enqueue
queue.add(20);
int frontElement = queue.remove(); // Dequeue, returns 10
```

  Queues are useful in scenarios like task scheduling, handling of asynchronous data (e.g., IO buffering), and breadth-first search algorithms.

Non-linear Data Structures: Non-linear data structures do not organize elements in a sequential order; instead, they are arranged in a hierarchical manner. Common non-linear data structures include trees and graphs.

- Trees: A tree is a hierarchical structure consisting of nodes, with a root node and children node forming a parent-child relationship. Binary trees, binary search trees (BST), AVL trees, and heap trees are examples. For instance, a simple binary tree:

```
class TreeNode {
    int data;
```

```
    TreeNode left, right;

    TreeNode(int d) {
        data = d;
        left = right = null;
    }
}

TreeNode root = new TreeNode(10);
root.left = new TreeNode(5);
root.right = new TreeNode(15);
```

Trees are utilized in databases, file systems, and network routing algorithms due to their hierarchical nature and efficient search, insert, and delete operations in balanced trees like AVL and red-black trees.

- Graphs: A graph is a collection of nodes (vertices) connected by edges. Graphs can be directed or undirected, weighted or unweighted. Graphs are represented using adjacency lists or adjacency matrices. For example, an adjacency list representation:

```
class Graph {
    private int V; // Number of vertices
    private LinkedList<Integer> adj[];

    Graph(int v) {
        V = v;
        adj = new LinkedList[v];
        for (int i = 0; i < v; ++i)
            adj[i] = new LinkedList<>();
    }

    void addEdge(int v, int w) { adj[v].add(w); } // Add w to v's list.
}

Graph g = new Graph(5);
g.addEdge(0, 1);
g.addEdge(0, 4);
g.addEdge(1, 2);
g.addEdge(1, 3);
g.addEdge(1, 4);
g.addEdge(2, 3);
g.addEdge(3, 4);
```

Graphs are pivotal in networking, social networks, recommendation systems, and various optimization problems solved using algorithms like Dijkstra's and Floyd-Warshall for shortest paths, and Prim's and Kruskal's for minimum spanning trees.

Selecting the appropriate data structure depends on the specific requirements of the application, such as the efficiency of operations like access, insertion, deletion, and the complexity of implementation. Proficiency in understanding and implementing data structures lays the groundwork for developing efficient and optimized software solutions.

1.5 Types of Algorithms

Algorithms can be classified in various ways based on their design paradigm, purpose, and implementation specifics. Understanding these classifications helps in choosing the appropriate algorithmic approach for solving a particular problem. Several key types of algorithms are widely recognized in computer science:

- **Divide and Conquer**
- **Dynamic Programming**
- **Greedy Algorithms**
- **Backtracking**
- **Branch and Bound**
- **Brute Force**
- **Randomized Algorithms**

Divide and Conquer algorithms work by recursively breaking down a problem into two or more sub-problems of the same type, until these become simple enough to be solved directly. The solutions to the sub-problems are then combined to give a solution to the original problem. The most common examples of divide and conquer algorithms are merge sort and quicksort.

```
void mergeSort(int arr[], int l, int r) {
    if (l < r) {
        int m = l + (r - l) / 2;
        mergeSort(arr, l, m);
        mergeSort(arr, m + 1, r);
        merge(arr, l, m, r);
    }
}

void merge(int arr[], int l, int m, int r) {
    int n1 = m - l + 1;
    int n2 = r - m;
    int L[] = new int[n1];
    int R[] = new int[n2];
    for (int i = 0; i < n1; i++)
        L[i] = arr[l + i];
```

```
    for (int j = 0; j < n2; j++)
        R[j] = arr[m + 1 + j];
    int i = 0, j = 0;
    int k = l;
    while (i < n1 && j < n2) {
        if (L[i] <= R[j]) {
            arr[k] = L[i];
            i++;
        } else {
            arr[k] = R[j];
            j++;
        }
        k++;
    }
    while (i < n1) {
        arr[k] = L[i];
        i++;
        k++;
    }
    while (j < n2) {
        arr[k] = R[j];
        j++;
        k++;
    }
}
```

Dynamic Programming (DP) is an optimization over plain recursion. The primary assumption in DP is that overlapping subproblems occur, and hence storing the results of these subproblems (memoization) to avoid redundancy leads to significant performance improvements. Common DP problems include the Fibonacci sequence and the knapsack problem.

```
int fib(int n, int[] memo) {
    if (n <= 1)
        return n;
    if (memo[n] != 0)
        return memo[n];
    memo[n] = fib(n-1, memo) + fib(n-2, memo);
    return memo[n];
}
```

Greedy Algorithms follow a problem-solving heuristic of making the locally optimal choice at each stage with the aim of finding a global optimum. Greedy algorithms do not always lead to the optimal solution, but they are easier to conceptualize and can be efficient for certain types of problems, such as the Minimum Spanning Tree (MST) using Prim's or Kruskal's algorithms.

```
int[] primMST(int graph[][]) {
    int V = graph.length;
    int[] parent = new int[V];
    int[] key = new int[V];
    boolean[] mstSet = new boolean[V];

    for (int i = 0; i < V; i++) {
```

```
        key[i] = Integer.MAX_VALUE;
        mstSet[i] = false;
    }

    key[0] = 0;
    parent[0] = -1;

    for (int count = 0; count < V - 1; count++) {
        int u = minKey(key, mstSet);
        mstSet[u] = true;
        for (int v = 0; v < V; v++)
            if (graph[u][v] != 0 && !mstSet[v] && graph[u][v] < key[v]) {
                parent[v] = u;
                key[v] = graph[u][v];
            }
    }
    return parent;
}

int minKey(int key[], boolean mstSet[]) {
    int min = Integer.MAX_VALUE, min_index = -1;
    for (int v = 0; v < key.length; v++)
        if (!mstSet[v] && key[v] < min) {
            min = key[v];
            min_index = v;
        }
    return min_index;
}
```

Backtracking algorithms solve problems incrementally, following a sequence of steps to build candidates to the solutions, and abandon each partial candidate ("backtracks") as soon as it determines that this candidate cannot possibly lead to a valid solution. This approach is commonly used in puzzle-solving, such as the N-Queens problem and Sudoku solvers.

```
boolean solveNQueens(int board[][], int col) {
    if (col >= board.length)
        return true;
    for (int i = 0; i < board.length; i++) {
        if (isSafe(board, i, col)) {
            board[i][col] = 1;
            if (solveNQueens(board, col + 1))
                return true;
            board[i][col] = 0;
        }
    }
    return false;
}

boolean isSafe(int board[][], int row, int col) {
    for (int i = 0; i < col; i++)
        if (board[row][i] == 1)
            return false;
    for (int i = row, j = col; i >= 0 && j >= 0; i--, j--)
        if (board[i][j] == 1)
            return false;
    for (int i = row, j = col; j >= 0 && i < board.length; i++, j--)
        if (board[i][j] == 1)
```

```
            return false;
    return true;
}
```

Branch and Bound is an optimization algorithm especially used for solving combinatorial and integer programming problems. It works by dividing the problem into subproblems (branching) and then evaluates the lower and upper bounds of the objective function within these subproblems to prune the solution space.

```
class KnapsackItem {
    int weight;
    int value;
    double ratio;

    KnapsackItem(int weight, int value) {
        this.weight = weight;
        this.value = value;
        this.ratio = (double)value / weight;
    }
}
```

- Branch and Bound Algorithms

- Commonly used in scheduling problems.

- Efficient for combinatorial optimization.

Brute Force algorithms try all possible solutions until a satisfactory solution is found, or the entire solution space is exhausted. Although they guarantee finding a solution, these algorithms can be computationally expensive and impractical for large input sizes. Examples include checking all possible arrangements of strings to find palindromes.

Randomized Algorithms use a degree of randomness as part of their logic. Typically these algorithms make random choices or employ a probabilistic approach to sample the problem's solution space, yielding high efficiency in many practical scenarios. Notable examples are QuickSort (when using a random pivot) and randomized primality tests.

These classifications help in recognizing the appropriate algorithmic strategy to solve different types of problems. Understanding the strengths and limitations of each type enables the selection of the best method for efficient problem-solving.

1.6 Analyzing Algorithms: Time and Space Complexity

Understanding how to analyze algorithms is a crucial skill in computer science. The efficiency of an algorithm is typically measured in terms of its time complexity and space complexity. Time complexity gives us an estimate of the running time of an algorithm, while space complexity tells us about the amount of memory it requires. This section provides an in-depth exploration of these concepts.

Time Complexity

Time complexity is a measure of the amount of computational time that an algorithm takes as a function of the input size. It is important to understand how the running time increases with the size of the input. The most common way to denote time complexity is through the Big O notation, which we will cover in detail later.

Consider a simple example of an algorithm to sum the numbers from 1 to n:

```
public int sum(int n) {
    int sum = 0;
    for (int i = 1; i <= n; i++) {
        sum += i;
    }
    return sum;
}
```

The running time of this algorithm can be analyzed by observing the loop. The loop runs n times, and each operation inside the loop (addition and assignment) takes a constant time. Therefore, the time complexity of this algorithm is $O(n)$, which means it scales linearly with the input size.

To illustrate a more complex example, consider the following program which involves a nested loop:

```
public void printPairs(int n) {
    for (int i = 1; i <= n; i++) {
        for (int j = 1; j <= n; j++) {
            System.out.println(i + ", " + j);
        }
    }
}
```

In this case, the outer loop runs n times, and for each iteration of the outer loop, the inner loop also runs n times. Therefore, the total number of iterations is $n \times n = n^2$. The time complexity of this algorithm is $O(n^2)$, which means it scales quadratically with the input size.

Space Complexity

Space complexity refers to the amount of memory an algorithm needs to run to completion. Like time complexity, space complexity is also expressed using Big O notation. Consider the following algorithm that creates and returns an array of size n:

```
public int[] createArray(int n) {
    int[] array = new int[n];
    for (int i = 0; i < n; i++) {
        array[i] = i;
    }
    return array;
}
```

The space complexity of this algorithm is $O(n)$ because it requires an additional space proportional to the size of the input array n. The space required for variables such as i and array pointer do not depend on n and thus, are considered constant.

Now consider an algorithm that involves recursion:

```
public int factorial(int n) {
    if (n == 0) {
        return 1;
    }
    return n * factorial(n - 1);
}
```

In this case, the space complexity is also $O(n)$ due to the depth of the recursion. Each recursive call adds a new layer to the call stack, and there are n recursive calls before the base case is reached.

Algorithm Analysis Using Big O Notation

Big O notation is a mathematical notation used to describe the upper bound of an algorithm's running time or space requirements in terms of the size of the input. It provides a high-level understanding of the algorithm's efficiency and helps in comparing different algorithms.

Common time complexities expressed in Big O notation include:

- $O(1)$: Constant time complexity.
- $O(\log n)$: Logarithmic time complexity.
- $O(n)$: Linear time complexity.
- $O(n \log n)$: Linearithmic time complexity.

- $O(n^2)$: Quadratic time complexity.
- $O(2^n)$: Exponential time complexity.
- $O(n!)$: Factorial time complexity.

Analyzing an algorithm involves examining its structure and determining which instructions are executed how many times, in terms of the input size. For example, in a loop that runs from 1 to n, the loop variable inspects every number, once contributing to an $O(n)$ complexity. Nested loops contribute multiplicatively to the complexity.

Consider the following sorting algorithm bubble sort:

```
public void bubbleSort(int[] array) {
    int n = array.length;
    for (int i = 0; i < n - 1; i++) {
        for (int j = 0; j < n - i - 1; j++) {
            if (array[j] > array[j + 1]) {
                int temp = array[j];
                array[j] = array[j + 1];
                array[j + 1] = temp;
            }
        }
    }
}
```

In the worst-case scenario, the inner loop runs $n - i - 1$ times for each iteration of the outer loop, leading to a total of $n(n - 1)/2$ comparisons. Hence, the worst-case time complexity is $O(n^2)$.

Understanding the intricacies of time and space complexity helps one design more efficient algorithms and choose the appropriate data structures for solving computational problems effectively.

1.7 Big O Notation: An Overview

Big O Notation is a mathematical notation used to describe the upper bound of an algorithm's running time. It provides a high-level understanding of the algorithm's efficiency by classifying performance in terms of the input size, denoted as n. The Big O Notation focuses on the behavior of the algorithm as the input size grows, abstracting away constant factors and lower-order terms that have negligible impact on the efficiency for large inputs.

Definition and Purpose: The formal definition of Big O Notation is given as follows: an algorithm is said to be $O(f(n))$ if there exist positive constants c and n_0 such that for all $n \geq n\_0$, the running time of the algorithm is at most c * f(n). The function f(n) represents the dominant term that dictates the algorithm's growth rate, and c is a constant scaling factor.

Consider the following example where an algorithm has a running time expressed as $T(n) = 5n^2 + 3n + 7$. For large values of n, the quadratic term 5n^2 dominates the expression, making the linear term 3n and the constant term 7 insignificant. Therefore, this algorithm is said to have a time complexity of O(n^2).

Common Big O Notations:

- O(1) - Constant Time: This denotes an algorithm whose running time remains constant irrespective of the input size. An example is accessing an element in an array by index.

```
int x = arr[0];
```

- O(n) - Linear Time: This represents an algorithm whose running time is directly proportional to the input size. An example is the traversal of an array.

```
for (int i = 0; i < n; i++) {
    // Some constant-time operation
}
```

- O(log n) - Logarithmic Time: This describes an algorithm whose running time grows logarithmically with the input size. A common example is binary search.

```
int binarySearch(int[] arr, int key) {
    int low = 0, high = arr.length - 1;
    while (low <= high) {
        int mid = (low + high) / 2;
        if (arr[mid] == key) return mid;
        else if (arr[mid] < key) low = mid + 1;
        else high = mid - 1;
    }
    return -1;
}
```

- O(n log n) - Linearithmic Time: Typically seen in efficient sorting algorithms like Merge Sort and Quick Sort.

```
void mergeSort(int[] arr, int left, int right) {
    if (left < right) {
        int mid = (left + right) / 2;
        mergeSort(arr, left, mid);
        mergeSort(arr, mid + 1, right);
        merge(arr, left, mid, right);
    }
}
```

- $O(n^2)$ - Quadratic Time: This denotes an algorithm whose running time is proportional to the square of the input size. An example is a simple comparison-based sort like Bubble Sort.

```
void bubbleSort(int[] arr) {
    int n = arr.length;
    for (int i = 0; i < n-1; i++) {
        for (int j = 0; j < n-i-1; j++) {
            if (arr[j] > arr[j+1]) {
                int temp = arr[j];
                arr[j] = arr[j+1];
                arr[j+1] = temp;
            }
        }
    }
}
```

Graphical Representation: Understanding the practical differences among these complexities can be enhanced by visualizing their growth using a graph. Consider a plot where the x-axis represents the input size n and the y-axis represents the running time:

- $O(1)$ appears as a horizontal line.
- $O(n)$ appears as a linearly increasing line.
- $O(\log n)$ appears as a curve that flattens as n increases.
- $O(n \log n)$ appears steeper than $O(n)$ but less steep than $O(n^2)$.
- $O(n^2)$ appears as a parabolically increasing curve.

Analyzing Worst-Case Complexity: The Big O Notation typically considers the worst-case scenario for an algorithm. By focusing on the worst-case performance, developers are ensured that the algorithm will never exceed this bound, providing a reliable measure of its efficiency. For example, in sorting algorithms like Quick Sort, although the average complexity is $O(n \log n)$, in the worst case, it can degrade to $O(n^2)$ if the pivot selection is consistently poor. This worst-case analysis helps in better understanding and choosing algorithms based on their most demanding scenarios.

In the context of data structures, consider the operations on a hash table. The average time complexity for lookups, insertions, and deletions is $O(1)$; however, in the worst case, when dealing with hash collisions, these operations can degrade to $O(n)$. Big O Notation thus provides insights into the possible performance pitfalls and aids in designing more robust applications.

Amortized Analysis: While Big O Notation emphasizes the worst-case scenario, amortized analysis evaluates the average time taken per operation over a sequence of operations. This method is particularly useful when analyzing data structures such as dynamic arrays, where certain operations like resizing affect the overall performance. For instance, in a dynamic array, while an individual insertion might occasionally take $O(n)$ time due to resizing, the amortized time complexity over a series of insertions remains $O(1)$.

Consider the following pseudocode for inserting elements into a dynamic array: Even though resizing operations are $O(n)$, the amortized

```
Input: Element e
Output: Updated Array
if current size == capacity then
    double the array capacity;
    copy elements to the new array;
insert e into the array;
```

time complexity of each insertion remains $O(1)$ because resizing happens infrequently.

Understanding Big O Notation is crucial for analyzing and comparing algorithms, ensuring efficient solutions to computational problems.

1.8 Choosing the Right Data Structure for Your Problem

Selecting the appropriate data structure for a given problem is critical to achieving efficient and effective solutions in software development. The choice of data structure affects the performance of algorithms, the simplicity of code, and the overall maintainability of the software. This section guides you through the decision-making process, outlining key considerations and providing examples in Java.

Factors to Consider

When choosing a data structure, the following factors need to be carefully evaluated:

- Operations: Identify the operations that need to be performed frequently. Are insertion, deletion, searching, or traversal operations needed? Understanding these requirements can help narrow down the choices.
- Data Characteristics: Consider the properties of the data, such as size, whether it is ordered or unordered, and if there are any unique constraints.
- Memory Usage: Analyze how much memory is available and how it will be managed. Some data structures are more memory-efficient than others.
- Complexity: Evaluate the time and space complexity of the data structure's operations to ensure they meet the performance requirements.
- Concurrency: If your application is multi-threaded, you may need data structures that support concurrent operations.

Common Data Structures and Their Use Cases

Below are common data structures and scenarios where each would be the most appropriate choice.

- Array:
  - Best For: Fixed-size collections, fast indexing.
  - Java Example:

```java
int[] numbers = {1, 2, 3, 4, 5};
int value = numbers[2]; // Accessing the third element
```

- ArrayList:
  - Best For: Dynamic-size collections requiring random access.

- Java Example:

```
ArrayList<String> names = new ArrayList<>();
names.add("Alice");
names.add("Bob");
String name = names.get(1); // Accessing the second element
```

- LinkedList:
  - Best For: Insertion and deletion at the ends or middle.
  - Java Example:

```
LinkedList<Integer> linkedList = new LinkedList<>();
linkedList.add(10);
linkedList.add(20);
int firstElement = linkedList.getFirst();
```

- Stack:
  - Best For: Last-in, first-out (LIFO) operations like function call management.
  - Java Example:

```
Stack<String> stack = new Stack<>();
stack.push("First");
stack.push("Second");
String top = stack.pop(); // "Second"
```

- Queue:
  - Best For: First-in, first-out (FIFO) operations like task scheduling.
  - Java Example:

```
Queue<Integer> queue = new LinkedList<>();
queue.add(1);
queue.add(2);
int head = queue.poll(); // 1
```

- HashMap:
  - Best For: Fast access to key-value pairs.
  - Java Example:

```
HashMap<String, Integer> map = new HashMap<>();
map.put("Alice", 30);
map.put("Bob", 25);
int age = map.get("Alice"); // 30
```

- TreeMap:

- Best For: Sorted key-value pairs.
- Java Example:

```
TreeMap<String, Integer> sortedMap = new TreeMap<>();
sortedMap.put(”Alice”, 30);
sortedMap.put(”Bob”, 25);
String firstKey = sortedMap.firstKey(); // ”Alice”
```

- PriorityQueue:
  - Best For: Elements with priorities, like task scheduling.
  - Java Example:

```
PriorityQueue<Integer> pq = new PriorityQueue<>();
pq.add(10);
pq.add(20);
int highestPriority = pq.poll(); // 10
```

Decision-Making Process

The process of deciding on the right data structure involves a structured approach:

Input: Problem requirements and constraints
Output: Optimal data structure

begin
- Identify the operations you need to perform frequently;
- Consider the properties of your data, such as size and uniqueness;
- Analyze time and space complexity of potential data structures;
- Evaluate memory usage and manageability;
- Account for concurrency needs;
- Select the data structure that meets all criteria optimally;

Example Scenario

Consider a scenario where you need to design a system to manage the seating arrangement in a theater. You need to support operations such as booking a seat, canceling a booking, checking seat availability, and outputting a list of available seats in order.

- Operations: Booking, canceling, checking availability, ordered listing.

- Data Characteristics: Seats are ordered and indexed.
- Best Choice: TreeSet (from java.util)

```
TreeSet<Integer> availableSeats = new TreeSet<>();
// Initialize seats
for (int i = 1; i <= 100; i++) {
    availableSeats.add(i);
}

// Book a seat
availableSeats.remove(10);

// Cancel a booking
availableSeats.add(10);

// Check available seats in order
for (int seat : availableSeats) {
    System.out.println("Seat " + seat + " is available");
}
```

The TreeSet data structure maintains the order of the elements, supports efficient insertion and deletion, and offers logarithmic time complexity for critical operations, meeting all the requirements optimally.

Effective software design heavily relies on the proper choice of data structures tailored to specific problem requirements. The ability to analyze problem constraints and efficiently select the optimal data structure can significantly enhance the performance and reliability of software applications.

1.9 Real-world Applications of Data Structures and Algorithms

Data structures and algorithms are not only fundamental to computer science but are also critical components of modern technology solutions. By leveraging appropriate data structures and algorithms, we can solve complex problems efficiently. This section elaborates on the real-world applications of data structures and algorithms, providing tangible examples that bring abstract concepts to life.

One ubiquitous data structure, the array, is used extensively in real-time systems for tasks that involve optimal time complexity access. In video games, for example, arrays store player statistics, game assets, and level data due to their efficient indexing and locality of reference properties.

Another widely-used data structure is the hash table. Hash tables provide average-case constant time complexity for insertions, deletions, and lookups, making them invaluable for applications requiring quick data retrieval. In databases, hash tables facilitate fast lookup of records using keys such as user IDs or transaction IDs. Consider an online banking system where customer transactions must be fetched quickly. Using a hash table to map transaction IDs to transaction details improves performance significantly.

```
import java.util.HashMap;

public class TransactionManager {
    private HashMap<String, Transaction> transactionTable;

    public TransactionManager() {
        transactionTable = new HashMap<>();
    }

    public void addTransaction(String transactionID, Transaction transaction) {
        transactionTable.put(transactionID, transaction);
    }

    public Transaction getTransaction(String transactionID) {
        return transactionTable.get(transactionID);
    }
}
```

Graphs and graph algorithms play a pivotal role in network-based applications such as social networks, communication networks, and transportation systems. Algorithms like Dijkstra's algorithm and A* search algorithm are used for finding the shortest path in routing and navigation systems. Social networking platforms use graphs to represent users and their relationships, enabling features like friend recommendations and connection queries.

```
Output of Dijkstra's Algorithm for Shortest Path:
Node: A, Shortest Distance: 0
Node: B, Shortest Distance: 5
Node: C, Shortest Distance: 3
Node: D, Shortest Distance: 7
```

```
public void dijkstra(Graph graph, Node source) {
    source.setDistance(0);
    PriorityQueue<Node> priorityQueue = new PriorityQueue<>();
    priorityQueue.add(source);

    while(!priorityQueue.isEmpty()) {
        Node current = priorityQueue.poll();

        for (Edge edge : current.getAdjacencies()) {
            Node neighbor = edge.getTarget();
            double newDist = current.getDistance() + edge.getWeight();

            if (newDist < neighbor.getDistance()) {
                priorityQueue.remove(neighbor);
                neighbor.setDistance(newDist);
```

```
                neighbor.setPrevious(current);
                priorityQueue.add(neighbor);
            }
        }
    }
}
```

In addition to graph algorithms, heap data structures (priority queues) are fundamental to various real-time applications that need to manage dynamically changing datasets. One notable application is in scheduling systems within operating systems (OS) where tasks are scheduled based on priority levels.

Trees, specifically binary search trees (BSTs), AVL trees, and B-trees, are employed effectively in database indexing to support efficient query processing. B-trees are particularly suited to databases and filesystems due to their balanced nature, ensuring logarithmic time complexity for insertions, deletions, and lookups.

```
public class BTree {
    private Node root;
    private int T;

    public BTree(int t) {
        this.T = t;
        root = new Node(t, true);
    }

    public void insert(int key) {
        Node r = root;
        if (r.n == 2 * T - 1) {
            Node s = new Node(T, false);
            root = s;
            s.C[0] = r;
            splitChild(s, 0, r);
            insertNonFull(s, key);
        } else {
            insertNonFull(r, key);
        }
    }

    private void insertNonFull(Node x, int key) {
        int i = x.n - 1;

        if (x.leaf) {
            while (i >= 0 && key < x.key[i]) {
                x.key[i + 1] = x.key[i];
                i--;
            }
            x.key[i + 1] = key;
            x.n = x.n + 1;
        } else {
            while (i >= 0 && key < x.key[i]) {
                i--;
            }
            i++;
            if (x.C[i].n == 2 * T - 1) {
```

```
                splitChild(x, i, x.C[i]);
                if (key > x.key[i]) {
                    i++;
                }
            }
            insertNonFull(x.C[i], key);
        }
    }

    private void splitChild(Node x, int i, Node y) {
        Node z = new Node(y.T, y.leaf);
        x.C[i + 1] = z;
        z.n = T - 1;

        for (int j = 0; j < T - 1; j++) {
            z.key[j] = y.key[j + T];
        }

        if (!y.leaf) {
            for (int j = 0; j < T; j++) {
                z.C[j] = y.C[j + T];
            }
        }
        y.n = T - 1;

        for (int j = x.n; j >= i + 1; j--) {
            x.C[j + 1] = x.C[j];
        }
        x.C[i + 1] = z;

        for (int j = x.n - 1; j >= i; j--) {
            x.key[j + 1] = x.key[j];
        }
        x.key[i] = y.key[T - 1];
        x.n = x.n + 1;
    }
}
```

Sorting algorithms are indispensable in various financial applications. For instance, the stock market requires efficient sorting algorithms to order transactions by timestamps or other criteria to enable real-time trading. Algorithms such as QuickSort and MergeSort are essential due to their efficiency and relatively simple implementation.

```
public class QuickSort {
    int partition(int arr[], int low, int high) {
        int pivot = arr[high];
        int i = (low-1);
        for (int j=low; j<high; j++) {
            if (arr[j] <= pivot) {
                i++;
                int temp = arr[i];
                arr[i] = arr[j];
                arr[j] = temp;
            }
        }
        int temp = arr[i+1];
        arr[i+1] = arr[high];
        arr[high] = temp;
```

```
        return i+1;
    }

    void sort(int arr[], int low, int high) {
        if (low < high) {
            int pi = partition(arr, low, high);

            sort(arr, low, pi-1);
            sort(arr, pi+1, high);
        }
    }
}
```

In cybersecurity, algorithms like search algorithms and encryption algorithms are crucial. For example, the RSA algorithm for public-key cryptography uses mathematical principles of number theory and is widely used for secure data transmission.

```
import java.math.BigInteger;
import java.security.SecureRandom;

public class RSA {
    private BigInteger modulus, privateKey, publicKey;

    public RSA(int bitlen) {
        SecureRandom random = new SecureRandom();
        BigInteger p = new BigInteger(bitlen / 2, 100, random);
        BigInteger q = new BigInteger(bitlen / 2, 100, random);
        modulus = p.multiply(q);
        BigInteger phi = (p.subtract(BigInteger.ONE)).multiply(q.subtract(BigInteger.
            ONE));
        publicKey = new BigInteger("65537"); // Common value for e
        privateKey = publicKey.modInverse(phi);
    }

    public BigInteger encrypt(BigInteger message) {
        return message.modPow(publicKey, modulus);
    }

    public BigInteger decrypt(BigInteger encrypted) {
        return encrypted.modPow(privateKey, modulus);
    }
}
```

Data structures and algorithms span across numerous domains, proving their efficacy by optimizing performance, reducing computational complexity, and ensuring efficient use of resources. Their real-world applications are vast and varied, underscoring the value of a robust understanding of these foundational concepts in computer science.

1.10 Future Trends in Data Structures and Algorithms

As the field of computer science evolves, so does the landscape of data structures and algorithms. This section explores some of the emerging trends shaping the future of data structures and algorithms. By analyzing these trends, we aim to provide insights into how they might influence the development and optimization of software systems in the years to come.

Parallel and Distributed Algorithms: With the advent of multicore processors and distributed computing environments, there is a pronounced shift towards parallel and distributed algorithms. Traditional sequential algorithms are being re-engineered to leverage the power of concurrency. MapReduce and similar frameworks exemplify this trend by dividing large datasets across many nodes, allowing for parallel processing.

For instance, consider the parallel implementation of the QuickSort algorithm using OpenMP.

```
void parallelQuickSort(int[] arr, int low, int high) {
    if (low < high) {
        int pivotIndex = partition(arr, low, high);
        #pragma omp parallel sections
        {
            #pragma omp section
            {
                parallelQuickSort(arr, low, pivotIndex - 1);
            }
            #pragma omp section
            {
                parallelQuickSort(arr, pivotIndex + 1, high);
            }
        }
    }
}
```

This code snippet demonstrates how the recursive QuickSort can be parallelized using OpenMP directives to enhance performance on multicore systems.

Cache-Efficient Algorithms: As processor speeds outstrip memory access times, cache-efficient algorithms are gaining prominence. These algorithms are designed to minimize cache misses by improving data locality. The Cache-Oblivious Model is one such approach, where algorithms are constructed without cache parameters but still function efficiently across different memory hierarchies.

A quintessential example is the cache-oblivious matrix multiplication algorithm. This algorithm optimizes the standard matrix multiplication by recursively breaking down the problem into smaller blocks to enhance cache performance.

Machine Learning Algorithms Integration: The rapid growth of machine learning is infiltrating traditional algorithmic problem-solving. Data structures and algorithms are increasingly being infused with machine learning models to optimize performance. For example, machine learning techniques are being employed to predict the best data structure or algorithm for a given problem context dynamically.

Consider an adaptive sorting algorithm that uses a neural network to decide between MergeSort and QuickSort based on input characteristics such as size and distribution.

```
String chooseSortAlgorithm(int[] arr) {
    NeuralNetwork nn = loadTrainedModel("sort_decision_model");
    double[] features = extractFeatures(arr);
    return nn.predict(features); # Returns "MergeSort" or "QuickSort"
}
```

This adaptability leads to more efficient data processing by selecting the most appropriate sorting algorithm on-the-fly.

Quantum Algorithms: Quantum computing represents another major frontier. Quantum algorithms leverage phenomena such as superposition and entanglement to solve problems that are impractical for classical computers. The Grover's Algorithm for unsorted database search and Shor's Algorithm for integer factorization are well-known examples.

As quantum computers inch closer to practical usability, we will witness a growing number of quantum algorithm implementations for classical problems. A straightforward example in quantum programming is the Grover's search algorithm.

```
# include <iostream>
# include <qiskit/QuantumCircuit>

void groversSearch() {
    QuantumCircuit qc(2); # Two qubits for search
    qc.h(0); # Apply Hadamard gate to both qubits
    qc.h(1);

    # Oracle and amplitude amplification steps would follow
    qc.measure_all();
    qc.run();
}
```

Here, groversSearch function sets up a quantum circuit with the basic initialization for Grover's algorithm.

Persistent Data Structures: Persistent data structures are becoming increasingly crucial in applications where immutability and historical data tracking are essential, such as version control systems and blockchain technologies. These structures ensure that previous versions of data are preserved and accessible, which is particularly beneficial for undo operations and audit trails.

For example, the persistent list supports push and pop operations without altering past versions:

```
class PersistentList {
    final int head;
    final PersistentList tail;

    PersistentList(int head, PersistentList tail) {
        this.head = head;
        this.tail = tail;
    }

    PersistentList push(int value) {
        return new PersistentList(value, this);
    }

    PersistentList pop() {
        return this.tail;
    }
}
```

This immutability is a pivotal feature, stripping away concerns about inadvertent data modification.

Advancements in data structures and algorithms are also spurred by the increasing importance of security, real-time processing, and the need to handle massive amounts of data. These trends underscore the need for continuous learning and adaptation within the field of computer science, ensuring that future software systems are more efficient, resilient, and capable of addressing ever-evolving challenges.

Chapter 2

Java Basics for Data Structures and Algorithms

This chapter covers the fundamental aspects of Java necessary for understanding and implementing data structures and algorithms. Beginning with an introduction to Java and its development environment, it progresses through basic syntax, data types, control flow statements, and loops. Additionally, it explores object-oriented programming concepts, arrays, collections, and exception handling. By the end of this chapter, readers will have acquired the essential Java skills required to implement and work with various data structures and algorithms effectively.

2.1 Introduction to Java

Java is a versatile and widely-used programming language, initially developed by Sun Microsystems in 1995 and later acquired by Oracle Corporation. It operates on the philosophy of "write once, run anywhere" (WORA), meaning that compiled Java code can run on any platform without recompilation. This cross-platform capability is supported by the Java Virtual Machine (JVM), which provides a runtime environment for executing Java bytecode. Java is designed to be object-oriented, concurrent, and secure, which makes it ideal for developing a wide range of applications, from mobile devices to enterprise servers and supercomputers.

History and Evolution

Java's development was initiated by James Gosling and his team under the "Green Project" at Sun Microsystems. The initial goal was to create a language for embedded systems; however, its scope expanded to include web applications and desktop applications due to its robust and portable nature. Since its inception, Java has undergone several enhancements and updates, the most notable versions being:

- **Java SE 1.0 (1996)**: The first official release, which introduced the core APIs and the AWT (Abstract Window Toolkit).
- **Java SE 1.2 (1998)**: Known as Java 2, it introduced the Swing framework, Collection Framework, and a pluggable look-and-feel.
- **Java SE 5 (2004)**: Introduced generics, metadata, enumerated types, and the enhanced for loop.
- **Java SE 8 (2014)**: Presented lambda expressions, the Stream API, and other functional programming constructs.
- **Java SE 11 (2018)**: A long-term support (LTS) release incorporating several performance improvements and new features like the var keyword for local variable type inference.

Java continues to evolve, maintaining a strong presence in both academic and professional environments due to its robust standard libraries, extensive community support, and strong performance.

Java Platform and JVM

The Java platform consists of the Java language, the Java compilation process, and the JVM. The Java language is used to write programs, which are then compiled into bytecode by the Java compiler. The JVM interprets this bytecode and executes it, making the Java platform capable of running on various hardware and operating systems. The architecture of the JVM allows it to optimize performance through Just-In-Time (JIT) compilation, where bytecode is compiled into native machine code during execution.

Figure **??** illustrates the typical Java platform architecture.

Key components of the Java platform include:

- **Java Standard Edition (SE)**: Provides the core functionality, including the standard libraries, tools, and virtual machine for desktop and server applications.
- **Java Enterprise Edition (EE)**: Extends Java SE with additional libraries and frameworks for building large-scale, multi-tiered, scalable applications.
- **Java Micro Edition (ME)**: Targets resource-constrained environments, such as mobile and embedded devices.

Features of Java

Java incorporates several features that contribute to its popularity and effectiveness as a programming language:

- **Object-Oriented**: Facilitates modular programming through encapsulation, inheritance, and polymorphism, promoting code reuse and maintainability.
- **Platform-Independent**: Utilizes the JVM to enable cross-platform execution of bytecode.
- **Robust and Secure**: Incorporates strong memory management, exception handling, and a security model that defines permissions at the bytecode level.
- **Multithreaded**: Supports concurrent execution of multiple threads, enabling efficient utilization of CPU resources.
- **High Performance**: Achieved through JIT compilers, which translate bytecode into native machine code at runtime.
- **Rich Standard Library**: Provides extensive APIs for I/O, networking, data structures, and more, facilitating rapid and efficient application development.

Java Development Kit (JDK) and Java Runtime Environment (JRE)

Developing Java applications requires the Java Development Kit (JDK), which includes the Java compiler, standard libraries, and other development tools. The JDK encompasses the following components:

- javac: The Java compiler that translates Java source code into bytecode.

- java: The launcher tool that starts the JVM and executes Java applications.
- javadoc: A documentation generator that creates HTML documentation from Java source code comments.
- jar: A tool for packaging Java class files and associated resources into a JAR (Java Archive) file.
- jdb: A debugger for Java programs.

The Java Runtime Environment (JRE) is a subset of the JDK and includes only the necessary components to run Java programs, such as the JVM, core libraries, and other supporting files. It is sufficient for executing Java applications but does not include development tools like the compiler.

Writing and Running a Simple Java Program

To illustrate the basic structure of a Java program, consider the classic "Hello, World!" example. The following code demonstrates a minimal Java program:

```
public class HelloWorld {
    public static void main(String[] args) {
        System.out.println("Hello, World!");
    }
}
```

In this example, the program defines a class named HelloWorld containing a main method, which serves as the entry point for the application. The System.out.println statement prints the string "Hello, World!" to the console.

To compile and run the program, follow these steps:

- Save the code in a file named HelloWorld.java.
- Open a terminal or command prompt and navigate to the directory containing the file.
- Compile the program using the following command:

```
javac HelloWorld.java
```

- If the compilation is successful, execute the program with this command:

```
java HelloWorld
```

The output should be:

```
Hello, World!
```

This example highlights the fundamental aspects of writing, compiling, and running a Java program. The class definition, method declaration, and the use of standard output illustrate core concepts that will be built upon in subsequent sections.

2.2 Setting Up Your Development Environment

To effectively write, compile, and run Java programs, it is imperative to set up a suitable development environment. This section provides a comprehensive guide to installing and configuring the necessary tools. We will focus on the Java Development Kit (JDK), Integrated Development Environments (IDEs), and setting environment variables.

Step 1: Install the Java Development Kit (JDK)

The JDK is an essential component comprising the Java Runtime Environment (JRE), an interpreter/loader (Java Virtual Machine), an archiver (jar), a compiler (javac), and other tools needed to develop Java applications.

1. **Download the JDK**:

    - Visit the official Oracle website: https://www.oracle.com/java/technologies/javase-downloads.html.
    - Select the latest version of the JDK and download the appropriate installer for your operating system (Windows, macOS, or Linux).

2. **Install the JDK**:

    - Run the downloaded installer and follow the on-screen instructions to complete the installation.
    - Verify the installation by opening a terminal or command prompt and typing:

```
javac -version
java -version
```

- You should see the installed version of the JDK and JVM.

Step 2: Set Environment Variables

To ensure that the JDK and its tools are accessible from any command prompt, set the environment variables appropriately.

1. **Setting environment variables on Windows**:

    - Open the Start Menu, search for Environment Variables, and select Edit the system environment variables.
    - Click on the Environment Variables button.
    - Under System Variables, click on New and add:
        - **Name**: JAVA_HOME
        - **Value**: Path to the JDK installation directory (e.g., C:\Program Files\Java\jdk-XX).
    - Find the Path variable, click Edit, and add the following path:
        - %\JAVA_HOME\bin
    - Click OK to save the changes.

2. **Setting environment variables on macOS/Linux**:

    - Open a terminal and edit the shell configuration file (e.g., .bashrc, .bash_profile, .zshrc):
    - Add the following lines to the file:

```
export JAVA_HOME=/Library/Java/JavaVirtualMachines/jdk-XX.jdk/Contents/Home
export PATH=$JAVA_HOME/bin:$PATH
```

    - Save the file and run source to apply the changes:

```
source ~/.bashrc
```

Step 3: Select an Integrated Development Environment (IDE)

A robust IDE can significantly enhance productivity by providing features like syntax highlighting, code completion, and debugging tools. Below are some widely-used IDEs for Java development:

1. **Eclipse**:

- Visit https://www.eclipse.org/downloads/ and download the Eclipse installer.
- Run the installer and select Eclipse IDE for Java Developers.
- Follow the installation instructions to set up Eclipse.

2. **IntelliJ IDEA**:
   - Download the Community Edition from https://www.jetbrains.com/idea/download/.
   - Run the installer and follow the on-screen instructions.

3. **NetBeans**:
   - Visit https://netbeans.apache.org/download/ and download the installer.
   - Follow the installation instructions to set up NetBeans IDE.

Step 4: Configure the IDE

Once the IDE is installed, configure it to work seamlessly with the JDK.

1. **Configuring Eclipse**:
   - Open Eclipse and navigate to Window > Preferences.
   - Expand Java and click on Installed JREs.
   - Click Add, select Standard VM, and specify the path to the JDK installation directory.
   - Click Finish and ensure that the newly added JRE is checked.

2. **Configuring IntelliJ IDEA**:
   - Open IntelliJ IDEA and navigate to File > Project Structure.
   - Under Project Settings, select Project.
   - Set the Project SDK to the installed JDK.
   - Apply the changes and click OK.

3. **Configuring NetBeans**:

- Open NetBeans and navigate to Tools > Java Platforms.
- Click Add Platform, select Java Standard Edition, and specify the path to the JDK installation directory.
- Finish the configuration and set the newly added JDK as the default platform.

With the JDK installed, environment variables set, and an IDE configured, your development environment is ready for Java programming. This setup will provide a robust foundation for writing, debugging, and executing Java code efficiently.

2.3 Basic Syntax and Structure of Java Programs

Java programs are structured into classes, methods, and blocks. Understanding this structure and the syntax is crucial for implementing data structures and algorithms effectively. In this section, we will discuss the fundamental elements that constitute a Java program, including classes, methods, variables, data types, and operators.

A basic Java program starts with a class definition. The class is the blueprint for objects and contains methods that define the behavior of the objects. The entry point of any Java application is the main method. Here is a simple example:

```
public class HelloWorld {
    public static void main(String[] args) {
        System.out.println("Hello, World!");
    }
}
```

In this example, HelloWorld is the class name, and it contains one method main. The main method is the entry point of the program and is always defined as public static void main(String[] args).

Classes and Methods

A class in Java is declared using the class keyword. It can contain fields, methods, constructors, and nested classes. Methods are functions that define the behavior of a class. Here is a more detailed example:

```
public class Calculator {
    // Field variable
    private int result;

    // Constructor
    public Calculator() {
        result = 0;
    }

    // Method to add two numbers
    public void add(int a, int b) {
        result = a + b;
    }

    // Method to get the result
    public int getResult() {
        return result;
    }

    // Main method
    public static void main(String[] args) {
        Calculator calc = new Calculator();
        calc.add(5, 3);
        System.out.println("The result is: " + calc.getResult());
    }
}
```

In this example, the Calculator class has a field result, a constructor Calculator(), and two methods, add and getResult. The main method creates an instance of Calculator and uses it to perform an addition.

Variables and Data Types

Variables in Java must be declared before they can be used. Each variable has a data type that determines what kind of data it can store. Java is a strongly-typed language, meaning that a variable type is known at compile time. Here are the basic data types:

- int - for integers.
- double - for floating-point numbers.
- char - for single characters.
- boolean - for true/false values.

Example of declaring variables:

```
public class DataTypesExample {
    public static void main(String[] args) {
```

```
        int num = 10;
        double price = 19.99;
        char grade = 'A';
        boolean isAvailable = true;

        System.out.println("Integer: " + num);
        System.out.println("Double: " + price);
        System.out.println("Char: " + grade);
        System.out.println("Boolean: " + isAvailable);
    }
}
```

This program declares variables of different types and prints their values.

Operators

Java provides a rich set of operators to manipulate variables. These include arithmetic operators, relational operators, logical operators, and bitwise operators. Here are some examples:

- Arithmetic operators: +, -, *, /, %
- Relational operators: ==, !=, >, <, >=, <=
- Logical operators: &&, ||, !
- Bitwise operators: &, |,ˆ, », «

Example of using operators:

```
public class OperatorsExample {
    public static void main(String[] args) {
        int a = 10;
        int b = 20;

        // Arithmetic Operators
        int sum = a + b;
        int diff = a - b;

        // Relational Operators
        boolean isEqual = a == b;
        boolean isGreater = a > b;

        // Logical Operators
        boolean andCondition = (a < b) && (a > 5);

        // Bitwise Operators
        int bitwiseAnd = a & b;

        System.out.println("Sum: " + sum);
        System.out.println("Difference: " + diff);
```

```
        System.out.println("Is Equal: " + isEqual);
        System.out.println("Is Greater: " + isGreater);
        System.out.println("AND Condition: " + andCondition);
        System.out.println("Bitwise AND: " + bitwiseAnd);
    }
}
```

This example demonstrates the usage of different types of operators. Understanding these basic elements is essential for writing any Java program and will be foundational for implementing more complex data structures and algorithms.

2.4 Variables, Data Types, and Operators

Variables in Java serve as storage locations in memory, each with a specific data type defining the kind of value it can hold. Declaring variables correctly and understanding their associated data types and operators are fundamental to programming and form the foundation for implementing data structures and algorithms in Java.

Variables and Data Types

Java provides a set of built-in data types, each with a specific size and range of values. These are categorized into two primary types: primitive types and reference types.

- **Primitive Data Types**: These are the most basic data types and are predefined in Java. They include:
  - byte - 8-bit signed integer
  - short - 16-bit signed integer
  - int - 32-bit signed integer
  - long - 64-bit signed integer
  - float - single-precision 32-bit IEEE 754 floating-point
  - double - double-precision 64-bit IEEE 754 floating-point
  - boolean - represents one bit of information, values can be true or false
  - char - a single 16-bit Unicode character
- **Reference Data Types**: These refer to objects and include arrays, classes, interfaces, etc. The reference variables store memory addresses where the objects are located.

```
int number; // variable declaration
number = 10; // variable initialization

double pi = 3.14159; // declaration and initialization in one line
boolean flag = true;
```

Operators

Java operators are symbols that perform operations on variables and values. They can be classified into several categories: arithmetic, relational, logical, bitwise, assignment, unary, and ternary operators.

Arithmetic Operators

These operators are used to perform basic arithmetic operations: addition, subtraction, multiplication, division, and modulus.

- + (Addition)
- - (Subtraction)
- * (Multiplication)
- / (Division)
- % (Modulus - remainder after division)

```
int a = 15, b = 5;
int addition = a + b; // 20
int subtraction = a - b; // 10
int multiplication = a * b; // 75
int division = a / b; // 3
int modulus = a % b; // 0
```

Relational Operators

These operators compare two values and return a boolean result (true or false).

- == (Equal to)
- != (Not equal to)
- > (Greater than)
- < (Less than)
- >= (Greater than or equal to)
- <= (Less than or equal to)

```
boolean result1 = (a == b); // false
boolean result2 = (a != b); // true
boolean result3 = (a > b); // true
boolean result4 = (a < b); // false
boolean result5 = (a >= b); // true
boolean result6 = (a <= b); // false
```

Logical Operators

These operators are used to combine multiple boolean expressions or operands.

- && (Logical AND)
- || (Logical OR)
- ! (Logical NOT)

```
boolean flag1 = true, flag2 = false;
boolean andResult = flag1 && flag2; // false
boolean orResult = flag1 || flag2; // true
boolean notResult = !flag1; // false
```

Bitwise Operators

Bitwise operators perform bit-level operations on integer data types.

- & (Bitwise AND)
- | (Bitwise OR)
- ^ (Bitwise XOR)
- ~ (Bitwise Complement)
- « (Left Shift)
- » (Right Shift)
- »> (Unsigned Right Shift)

```
int x = 6; // binary: 110
int y = 4; // binary: 100

int andResult = x & y; // binary: 100, decimal: 4
int orResult = x | y; // binary: 110, decimal: 6
int xorResult = x ^ y; // binary: 010, decimal: 2
int complementResult = ~x; // binary: 001, decimal: -7 (in two's complement)
int leftShift = x << 1; // binary: 1100, decimal: 12
int rightShift = x >> 1; // binary: 011, decimal: 3
```

Assignment Operators

These operators assign values to variables.

- = (Simple assignment)
- += (Add and assign)
- -= (Subtract and assign)
- *= (Multiply and assign)
- /= (Divide and assign)
- %= (Modulus and assign)

```
int num = 10;
num += 5; // equivalent to num = num + 5; result: 15
num -= 3; // equivalent to num = num - 3; result: 12
num *= 2; // equivalent to num = num * 2; result: 24
num /= 4; // equivalent to num = num / 4; result: 6
num %= 3; // equivalent to num = num % 3; result: 0
```

Unary Operators

Unary operators require only one operand and perform operations such as incrementing/decrementing a value by one, negating an expression, or inverting the value of a boolean.

- + (Unary plus)
- - (Unary minus)
- ++ (Increment)
- – (Decrement)
- ! (Logical complement)

```
int u = 5;
u++; // equivalent to u = u + 1; result: 6
u--; // equivalent to u = u - 1; result: 5

boolean boolVal = true;
boolean notBoolVal = !boolVal; // false
```

Ternary Operator

The ternary operator is a shorthand for the if-else statement and is represented by the symbol ?:. It takes three operands.

```
int v = 10;
int result = (v > 5) ? v : 0; // Since v > 5, result is assigned the value of v, which is
    10
```

Understanding variables, data types, and operators is critical for efficient programming in Java. As we delve deeper into data structures and algorithms, these basics will be the foundation for more complex manipulations and operations.

2.5 Control Flow Statements (if, else, switch)

Control flow statements in Java allow you to dictate the order in which statements are executed based on certain conditions. These constructs are fundamental for implementing decision-making logic in programs. This section details the use of if, else, and switch statements to control the flow of execution in Java applications.

The if statement evaluates a boolean expression. If the expression evaluates to true, the code block within the if statement is executed. If the expression evaluates to false, the block is skipped.

```
int num = 10;
if (num > 5) {
    System.out.println("The number is greater than 5.");
}
```

In this example, the condition $num > 5$ evaluates to true, so the message "The number is greater than 5." is printed to the console.

The else statement is used in conjunction with if to provide an alternative path of execution when the if condition evaluates to false.

```
int num = 3;
if (num > 5) {
    System.out.println("The number is greater than 5.");
} else {
    System.out.println("The number is 5 or less.");
}
```

Here, since the condition $num > 5$ is false, the message "The number is 5 or less." is printed to the console.

if statements can be chained using else if to handle multiple conditions.

```
int num = 7;
if (num > 10) {
```

```
    System.out.println("The number is greater than 10.");
} else if (num > 5) {
    System.out.println("The number is greater than 5 but 10 or less.");
} else {
    System.out.println("The number is 5 or less.");
}
```

In this case, since num is 7, the second condition num > 5 evaluates to true and the corresponding message is printed: "The number is greater than 5 but 10 or less."

Java's switch statement allows you to execute one code block among many based on the value of a single expression. This can be more readable than using multiple if-else statements when evaluating a single variable against several constant values.

```
int day = 3;
switch (day) {
    case 1:
        System.out.println("Monday");
        break;
    case 2:
        System.out.println("Tuesday");
        break;
    case 3:
        System.out.println("Wednesday");
        break;
    case 4:
        System.out.println("Thursday");
        break;
    case 5:
        System.out.println("Friday");
        break;
    case 6:
        System.out.println("Saturday");
        break;
    case 7:
        System.out.println("Sunday");
        break;
    default:
        System.out.println("Invalid day");
        break;
}
```

In this switch-case example, the day variable is evaluated. Since day is 3, the message "Wednesday" is printed.

The break statement is crucial in a switch block to terminate the current case and prevent fall-through, where subsequent cases are executed even if their conditions are not met. Without break, each subsequent case will execute until another break is encountered or the switch block ends.

switch blocks also support string and enum types starting from Java 7, making them versatile in various contexts.

```
String season = "Summer";
switch (season) {
    case "Spring":
        System.out.println("Flowers bloom in Spring.");
        break;
    case "Summer":
        System.out.println("It's hot in Summer.");
        break;
    case "Fall":
        System.out.println("Leaves fall in Autumn.");
        break;
    case "Winter":
        System.out.println("It's cold in Winter.");
        break;
    default:
        System.out.println("Invalid season");
        break;
}
```

The above example evaluates the season variable and prints "It's hot in Summer." because the season value is "Summer".

Utilizing flow control statements efficiently in Java is essential for creating programs that can respond dynamically to varied inputs and conditions.

2.6 Loops (for, while, do-while)

Loops are control structures that allow repeated execution of a block of code as long as a given condition is true. Java provides three primary types of loops: for, while, and do-while loops. Each of these looping constructs serves different use cases and has unique characteristics.

The for Loop

A for loop is generally used when the number of iterations is known beforehand. Its syntax consists of three parts: initialization, condition, and update. These components are enclosed in parentheses and separated by semicolons.

```
// For loop syntax
for (initialization; condition; update) {
    // Code to be executed
}
```

Let's consider an example that prints numbers from 1 to 5:

```
for (int i = 1; i <= 5; i++) {
    System.out.println(i);
}
```

The above loop initializes the variable i to 1, checks if i is less than or equal to 5, and prints i. After each iteration, i is incremented by 1. The loop terminates when i exceeds 5. The output will be:

```
1
2
3
4
5
```

The while Loop

The while loop is typically used when the condition must be checked before executing the loop body. The syntax of the while loop is simpler than the for loop, consisting of only a condition.

```
// While loop syntax
while (condition) {
    // Code to be executed
}
```

Here is an example of a while loop that accomplishes the same task as the previous for loop:

```
int i = 1;
while (i <= 5) {
    System.out.println(i);
    i++;
}
```

In this case, the variable i is initialized outside the loop. The condition i <= 5 is checked before each iteration, and i is incremented within the loop body. The output will again be:

```
1
2
3
4
5
```

The do-while Loop

Unlike the while loop, the do-while loop guarantees that the loop body executes at least once, regardless of whether the condition is true. This feature is due to the condition being evaluated after the loop body has executed.

```
// Do-while loop syntax
do {
    // Code to be executed
} while (condition);
```

Consider the following do-while loop example:

```
int i = 1;
```

```
do {
    System.out.println(i);
    i++;
} while (i <= 5);
```

As with the while loop, the variable i is initialized outside the loop. The do-while loop prints i and then increments i. After each iteration, it checks whether i is less than or equal to 5. The result will be:

```
1
2
3
4
5
```

Usage Considerations

Choosing the appropriate loop depends on the specific requirements of the task. Use for loops when the number of iterations is predefined, while loops when the number of iterations is unknown and based on a condition, and do-while loops when at least one iteration is required regardless of the condition.

It is also essential to avoid common pitfalls such as infinite loops, which occur when the loop's termination condition is never met. For instance, the following code results in an infinite loop:

```
int i = 1;
while (i <= 5) {
    System.out.println(i);
    // Missing increment of i
}
```

To prevent this, ensure all necessary updates to loop variables are correctly implemented. Proper use of loops can greatly enhance the efficiency and readability of your code, making them a powerful tool in Java programming.

2.7 Methods and Modular Programming

Methods in Java are blocks of code that perform a specific task, encapsulated into a reusable unit. They enable modular programming by allowing the division of complex problems into simpler, manageable sub-problems. Within this section, we will examine the syntax and usage of methods, explore their applications in modular programming, and understand the core principles behind method overloading and recursion.

Defining Methods

A basic method in Java is defined with the following structure:

```
accessModifier returnType methodName(parameters) {
    // method body
    // statements
}
```

accessModifier can be public, protected, default (no keyword), or private, which determine the visibility scope. The returnType specifies the type of value the method returns. For methods that do not return any value, the return type is void.

An example method that adds two integers:

```
public int add(int a, int b) {
    return a + b;
}
```

Method Invocation

To utilize a method, you invoke it by its name followed by parentheses. If parameters are required, they are provided within the parentheses.

```
public static void main(String[] args) {
    int sum = add(5, 10);
    System.out.println("Sum: " + sum);
}

public static int add(int a, int b) {
    return a + b;
}
```

Parameters and Arguments

Parameters are variables listed in the method definition, whereas arguments are the actual values passed to the method. Java supports both pass-by-value (for primitives) and pass-by-reference (for objects).

Method Overloading

Method overloading allows multiple methods in the same class to have the same name but different parameter lists (different type, number, or both). It enhances polymorphism by enabling different behaviors depending on the argument list.

```
public static int add(int a, int b) {
    return a + b;
}

public static double add(double a, double b) {
    return a + b;
}
```

```
public static int add(int a, int b, int c) {
    return a + b + c;
}
```

The Java compiler differentiates these overloaded methods based on their parameter types and numbers.

Return Types

Every method's return type must either be a primitive data type or an object. For methods with no return value, the type is void. Return types enforce the type safety within your programs.

```
public static double calculateAverage(int sum, int count) {
    if (count == 0) return 0;
    return (double) sum / count;
}
```

Recursion

A recursive method is one that calls itself to solve a smaller instance of the same problem. Recursive solutions can be elegant and concise. However, they must have a termination condition to prevent infinite recursion.

```
public static int factorial(int n) {
    if (n <= 1) return 1;
    return n * factorial(n - 1);
}
```

This example computes the factorial of a number using recursion.

Encapsulation and Information Hiding

Methods enable encapsulation by exposing only required functionalities and hiding internal implementation details. This principle of information hiding supports modular programming, making code maintenance and debugging more manageable.

Modular Programming

Modular programming involves dividing a program into separate, interchangeable modules, each performing a specific task. Methods play a crucial role in this paradigm by enabling code reuse and independence.

Consider the following example:

```
public class MathOperations {
    public static int add(int a, int b) {
        return a + b;
    }

    public static int subtract(int a, int b) {
```

```
        return a - b;
    }

    public static int multiply(int a, int b) {
        return a * b;
    }

    public static double divide(int a, int b) {
        if (b == 0) throw new IllegalArgumentException("Division by zero");
        return (double) a / b;
    }
}
```

Here, the MathOperations class contains methods implementing basic arithmetic operations. Each method is tested and executed independently, illustrating modular programming.

The benefits include:

- Enhanced code readability
- Improved maintainability
- Reusability of individual methods or classes
- Ease of testing and debugging

By adhering to these concepts and best practices, you can leverage methods to structure complex programs into manageable, logical units, optimizing both development and maintenance efforts.

2.8 Object-Oriented Programming in Java

Object-Oriented Programming (OOP) is a paradigm that organizes software design around data, or objects, rather than functions and logic. In Java, OOP principles encompass four main concepts: encapsulation, inheritance, polymorphism, and abstraction. These principles allow developers to build modular, scalable, and maintainable code.

Encapsulation restricts access to some of an object's components, which means that the internal representation of an object is hidden from the outside. This is achieved using access modifiers, the most common being private, public, and protected. Access to the object's data is provided through public methods known as getter and setter methods.

```
public class EncapsulationExample {
    private String name;
    private int age;

    public String getName() {
        return name;
    }

    public void setName(String name) {
        this.name = name;
    }

    public int getAge() {
        return age;
    }

    public void setAge(int age) {
        this.age = age;
    }
}
```

Inheritance is a mechanism wherein a new class is derived from an existing class. The derived class, called the subclass, inherits fields and methods from the existing class, known as the superclass. This promotes code reuse and establishes a natural hierarchy. In Java, inheritance is implemented using the extends keyword.

```
class Animal {
    void eat() {
        System.out.println("This animal eats food.");
    }
}

class Dog extends Animal {
    void bark() {
        System.out.println("The dog barks.");
    }
}

public class TestInheritance {
    public static void main(String args[]) {
        Dog dog = new Dog();
        dog.eat();
        dog.bark();
    }
}
```

The output of the above example would be:

```
This animal eats food.
The dog barks.
```

Polymorphism allows an object to take on many forms. The most common use of polymorphism in OOP is when a parent class reference is used to refer to a child class object. The mechanism is split into two types: compile-time (method overloading) and run-time (method overriding).

```
class Bird {
    void sound() {
        System.out.println("This bird makes a sound.");
    }
}

class Sparrow extends Bird {
    void sound() {
        System.out.println("The sparrow chirps.");
    }
}

public class TestPolymorphism {
    public static void main(String args[]) {
        Bird myBird = new Sparrow(); // Run-time polymorphism
        myBird.sound(); // Calls the overridden method in Sparrow class
    }
}
```

The output of the above example would be:

```
The sparrow chirps.
```

Abstraction is the concept of hiding the complex implementation details and showing only the essential features of the object. Abstraction can be achieved with either abstract classes or interfaces. An abstract class cannot be instantiated and may contain abstract methods (methods without a body).

```
abstract class Shape {
    abstract void draw();
}

class Circle extends Shape {
    void draw() {
        System.out.println("Drawing a circle.");
    }
}

public class TestAbstraction {
    public static void main(String args[]) {
        Shape myShape = new Circle();
        myShape.draw();
    }
}
```

The output of the above example would be:

```
Drawing a circle.
```

Additionally, Java supports **Interfaces**, which are similar to abstract classes but can contain only abstract methods (until Java 8 where default methods were introduced). Interfaces are used to achieve full abstraction and multiple inheritance in Java.

```
interface Drawable {
    void draw();
}

class Rectangle implements Drawable {
    public void draw() {
        System.out.println("Drawing a rectangle.");
    }
}

public class TestInterface {
    public static void main(String args[]) {
        Drawable myDrawable = new Rectangle();
        myDrawable.draw();
    }
}
```

The output of the above example would be:

```
Drawing a rectangle.
```

By leveraging the principles of OOP in Java, developers can create robust and flexible software designs that facilitate easy maintenance, reuse, and scalability. The combination of encapsulation, inheritance, polymorphism, and abstraction forms the cornerstone of modern software development in Java.

2.9 Working with Arrays and Collections

In Java, arrays and collections are fundamental tools used for storing and manipulating data. They offer various functionalities and efficiencies, which make them indispensable when implementing data structures and algorithms. This section will delve into the use of arrays and collections, explaining their syntax, operations, and applicable scenarios.

Arrays are fixed-size data structures that are homogeneous, meaning they can store elements of the same data type. The syntax to declare an array in Java is as follows:

```
// Syntax for declaring an array
int[] myArray;
// Initializing the array with a size of 10
myArray = new int[10];
```

Alternatively, an array can be both declared and initialized in a single line:

```
// Declaration and initialization of an array
```

```
int[] myArray = new int[10];
```

To assign values to the array elements, you can use the following notation:

```
// Assigning values to an array
myArray[0] = 1;
myArray[1] = 2;
// Continue assigning values as needed
```

Array initialization can also be done directly with values:

```
// Direct initialization
int[] myArray = {1, 2, 3, 4, 5};
```

Accessing array elements is done using their index, starting from 0 for the first element:

```
// Accessing elements of an array
int firstElement = myArray[0];
int secondElement = myArray[1];
```

A common use case for arrays is iteration to perform operations on each element. This can be achieved using loops:

```
// Iterating through an array using a for loop
for (int i = 0; i < myArray.length; i++) {
    System.out.println(myArray[i]);
}
```

Collections, unlike arrays, are part of the Java Collections Framework (JCF) and provide more flexible and powerful tools for data handling. Collections can grow or shrink in size dynamically and offer various methods for data manipulation. The main collections interfaces are List, Set, and Map.

The ArrayList class, implementing the List interface, is a widely used collection that resizes automatically. Here is how to initialize and use an ArrayList:

```
// Importing the ArrayList class
import java.util.ArrayList;

// Creating an ArrayList
ArrayList<Integer> myList = new ArrayList<>();

// Adding elements to the ArrayList
myList.add(1);
myList.add(2);
myList.add(3);

// Accessing elements using get method
int firstElement = myList.get(0);
```

```
// Iterating through ArrayList
for (int i = 0; i < myList.size(); i++) {
    System.out.println(myList.get(i));
}

// Alternatively, using an enhanced for loop
for (int element : myList) {
    System.out.println(element);
}
```

HashSet is a collection from the Set interface that stores unique elements and provides efficient operations. An example usage is shown below:

```
// Importing the HashSet class
import java.util.HashSet;

// Creating a HashSet
HashSet<String> mySet = new HashSet<>();

// Adding elements to the HashSet
mySet.add("element1");
mySet.add("element2");
mySet.add("element3");

// Checking if the HashSet contains an element
boolean containsElement1 = mySet.contains("element1");

// Iterating through HashSet
for (String element : mySet) {
    System.out.println(element);
}
```

HashMap implements the Map interface and is used to store key-value pairs. Here is an example of a HashMap in use:

```
// Importing the HashMap class
import java.util.HashMap;

// Creating a HashMap
HashMap<String, Integer> myMap = new HashMap<>();

// Putting key-value pairs in the HashMap
myMap.put("key1", 1);
myMap.put("key2", 2);

// Accessing a value using its key
int value1 = myMap.get("key1");

// Iterating through the HashMap
for (Map.Entry<String, Integer> entry : myMap.entrySet()) {
    System.out.println("Key: " + entry.getKey() + ", Value: " + entry.getValue());
}
```

Collections provide built-in methods that offer more functionality compared to arrays. Some commonly used methods include:

- add() - Adds an element to the collection.
- remove() - Removes an element from the collection.
- contains() - Checks if the collection contains a specified element.
- size() - Returns the number of elements in the collection.

It is crucial to understand the differences between arrays and collections to choose the appropriate data structure. Arrays offer fast access time due to their fixed size but lack flexibility. Collections, part of the JCF, provide flexible and powerful mechanisms for data manipulation, with dynamically resizable storage and a variety of built-in methods.

2.10 Handling Exceptions

Java provides a robust and versatile mechanism for handling errors and exceptional conditions, known as exception handling. Understanding and effectively utilizing this feature is crucial for creating robust and reliable Java applications, especially when dealing with complex data structures and algorithms.

An exception is an event that disrupts the normal flow of a program's execution. When an exception occurs, Java creates an object representing the exception and then "throws" it. The thrown exception can be "caught" by the surrounding code, which can then take appropriate action. If exceptions are not properly handled, the program may terminate abruptly.

Types of Exceptions:

Java exceptions fall into three main categories:

- **Checked Exceptions:** These are exceptions that are checked at compile-time. Examples include FileNotFoundException and IOException. These exceptions must be either caught or declared in the method signature using the throws keyword.
- **Unchecked Exceptions:** These exceptions are not checked at compile-time but are instead checked at runtime. They are represented by the RuntimeException class and its subclasses, such as NullPointerException and ArithmeticException. Handling these exceptions is optional.

- **Errors:** These are serious issues not typically handled by applications. They are represented by the Error class and its subclasses, such as OutOfMemoryError. Errors usually indicate problems with the JVM itself or hardware issues.

Basic Try-Catch-Finally:

The primary constructs for handling exceptions in Java are try, catch, and finally blocks. A try block encloses code that might throw an exception, while the catch block contains code to handle the exception. The finally block contains code that will execute regardless of whether an exception was thrown or caught.

Here is the general syntax:

```
try {
    // Code that may throw an exception
} catch (ExceptionType1 e1) {
    // Handle exception of type ExceptionType1
} catch (ExceptionType2 e2) {
    // Handle exception of type ExceptionType2
} finally {
    // Code that will always execute
}
```

Example of Exception Handling:

Consider a simple example where an array might cause an ArrayIndexOutOfBoundsException:

```
public class ExceptionExample {
    public static void main(String[] args) {
        int[] array = new int[5];
        try {
            array[10] = 30; // This will throw ArrayIndexOutOfBoundsException
        } catch (ArrayIndexOutOfBoundsException e) {
            System.out.println("Exception caught: " + e);
        } finally {
            System.out.println("Finally block executed.");
        }
    }
}
```

The above code attempts to assign a value to an index that is out of bounds of the array. The catch block handles the exception, and the finally block ensures that the clean-up code runs irrespective of whether an exception was thrown.

Throwing Exceptions:

In addition to catching exceptions, Java allows you to throw exceptions explicitly using the throw keyword. This is useful for custom exception handling.

```
public class ExceptionExample {
    public static void main(String[] args) {
        try {
            checkAge(15);
        } catch (IllegalArgumentException e) {
            System.out.println("Exception caught: " + e);
        }
    }

    static void checkAge(int age) {
        if (age < 18) {
            throw new IllegalArgumentException("Age must be 18 or older.");
        }
    }
}
```

In this example, the checkAge method throws an IllegalArgumentException if the age is less than 18. This exception is caught in the main method and handled appropriately.

Creating Custom Exceptions:

Java also allows the creation of custom exception classes. Custom exceptions are useful when you need to handle application-specific errors.

```
class CustomException extends Exception {
    public CustomException(String message) {
        super(message);
    }
}

public class CustomExceptionExample {
    public static void main(String[] args) {
        try {
            validateNumber(-1);
        } catch (CustomException e) {
            System.out.println("Exception caught: " + e.getMessage());
        }
    }

    static void validateNumber(int number) throws CustomException {
        if (number < 0) {
            throw new CustomException("Number cannot be negative.");
        }
    }
}
```

In this example, the CustomException class extends Exception. The validateNumber method throws CustomException when a negative number is passed.

Multi-Catch Block:

From Java 7 onwards, you can use a multi-catch block to handle multiple exceptions in a single catch block. This reduces code duplication and enhances readability.

```
public class MultiCatchExample {
    public static void main(String[] args) {
        try {
            int[] array = new int[5];
            array[10] = 30; // May throw ArrayIndexOutOfBoundsExceptior.
            int result = 10 / 0; // May throw ArithmeticException
        } catch (ArrayIndexOutOfBoundsException | ArithmeticException e) {
            System.out.println("Exception caught: " + e);
        }
    }
}
```

In this example, a single catch block handles both ArrayIndexOutOfBoundsException and ArithmeticException.

Effective exception handling ensures that your Java programs can handle unforeseen errors gracefully, one of the essential skills when dealing with data structures and algorithms. Utilizing these constructs, you can build robust and stable applications able to handle various runtime anomalies competently.

2.11 Java Standard Library Overview

The Java Standard Library, also known as the Java Development Kit (JDK) API, is a comprehensive set of classes and interfaces that provide a wide range of functionalities, enabling developers to write complex programs with minimal effort. Understanding the Java Standard Library is crucial for developing robust and efficient data structures and algorithms in Java. This section explores some key components of the Java Standard Library relevant to our study of data structures and algorithms.

java.lang Package: The java.lang package is automatically imported into every Java program and includes fundamental classes that are essential for the language. Key classes in this package include:

- Object: The root class of the Java class hierarchy. Every class in Java inherits from Object.
- System: Contains several useful class fields and methods. Notably, it provides access to the system input and output.
- Math: Provides methods for performing basic numeric operations such as exponentiation, logarithms, and trigonometric functions.

- String: Represents a sequence of characters. Strings in Java are immutable.

java.util Package: The java.util package includes classes that contain the collection framework, event model, date and time facilities, and miscellaneous utility classes. This package is crucial for implementing data structures and algorithms. Key classes and interfaces include:

- Collection: The root interface of the collection hierarchy.
- List: An ordered collection (also known as a sequence). Implementations include ArrayList and LinkedList.
- Set: A collection that cannot contain duplicate elements. Implementations include HashSet and TreeSet.
- Map: An object that maps keys to values, with no duplicate keys allowed. Implementations include HashMap and TreeMap.

java.io Package: The java.io package contains classes that support system input and output through data streams, serialization, and the file system. Key classes include:

- File: Represents a file or directory path in the file system.
- InputStream and OutputStream: Abstract classes for reading from and writing to byte streams, respectively.
- Reader and Writer: Abstract classes for reading from and writing to character streams, respectively.

```
import java.io.BufferedReader;
import java.io.FileReader;
import java.io.IOException;

public class FileReadingExample {
    public static void main(String[] args) {
        try (BufferedReader br = new BufferedReader(new FileReader("example.txt")))
            {
            String line;
            while ((line = br.readLine()) != null) {
                System.out.println(line);
            }
        } catch (IOException e) {
            e.printStackTrace();
        }
    }
}
```

java.nio Package: The java.nio package, introduced in Java 1.4, offers a new set of abstractions for dealing with I/O operations, commonly referred to as New Input/Output (NIO). It includes:

- Buffer: Classes that handle data of specific types such as ByteBuffer, CharBuffer, etc.
- Channel: Interfaces that represent connections to entities capable of performing I/O operations, such as reading and writing files.

java.time Package: The java.time package, introduced in Java 8, provides a comprehensive model for date and time manipulation. This package includes:

- LocalDate, LocalTime, LocalDateTime: Classes representing different levels of time complexity without timezone information.
- ZonedDateTime: Represents a date-time with a time-zone in the ISO-8601 calendar system.

Example of Using java.time:

```
import java.time.LocalDate;
import java.time.LocalTime;
import java.time.LocalDateTime;

public class DateTimeExample {
    public static void main(String[] args) {
        LocalDate today = LocalDate.now();
        LocalTime now = LocalTime.now();
        LocalDateTime currentDateTime = LocalDateTime.now();

        System.out.println("Current Date: " + today);
        System.out.println("Current Time: " + now);
        System.out.println("Current Date and Time: " + currentDateTime);
    }
}
```

java.net Package: The java.net package provides the classes for implementing networking applications. These classes are essential for communicating over the network and include:

- URL: Represents a Uniform Resource Locator, allowing access to resources on the web.
- Socket: Provides a way to communicate with other computers using TCP/IP protocols.
- ServerSocket: Waits for requests to come in over the network.

java.util.concurrent Package: The java.util.concurrent package contains various utility classes commonly useful in concurrent programming. This package includes:

- ExecutorService: A framework for managing and controlling asynchronous task execution.
- ConcurrentHashMap: A thread-safe variant of HashMap.
- CountDownLatch, Semaphore, CyclicBarrier: Utilities that provide synchronization capabilities.

Example of Using ExecutorService:

```
import java.util.concurrent.ExecutorService;
import java.util.concurrent.Executors;

public class ExecutorServiceExample {
    public static void main(String[] args) {
        ExecutorService executor = Executors.newFixedThreadPool(3);

        Runnable task1 = () -> System.out.println("Task 1");
        Runnable task2 = () -> System.out.println("Task 2");
        Runnable task3 = () -> System.out.println("Task 3");

        executor.submit(task1);
        executor.submit(task2);
        executor.submit(task3);

        executor.shutdown();
    }
}
```

Understanding the Java Standard Library enhances your ability to efficiently solve problems and implement sophisticated data structures and algorithms. Encouraging familiarity with these robust and versatile classes will significantly aid in the development of efficient, error-free Java applications.

2.12 Writing and Running Java Programs

To effectively implement data structures and algorithms in Java, it is crucial to understand how to write and run Java programs. This section will cover the necessary steps and provide a detailed walkthrough of the process, ensuring you can build, compile, and execute your Java programs with ease.

Writing Java Programs

Java programs are written in plain text files with a .java extension. Each Java program consists of at least one class and a main method, which serves as the entry point for the application.

The basic structure of a Java program is illustrated below:

```
public class HelloWorld {
    public static void main(String[] args) {
        System.out.println("Hello, World!");
    }
}
```

In this code snippet:

- public class HelloWorld defines a public class named HelloWorld. In Java, every application must have at least one class definition.
- public static void main(String[] args) is the main method, which is the entry point for any Java application. The main method must be public, static, return void, and accept a single argument: an array of String objects.
- System.out.println("Hello, World!"); prints the string "Hello, World!" to the console. The System class provides the standard input, output, and error streams.

Compiling Java Programs

Before a Java program can be run, it must be compiled into bytecode, which is then executed by the Java Virtual Machine (JVM). The Java Development Kit (JDK) provides the javac compiler for this purpose.

To compile the HelloWorld.java program, use the following command in your terminal or command prompt:

```
javac HelloWorld.java
```

If the program is free from syntax errors, the compiler generates a HelloWorld.class file, which contains the bytecode.

Running Java Programs

Once compiled, the Java program can be executed using the java command, followed by the name of the class containing the main method (without the .class extension):

```
java HelloWorld
```

Executing this command will produce the following output:

```
Hello, World!
```

Key Java Development Tools

The Java Development Kit (JDK) provides several essential tools for Java development:

- javac: The Java compiler, which converts source code into bytecode.
- java: The launcher for executing Java applications.
- javadoc: A documentation generator that creates HTML documentation from Java source code.
- jar: A tool for packaging compiled Java classes into a JAR (Java ARchive) file.
- jdb: The Java Debugger, which helps in tracking down and fixing bugs in Java programs.

Example: Compiling and Running a Program with Multiple Classes

Consider a more complex example with multiple classes. We will create a simple program that models a basic arithmetic operation (addition). The program will comprise two classes: Calculator and MainApp.

```
// Calculator.java
public class Calculator {
    public int add(int a, int b) {
        return a + b;
    }
}
```

```
// MainApp.java
public class MainApp {
    public static void main(String[] args) {
        Calculator calc = new Calculator();
        int sum = calc.add(5, 3);
        System.out.println("Sum: " + sum);
```

```
    }
}
```

To compile and run this program, follow these steps:

1. Save the above code snippets in two separate files named Calculator.java and MainApp.java.

2. Open your terminal or command prompt and navigate to the directory containing the files.

3. Compile both classes using the javac command:

```
javac Calculator.java MainApp.java
```

4. Execute the program using the java command and specify the class containing the main method:

```
java MainApp
```

This will generate the following output:

```
Sum: 8
```

Understanding the process of writing, compiling, and running Java programs is fundamental for implementing data structures and algorithms effectively. By mastering these steps, you will be well-prepared to tackle more complex programming challenges and build efficient, reliable Java applications.

Chapter 3

Arrays and Strings

This chapter introduces arrays and strings, fundamental data structures in programming. It begins by explaining the concept and operations of one-dimensional and multi-dimensional arrays, and explores dynamic arrays and their manipulation. The chapter then delves into array traversal, searching, and sorting algorithms. Following this, the focus shifts to strings, covering basic operations, manipulations, and searching algorithms. By the end, readers will understand how to efficiently work with arrays and strings to solve various computational problems.

3.1 Introduction to Arrays

An array is a data structure that allows storage of elements of the same data type in a contiguous block of memory. Arrays provide efficient random access to their elements, making them an essential tool in many programming problems. In Java, arrays are objects, with a flexible and diverse set of operations and functionalities.

The syntax for declaring an array in Java involves specifying the data type followed by square brackets and the array name. The array can be initialized at the time of declaration or separately.

```
int[] numbers; // Declaration of an array of integers
numbers = new int[5]; // Initialization of array with size 5
```

In the code snippet above, numbers is declared as an array of integers.

The new keyword allocates memory for the array, specifying that the array will hold 5 integers. Individual elements of the array can be accessed using their index, which starts from 0.

```
numbers[0] = 10; // Assign value to the first element
System.out.println(numbers[0]); // Output: 10
```

Elements in the array can be assigned and accessed using their respective indices. This characteristic enables quick data retrieval but requires careful management of index bounds to avoid ArrayIndexOutOfBoundsException.

Arrays can also be initialized using literals at the time of declaration, providing a shorthand for initializing arrays with predefined values.

```
int[] primes = {2, 3, 5, 7, 11}; // Declaration and initialization
```

With this notation, the array primes is declared and immediately initialized with the values 2, 3, 5, 7, and 11.

Java supports arrays of primitive types as well as arrays of objects. For instance, it is possible to create an array of strings.

```
String[] fruits = {"Apple", "Banana", "Cherry"};
System.out.println(fruits[1]); // Output: Banana
```

Arrays play a crucial role in algorithm implementations due to their ability to store multiple values efficiently. Several operations such as traversal, insertion, deletion, and searching can be performed on arrays. In array traversal, each element is accessed and processed. The following is a typical traversal loop for an array.

```
for (int i = 0; i < numbers.length; i++) {
    System.out.println(numbers[i]);
}
```

The for loop iterates over each element of the array numbers and prints its value. The length property of the array provides the number of elements in the array, ensuring that the loop runs correctly within bounds.

Arrays are static in Java, meaning their size cannot be altered after creation. This can lead to inefficient memory use if the array is either over-allocated or under-allocated. This problem is addressed by dynamic arrays, which will be covered in subsequent sections.

Arrays in Java are versatile and can be multi-dimensional. A common multi-dimensional array is the two-dimensional array, often used to represent matrices.

```
int[][] matrix = new int[3][3]; // Declaration and initialization of a 3x3 matrix
matrix[0][0] = 1; // Assign value to the first row and first column
```

In the example, matrix is a two-dimensional array with 3 rows and 3 columns. Elements are accessed using two indices. The following code snippet demonstrates iteration over a two-dimensional array to print its elements.

```
for (int row = 0; row < matrix.length; row++) {
    for (int col = 0; col < matrix[row].length; col++) {
        System.out.print(matrix[row][col] + " ");
    }
    System.out.println();
}
```

Each element in the two-dimensional array matrix is accessed using the row and column indices within nested for loops. This technique ensures that all elements are processed in a systematic manner.

Array operations go beyond just storing and retrieving elements. Computational problems often require modifying the array structure, performing complex operations efficiently. In the coming sections, we will delve deeper into various array operations such as insertion, deletion, searching, and sorting, as well as explore dynamic arrays to understand their flexibility and use-cases.

3.2 One-dimensional Arrays

One-dimensional arrays are a fundamental data structure in programming. They represent a contiguous block of memory divided into discrete elements, each of which can be accessed directly using an index. In Java, arrays are objects that store multiple variables of the same type, accessible through index positions starting from zero.

To declare a one-dimensional array in Java, specify the data type of its elements followed by square brackets and the array name. To instantiate the array, use the new keyword along with the size of the array. Here is an example of initializing a one-dimensional integer array with 5 elements:

```
int[] array = new int[5];
```

This snippet initializes an integer array named array with size 5, where each element defaults to 0. Elements can be assigned values using their respective indices:

```
array[0] = 10;
array[1] = 20;
array[2] = 30;
array[3] = 40;
array[4] = 50;
```

You can also declare and initialize an array in a single line with an array initializer:

```
int[] array = {10, 20, 30, 40, 50};
```

Accessing array elements is done using indices within square brackets. For example, array[2] returns the value 30. Attempting to access an index outside the array bounds results in an ArrayIndexOutOfBoundsException.

One common operation is iterating over the array elements, typically using a for loop or enhanced for loop:

```
for (int i = 0; i < array.length; i++) {
    System.out.println(array[i]);
}

for (int element : array) {
    System.out.println(element);
}
```

Arrays in Java are fixed in size, meaning the number of elements cannot change once the array has been created. This limitation necessitates dynamic arrays or lists for situations requiring resizable structures, covered in later sections.

To copy elements of one array into another, methods such as System.arraycopy or Arrays.copyOf can be employed. The System.arraycopy method copies a specified range from the source array to the destination array:

```
int[] sourceArray = {1, 2, 3, 4, 5};
int[] destinationArray = new int[5];
System.arraycopy(sourceArray, 0, destinationArray, 0, 5);
```

Alternatively, Arrays.copyOf allows copying and resizing simultaneously:

```
int[] sourceArray = {1, 2, 3, 4, 5};
int[] newArray = Arrays.copyOf(sourceArray, 7);
\end{lstisting}

With \texttt{newArray} containing: \{1, 2, 3, 4, 5, 0, 0\}.

Arrays also support utility methods in the \texttt{java.util.Arrays} class, such as \
    texttt{sort}, \texttt{fill}, \texttt{equals}, and \texttt{toString} for sorting,
```

```
filling, comparing, and converting arrays to strings respectively:

\begin{lstlisting}
int[] values = {3, 1, 4, 1, 5};
Arrays.sort(values);
System.out.println(Arrays.toString(values));
```

The above code sorts values in ascending order and prints [1, 1, 3, 4, 5].

Understanding one-dimensional arrays forms a critical foundation in data structure and algorithm development, as they provide the basis for more complex structures like dynamic arrays, matrices, and various collection types.

3.3 Multi-dimensional Arrays

Multi-dimensional arrays extend the concept of one-dimensional arrays by allowing arrays of arrays. This capability is particularly useful for representing data in tabular form, such as matrices or grids, and for solving complex problems that involve multiple dimensions. In Java, multi-dimensional arrays are essentially arrays of arrays, and they can be declared and manipulated in various ways.

To declare a two-dimensional array, you use a syntax similar to the declaration of one-dimensional arrays but with multiple pairs of square brackets. For instance, to declare a two-dimensional array of integers, you use:

```
int[][] matrix;
```

To create a two-dimensional array with specified dimensions, you use the new keyword. For example, to create a 3x3 matrix:

```
matrix = new int[3][3];
```

In this example, matrix is a two-dimensional array with three rows and three columns. The elements of the two-dimensional array can be accessed using two indices. For instance, to access the element in the second row and the third column, you use:

```
int element = matrix[1][2];
```

Here, the indices start from 0, so matrix[1][2] accesses the element in the second row and third column of the matrix.

You can also initialize a two-dimensional array directly at the time of declaration:

```
int[][] matrix = {
    {1, 2, 3},
    {4, 5, 6},
    {7, 8, 9}
};
```

In this example, matrix is a 3x3 array with pre-defined values.

Java also supports multi-dimensional arrays with more than two dimensions. For instance, a three-dimensional array can be declared and initialized as follows:

```
int[][][] cube = new int[3][3][3];
```

Each element in a three-dimensional array is accessed using three indices:

```
cube[1][2][0] = 5;
```

As with two-dimensional arrays, you can initialize three-dimensional arrays with predefined values. However, nested initialization tends to become cumbersome, so it is often done in stages:

```
int[][][] cube = {
    {
        {1, 2, 3},
        {4, 5, 6},
        {7, 8, 9}
    },
    {
        {10, 11, 12},
        {13, 14, 15},
        {16, 17, 18}
    },
    {
        {19, 20, 21},
        {22, 23, 24},
        {25, 26, 27}
    }
};
```

An important consideration when working with multi-dimensional arrays is that they can be jagged, meaning that the sub-arrays might have different lengths. For instance, a two-dimensional jagged array in Java can be created as follows:

```
int[][] jaggedArray = new int[3][];
jaggedArray[0] = new int[4];
jaggedArray[1] = new int[2];
jaggedArray[2] = new int[3];
```

In this example, jaggedArray is a two-dimensional array with three rows, where the first row has four elements, the second row has two elements, and the third row has three elements.

Traversing multi-dimensional arrays typically involves nested loops. For a two-dimensional array, you use a pair of nested for loops:

```
for (int i = 0; i < matrix.length; i++) {
    for (int j = 0; j < matrix[i].length; j++) {
        System.out.print(matrix[i][j] + " ");
    }
    System.out.println();
}
```

For a three-dimensional array, you extend this concept using three nested for loops:

```
for (int i = 0; i < cube.length; i++) {
    for (int j = 0; j < cube[i].length; j++) {
        for (int k = 0; k < cube[i][j].length; k++) {
            System.out.print(cube[i][j][k] + " ");
        }
        System.out.println();
    }
    System.out.println();
}
```

Multi-dimensional arrays are integral in various computational problems, particularly in fields such as computer graphics, numerical simulations, and data analysis. Understanding their structure and how to manipulate them effectively allows for more complex and efficient data representations.

3.4 Dynamic Arrays

Dynamic arrays, unlike static arrays, can grow and shrink as the elements are added or removed, providing more flexibility in managing collections of elements. This section discusses the core principles behind dynamic arrays, their implementation in Java, and the various operations typically performed on them, such as insertion, deletion, and resizing.

Implementation Principles:

To implement a dynamic array, the underlying principle is to use a resizable array that can accommodate more elements than initially allocated. A common technique involves using an initial fixed-size array. Once this array fills up, a new array with a larger capacity is created, and existing elements are copied to this new array. Here is a step-by-step explanation of how a dynamic array might function internally:

1. **Initial Allocation:** A fixed-size array is created with an initial capacity.

```
class DynamicArray {
    private int[] array;
    private int size;

    public DynamicArray(int initialCapacity) {
        array = new int[initialCapacity];
        size = 0;
    }
}
```

2. **Adding Elements:** When an element is added, it's placed in the next available position in the array. If the array is full, the capacity is doubled before adding the new element.

```
public void add(int element) {
    if (size == array.length) {
        resizeArray();
    }
    array[size] = element;
    size++;
}

private void resizeArray() {
    int newCapacity = array.length * 2;
    int[] newArray = new int[newCapacity];
    for (int i = 0; i < array.length; i++) {
        newArray[i] = array[i];
    }
    array = newArray;
}
```

When the array reaches its capacity, a new array with doubled capacity is created, and elements are copied into this new array. This ensures that the add operation remains efficient.

3. **Removing Elements:** Removing elements involves shifting all subsequent elements one position to the left to fill the gap. Optionally, the size of the underlying array can be reduced if the current usage drops below a certain threshold.

```
public void remove(int index) {
    if (index >= size || index < 0) {
        throw new ArrayIndexOutOfBoundsException();
    }
    for (int i = index; i < size - 1; i++) {
        array[i] = array[i + 1];
    }
    size--;
}
```

Dynamic Resizing and Amortized Cost:

Dynamic arrays offer average-case $O(1)$ time complexity for insertion operations, despite occasional resizing operations. The amortized analysis reveals how the cost balances out over multiple operations. Each resizing operation, which involves copying all elements to a new array, has a time complexity of $O(n)$. However, since the array size doubles each time it is resized, the number of such operations is logarithmic with respect to the number of insertions. Therefore, the average, or amortized, cost per insertion remains $O(1)$.

Advantages and Trade-offs:

The primary advantages of dynamic arrays over static arrays include their flexible size and ease of use for many practical applications. However, these benefits come with trade-offs:

- **Memory Overhead:** Dynamic arrays may allocate extra memory to accommodate future growth, leading to unused space.
- **Occasional High-cost Operations:** Resizing operations, although infrequent, have a higher time complexity than simple insertions.

Practical Implementation in Java:

Java's standard library provides a dynamic array implementation in the form of the ArrayList class. This class abstracts the complexities described above and provides a user-friendly interface for dynamic arrays.

```
import java.util.ArrayList;

public class DynamicArrayExample {
    public static void main(String[] args) {
        ArrayList<Integer> dynamicArray = new ArrayList<>(initialCapacity);

        // Adding elements
        dynamicArray.add(10);
        dynamicArray.add(20);

        // Removing elements
        dynamicArray.remove(0);
    }
}
```

Mastering dynamic arrays involves understanding their underlying resizing mechanisms, performance trade-offs, and practical implementation. Their dynamic nature makes them a fundamental tool in effective data management.

3.5 Array Operations: Insertion and Deletion

In programming, arrays are essential data structures used to store collections of elements. Two fundamental operations often performed on arrays are insertion and deletion. Understanding these operations is crucial for manipulating arrays effectively. This section provides a comprehensive examination of insertion and deletion operations in one-dimensional arrays.

Insertion Operation:

Insertion in an array involves adding an element at a specific index. The complexity of this operation varies based on the position where the new element is inserted. There are three primary scenarios:

- Insertion at the beginning.
- Insertion at the end.
- Insertion at an arbitrary position.

Given an array arr of size n, the general algorithm for insertion at index pos can be formulated as follows:

Algorithm 2: Insertion in an Array

Input: Array $\mathrm{arr}[0 \,..\, \text{n-1}]$, Size n, Element elem, Position pos
Output: Array $\mathrm{arr}[0 \,..\, \mathrm{n}]$, Size $\mathrm{n{+}1}$

```
begin
    if pos < 0 or pos > n then
        return Error ;                         // Invalid position
    for i = n down to pos do
        arr[i] = arr[i - 1];
    arr[pos] = elem; n = n + 1;
```

The implementation of this algorithm in Java is as follows:

```java
public static int[] insertElement(int[] arr, int n, int elem, int pos) {
    if (pos < 0 || pos > n) {
        throw new IllegalArgumentException("Invalid position");
    }
    int[] newArr = new int[n + 1];
    for (int i = 0; i < pos; i++) {
        newArr[i] = arr[i];
    }
    newArr[pos] = elem;
    for (int i = pos + 1; i < n + 1; i++) {
        newArr[i] = arr[i - 1];
```

```
    }
    return newArr;
}
```

The complexity of the insertion operation primarily depends on the number of elements that need to be shifted. The worst-case complexity is $O(n)$, which occurs when the insertion is at the beginning of the array, necessitating the shift of all the existing elements.

Deletion Operation:

Deletion from an array involves removing an element from a specified index, followed by the repositioning of subsequent elements to fill the gap. Similar to insertion, the complexity of deletion depends on the index of the element being removed. There are three main scenarios:

- Deletion from the beginning.
- Deletion from the end.
- Deletion from an arbitrary position.

Given an array arr of size n, the general algorithm for deletion at index pos is as follows:

Algorithm 3: Deletion from an Array

```
Input: Array arr[0 .. n-1], Size n, Position pos
Output: Array arr[0 .. n-2], Size n-1
begin
    if pos < 0 or pos >= n then
        return Error ;                          // Invalid position
    for i = pos to n-2 do
        arr[i] = arr[i + 1];
    n = n - 1;
```

The implementation of this algorithm in Java is as follows:

```
public static int[] deleteElement(int[] arr, int n, int pos) {
    if (pos < 0 || pos >= n) {
        throw new IllegalArgumentException("Invalid position");
    }
    int[] newArr = new int[n - 1];
    for (int i = 0; i < pos; i++) {
        newArr[i] = arr[i];
    }
    for (int i = pos; i < n - 1; i++) {
        newArr[i] = arr[i + 1];
    }
```

```
    return newArr;
}
```

Similar to insertion, the deletion operation's worst-case complexity is $O(n)$, occurring when the deletion is performed at the beginning of the array, requiring the shift of all remaining elements.

Example:

Consider an array $\text{arr} = [1,\ 2,\ 3,\ 4,\ 5]$, and implement insertion and deletion operations as follows:

```
public static void main(String[] args) {
    int[] arr = {1, 2, 3, 4, 5};
    int n = arr.length;

    // Insert element 10 at position 2
    arr = insertElement(arr, n, 10, 2);
    n = arr.length;
    System.out.println("Array after insertion: " + Arrays.toString(arr));

    // Delete element at position 3
    arr = deleteElement(arr, n, 3);
    n = arr.length;
    System.out.println("Array after deletion: " + Arrays.toString(arr));
}
```

Output:

```
Array after insertion: [1, 2, 10, 3, 4, 5]
Array after deletion: [1, 2, 10, 4, 5]
```

This approach ensures that elements are managed efficiently within the constraints of the array structure.

3.6 Array Traversal

Array traversal refers to the process of accessing each element of an array systematically, typically in a sequential order. Traversal is a fundamental operation that serves as a building block for more complex algorithms involving arrays. Understanding array traversal thoroughly is essential for performing operations such as searching, sorting, and manipulating array elements efficiently.

In Java, array traversal can be achieved using a variety of looping constructs such as for loops, while loops, and enhanced for loops (also known as foreach loops). We shall explore each method with detailed explanations and code examples.

```
// Example of traversing an array using a for loop
int[] numbers = {4, 8, 15, 16, 23, 42};
for (int i = 0; i < numbers.length; i++) {
    System.out.println(numbers[i]);
}
```

In the above code snippet, a for loop is used to iterate over the numbers array. The loop initializes an index variable i to 0 and increments it after each iteration until it reaches the length of the array. During each iteration, the current element is accessed using the index i, and its value is printed.

Traversing an array using a while loop follows a similar logic but uses a different syntax:

```
// Example of traversing an array using a while loop
int[] numbers = {4, 8, 15, 16, 23, 42};
int i = 0;
while (i < numbers.length) {
    System.out.println(numbers[i]);
    i++;
}
```

In this example, the index variable i is initialized before the loop starts and incremented within the loop after accessing each element of the array. The loop continues as long as i is less than the length of the array.

The enhanced for loop, or foreach loop, provides a more concise way to traverse arrays:

```
// Example of traversing an array using an enhanced for loop
int[] numbers = {4, 8, 15, 16, 23, 42};
for (int num : numbers) {
    System.out.println(num);
}
```

Here, the foreach loop iterates through each element in the numbers array directly, eliminating the need for an index variable. The variable num takes on the value of each element in the array one at a time.

Array traversal is not limited to one-dimensional arrays; multi-dimensional arrays can also be traversed. For a two-dimensional array, nested loops are typically used:

```
// Example of traversing a two-dimensional array
int[][] matrix = {
    {1, 2, 3},
    {4, 5, 6},
    {7, 8, 9}
};
for (int i = 0; i < matrix.length; i++) {
```

```
    for (int j = 0; j < matrix[i].length; j++) {
        System.out.println(matrix[i][j]);
    }
}
```

In this example, the outer loop traverses each row of the matrix, while the inner loop traverses each column within the current row. The variables i and j serve as indices to access elements of the two-dimensional array.

Traversal operations are often the substrate on which more complex array algorithms are built. For instance, to find the maximum value in an array, traversal is used to examine each element:

```
// Example of finding the maximum value in an array
int[] numbers = {4, 8, 15, 16, 23, 42};
int max = numbers[0];
for (int i = 1; i < numbers.length; i++) {
    if (numbers[i] > max) {
        max = numbers[i];
    }
}
System.out.println("The maximum value is: " + max);
```

Here, we initialize the variable max with the first element of the numbers array. As we traverse the array starting from the second element, we update max whenever we find an element larger than the current max.

Similarly, summing all elements of an array requires traversal:

```
// Example of summing the values in an array
int[] numbers = {4, 8, 15, 16, 23, 42};
int sum = 0;
for (int num : numbers) {
    sum += num;
}
System.out.println("The sum of the array elements is: " + sum);
```

In this code, the foreach loop iterates through each element in the numbers array, adding each value to sum. After the loop completes, sum contains the total of all array elements.

For various applications, it may be necessary to traverse an array in reverse order. This can be achieved using a for loop initialized to the last index of the array:

```
// Example of traversing an array in reverse order
int[] numbers = {4, 8, 15, 16, 23, 42};
for (int i = numbers.length - 1; i >= 0; i--) {
    System.out.println(numbers[i]);
}
```

Here, the loop initializes i to numbers.length - 1, which is the index of the last element. The loop decrements i after each iteration, accessing elements from the end to the beginning.

Understanding array traversal is crucial not only for direct array operations but also as a foundation for advanced algorithms in sorting, searching, and data manipulation. Proficiency in array traversal techniques ensures efficient and effective problem-solving capabilities in Java programming.

3.7 Array Searching Algorithms

Array searching algorithms are essential to efficiently locate elements in a collection. Here, we will discuss two primary types of array searching techniques: linear search and binary search. Understanding these algorithms is crucial for developing proficiency in data manipulation and retrieval tasks.

Linear Search

Linear search, often referred to as sequential search, is the simplest searching algorithm. It checks each element of the array sequentially until the desired element is found or the end of the array is reached. Below is the implementation of a linear search algorithm in Java:

```
public class LinearSearch {
    public static int linearSearch(int[] arr, int key) {
        for (int i = 0; i < arr.length; i++) {
            if (arr[i] == key) {
                return i; // Element found
            }
        }
        return -1; // Element not found
    }

    public static void main(String[] args) {
        int[] array = {2, 4, 0, 1, 9};
        int result = linearSearch(array, 1);
        System.out.println("Element found at index: " + result);
    }
}
```

```
Element found at index: 3
```

In the linearSearch function, we iterate over the entire array using a for-loop. Each element is compared with the key. If a match is found, the index of that element is returned. If no match is found after the loop terminates, the function returns -1.

Binary Search

Binary search is a more efficient algorithm compared to linear search but requires the array to be sorted. It follows a divide-and-conquer strategy to reduce the search space by half in each step. Binary search can be implemented iteratively or recursively.

Below is the implementation of an iterative binary search algorithm in Java:

```
public class BinarySearch {
    public static int binarySearch(int[] arr, int key) {
        int left = 0, right = arr.length - 1;
        while (left <= right) {
            int mid = left + (right - left) / 2;
            if (arr[mid] == key) {
                return mid; // Element found
            } else if (arr[mid] < key) {
                left = mid + 1; // Search right half
            } else {
                right = mid - 1; // Search left half
            }
        }
        return -1; // Element not found
    }

    public static void main(String[] args) {
        int[] array = {0, 1, 2, 4, 9};
        int result = binarySearch(array, 4);
        System.out.println("Element found at index: " + result);
    }
}
```

```
Element found at index: 3
```

In the binarySearch function, we maintain two pointers: left and right, which represent the bounds of the segment currently being searched. The midpoint mid is calculated, and the middle element is compared with the key. If the key matches the middle element, the index is returned. If the key is greater than the middle element, we adjust the left pointer to narrow the search to the right subarray. Conversely, if the key is less than the middle element, we adjust the right pointer to focus on the left subarray. This process continues iteratively until the key is found or the search space is exhausted.

Alternatively, binary search can be implemented recursively, as shown below:

```
public class RecursiveBinarySearch {
    public static int binarySearch(int[] arr, int left, int right, int key) {
        if (left <= right) {
            int mid = left + (right - left) / 2;
            if (arr[mid] == key) {
                return mid; // Element found
            } else if (arr[mid] < key) {
                return binarySearch(arr, mid + 1, right, key); // Search right half
            } else {
```

```
            return binarySearch(arr, left, mid - 1, key); // Search left half
        }
    }
    return -1; // Element not found
}

public static void main(String[] args) {
    int[] array = {0, 1, 2, 4, 9};
    int result = binarySearch(array, 0, array.length - 1, 4);
    System.out.println("Element found at index: " + result);
}
}
```

```
Element found at index: 3
```

In the recursive implementation, the base case checks whether the left pointer exceeds the right pointer. If the segment is valid (i.e., left is still not greater than right), the midpoint mid is calculated, and the same comparisons as in the iterative approach are made. Depending on the result of these comparisons, the function calls itself recursively, adjusting the search bounds accordingly.

Both linear and binary search algorithms play critical roles in different scenarios. Linear search is simpler and can be applied to unsorted data, making it more versatile despite its higher time complexity. Binary search, on the other hand, offers significant performance advantages on sorted data with its logarithmic time complexity. Understanding when and how to apply these algorithms is fundamental to creating efficient and effective solutions to array searching problems.

3.8 Array Sorting Algorithms

Sorting is an essential operation in computer science, as it organizes data into a specific order, thereby facilitating efficient searching and manipulation. Several sorting algorithms have been developed, each with its unique characteristics, time complexity, and suitability for different types of data and performance requirements. This section explores the fundamental algorithms used to sort arrays: Bubble Sort, Selection Sort, Insertion Sort, Merge Sort, Quick Sort, and Heap Sort.

Bubble Sort: This is a simple comparison-based algorithm where adjacent elements are compared and swapped if they are in the wrong order. Despite its simplicity, it is not efficient for large datasets due to its O(n^2) time complexity.

```
public void bubbleSort(int[] array) {
    int n = array.length;
```

```
    boolean swapped;
    for (int i = 0; i < n - 1; i++) {
        swapped = false;
        for (int j = 0; j < n - i - 1; j++) {
            if (array[j] > array[j + 1]) {
                // Swap array[j] and array[j + 1]
                int temp = array[j];
                array[j] = array[j + 1];
                array[j + 1] = temp;
                swapped = true;
            }
        }
        // If no two elements were swapped, the array is sorted
        if (!swapped) break;
    }
}
```

Selection Sort: This algorithm repeatedly picks the smallest element from the unsorted portion and moves it to the sorted portion. It also has an O(n^2) time complexity but performs well for small arrays or when the cost of swapping is low.

```
public void selectionSort(int[] array) {
    int n = array.length;
    for (int i = 0; i < n - 1; i++) {
        // Find the minimum element in the unsorted portion
        int minIdx = i;
        for (int j = i + 1; j < n; j++) {
            if (array[j] < minIdx) {
                minIdx = j;
            }
        }
        // Swap the found minimum element with the first element
        int temp = array[minIdx];
        array[minIdx] = array[i];
        array[i] = temp;
    }
}
```

Insertion Sort: This algorithm builds the sorted array one element at a time by repeatedly taking the next element and inserting it into its correct position. It is efficient for small datasets or partially sorted arrays, with a time complexity of O(n^2).

```
public void insertionSort(int[] array) {
    int n = array.length;
    for (int i = 1; i < n; ++i) {
        int key = array[i];
        int j = i - 1;

        // Move elements that are greater than key to one position ahead
        while (j >= 0 && array[j] > key) {
            array[j + 1] = array[j];
            j = j - 1;
        }
        array[j + 1] = key;
    }
}
```

Merge Sort: This is a divide-and-conquer algorithm that divides the array into halves, recursively sorts each half, and then merges the sorted halves. It has a time complexity of O($n \log n$), making it efficient for large datasets.

```
public void mergeSort(int[] array, int left, int right) {
    if (left < right) {
        int mid = (left + right) / 2;

        // Recursively sort each half
        mergeSort(array, left, mid);
        mergeSort(array, mid + 1, right);

        // Merge the sorted halves
        merge(array, left, mid, right);
    }
}

private void merge(int[] array, int left, int mid, int right) {
    // Find sizes of two subarrays
    int n1 = mid - left + 1;
    int n2 = right - mid;

    // Create temporary arrays
    int[] L = new int[n1];
    int[] R = new int[n2];

    // Copy data to temporary arrays
    for (int i = 0; i < n1; i++) {
        L[i] = array[left + i];
    }
    for (int j = 0; j < n2; j++) {
        R[j] = array[mid + 1 + j];
    }

    // Merge the temporary arrays

    // Initial indexes of the first and second subarrays
    int i = 0, j = 0;

    // Initial index of the merged subarray
    int k = left;
    while (i < n1 && j < n2) {
        if (L[i] <= R[j]) {
            array[k] = L[i];
            i++;
        } else {
            array[k] = R[j];
            j++;
        }
        k++;
    }

    // Copy remaining elements of L[] if any
    while (i < n1) {
        array[k] = L[i];
        i++;
        k++;
```

```
    }

    // Copy remaining elements of R[] if any
    while (j < n2) {
        array[k] = R[j];
        j++;
        k++;
    }
}
```

Quick Sort: Another divide-and-conquer algorithm, Quick Sort selects a pivot element and partitions the array into two sub-arrays, independently sorting each sub-array. Its average time complexity is O($n \log n$), but it can degrade to O(n^2) in the worst case.

```
public void quickSort(int[] array, int low, int high) {
    if (low < high) {
        int pi = partition(array, low, high);

        // Recursively sort the partitions
        quickSort(array, low, pi - 1);
        quickSort(array, pi + 1, high);
    }
}

private int partition(int[] array, int low, int high) {
    int pivot = array[high];
    int i = (low - 1); // Index of smaller element
    for (int j = low; j < high; j++) {
        // If the current element is smaller than or equal to pivot
        if (array[j] <= pivot) {
            i++;

            // Swap array[i] and array[j]
            int temp = array[i];
            array[i] = array[j];
            array[j] = temp;
        }
    }

    // Swap array[i + 1] and array[high] (or pivot)
    int temp = array[i + 1];
    array[i + 1] = array[high];
    array[high] = temp;

    return i + 1;
}
```

Heap Sort: This algorithm uses the heap data structure to sort elements. It involves building a max heap from the array and then repeatedly extracting the maximum element and rebuilding the heap. Heap Sort has a time complexity of O($n \log n$) and is efficient for large datasets.

```
public void heapSort(int[] array) {
    int n = array.length;
```

```
    // Build heap (rearrange array)
    for (int i = n / 2 - 1; i >= 0; i--) {
        heapify(array, n, i);
    }

    // One by one extract an element from heap
    for (int i = n - 1; i >= 0; i--) {
        // Move current root to end
        int temp = array[0];
        array[0] = array[i];
        array[i] = temp;

        // Call max heapify on the reduced heap
        heapify(array, i, 0);
    }
}

private void heapify(int[] array, int n, int i) {
    int largest = i; // Initialize the largest as root
    int left = 2 * i + 1; // Left child
    int right = 2 * i + 2; // Right child

    // If left child is larger than root
    if (left < n && array[left] > array[largest]) {
        largest = left;
    }

    // If right child is larger than largest so far
    if (right < n && array[right] > array[largest]) {
        largest = right;
    }

    // If largest is not root
    if (largest != i) {
        int swap = array[i];
        array[i] = array[largest];
        array[largest] = swap;

        // Recursively heapify the affected sub-tree
        heapify(array, n, largest);
    }
}
```

Understanding these sorting algorithms, their implementations, and their time complexities provides a strong foundation for tackling more complex data structures and algorithms. It is crucial to select the appropriate sorting algorithm based on the specific requirements and constraints of the task.

3.9 Introduction to Strings

Strings are fundamental data structures widely used in programming. A string is defined as a sequence of characters, typically used to represent textual data. In Java, strings are immutable objects, meaning that once a string object is created, its value cannot be changed. This immutability property provides several advantages, such as safety and efficiency, particularly in multithreaded environments where strings are often shared.

Strings in Java are instances of the String class, which is part of the java.lang package. The String class provides numerous methods for handling and manipulating textual data.

Creating a new string in Java can be done in several ways:

```
// Using string literals
String str1 = "Hello, World!";
// Using the new keyword
String str2 = new String("Hello, World!");
// From a character array
char[] charArray = {'H', 'e', 'l', 'l', 'o'};
String str3 = new String(charArray);
```

When using string literals, the Java Virtual Machine (JVM) maintains a pool of strings. This interning mechanism ensures that identical string literals reference the same object, enhancing memory efficiency.

One of the primary methods of the String class is the length() method, which returns the number of characters in the string:

```
String str = "Hello, World!";
int length = str.length(); // length will be 13
```

Since strings are immutable, all string manipulation methods in the String class return new string objects rather than modifying the existing string. Common string operations include concatenation, substring extraction, and character access.

String concatenation can be performed using the + operator or the concat() method:

```
String str1 = "Hello";
String str2 = "World";
String result1 = str1 + ", " + str2 + "!"; // result1 will be "Hello, World!"
String result2 = str1.concat(", ").concat(str2).concat("!"); // result2 will be "Hello,
     World!"
```

To extract a substring, the substring() method is used. This method returns a new string that is a substring of the existing string, defined by the start and end indices:

```
String str = "Hello, World!";
String substr = str.substring(7, 12); // substr will be "World"
```

Character access within a string is facilitated by the charAt() method, which retrieves the character at a specified index:

```
String str = "Hello, World!";
char character = str.charAt(1); // character will be 'e'
```

The String class also includes methods for case conversion, such as toUpperCase() and toLowerCase():

```
String str = "Hello, World!";
String upperStr = str.toUpperCase(); // upperStr will be "HELLO, WORLD!"
String lowerStr = str.toLowerCase(); // lowerStr will be "hello, world!"
```

Checking string equality is a common operation, which can be performed using the equals() and equalsIgnoreCase() methods. The equals() method compares the content of two strings for exact equality, while the equalsIgnoreCase() method disregards case differences:

```
String str1 = "Hello";
String str2 = "hello";
boolean isEqual = str1.equals(str2); // isEqual will be false
boolean isEqualIgnoreCase = str1.equalsIgnoreCase(str2); // isEqualIgnoreCase will be
    true
```

Strings can also be split into an array of substrings based on a specified delimiter using the split() method:

```
String str = "apple,banana,cherry";
String[] fruits = str.split(","); // fruits will be ["apple", "banana", "cherry"]
```

Further, the StringBuilder and StringBuffer classes are mutable alternatives to String, allowing for efficient string modifications. StringBuilder is unsynchronized and faster, suitable for single-threaded contexts, while StringBuffer is synchronized and thread-safe for use in multithreaded scenarios.

To illustrate the use of StringBuilder, consider the following example:

```
StringBuilder sb = new StringBuilder();
sb.append("Hello");
sb.append(", ");
sb.append("World!");
String result = sb.toString(); // result will be "Hello, World!"
```

The operations discussed provide a basis for manipulating and working with strings in Java. Developing an understanding of these methods is crucial for effective and efficient handling of textual data in your programs.

3.10 String Operations and Manipulations

String operations and manipulations are crucial in any programming language as they enable the manipulation of text data. Effective handling of strings can significantly optimize the performance of string-related tasks. This section explores various string operations such as concatenation, substring extraction, and modification. We will elaborate on Java methods provided by the String class and their applications.

Concatenation refers to the process of joining two or more strings end-to-end. Java provides two primary ways to concatenate strings: using the + operator and the concat() method.

```
String str1 = "Hello";
String str2 = "World";
String result1 = str1 + " " + str2;
String result2 = str1.concat(" ").concat(str2);
System.out.println(result1); // Output: Hello World
System.out.println(result2); // Output: Hello World
```

Both methods result in the string "Hello World", demonstrating that concatenation can be done efficiently using either approach. However, the + operator can be more intuitive and concise for simple concatenations.

Substring extraction involves obtaining a part of a string. The substring() method is primarily used for this purpose.

```
String str = "Data Structures";
String subStr1 = str.substring(5); // Output: "Structures"
String subStr2 = str.substring(5, 13); // Output: "Structur"
```

The first substring() call extracts the substring from index 5 to the end of the string, while the second call extracts characters from index 5 to 12 (index 13 is exclusive).

String modification involves replacing characters or substrings within a string. The replace() and replaceAll() methods facilitate this task.

```
String str = "abracadabra";
String modifiedStr1 = str.replace('a', 'o'); // Output: "obrocodobro"
String modifiedStr2 = str.replaceAll("bra", "zoo"); // Output: "azoozoodazoo"
```

In the above code, replace() replaces all occurrences of the character 'a' with 'o', and replaceAll() replaces the substring "bra" with "zoo".

Java also provides methods to change the case of characters within a string. The toUpperCase() and toLowerCase() methods are used to convert a string to uppercase and lowercase, respectively.

```
String str = "Programming";
String upperStr = str.toUpperCase(); // Output: "PROGRAMMING"
String lowerStr = str.toLowerCase(); // Output: "programming"
```

The Java String API includes several more methods for trimming and splitting strings. Trimming removes leading and trailing whitespace, accomplished with trim():

```
String str = " Leading and trailing spaces ";
String trimmedStr = str.trim(); // Output: "Leading and trailing spaces"
```

For splitting a string based on a delimiter, the split() method is used. It divides the string into an array of substrings.

```
String str = "apple,banana,cherry";
String[] fruits = str.split(",");
// Output: ["apple", "banana", "cherry"]
```

The split() method uses a regular expression as its argument to define the delimiter.

Another important aspect of string manipulations involves checking the presence of certain characters or substrings. The contains() method checks if a string contains a specific sequence of characters.

```
String str = "Data Structures";
boolean hasData = str.contains("Data"); // Output: true
boolean hasAlgo = str.contains("Algo"); // Output: false
```

Similarly, checking whether a string starts or ends with a particular substring is done using startsWith() and endsWith():

```
String str = "Introduction to Algorithms";
boolean startsWithIntro = str.startsWith("Introduction"); // Output: true
boolean endsWithData = str.endsWith("Data"); // Output: false
```

Advanced string manipulations might require more efficient string operations, for which the StringBuilder class can be particularly useful. Unlike the String class, StringBuilder is mutable, allowing modifications to strings without creating new objects. This can improve performance significantly when dealing with frequent string concatenations or modifications.

```
StringBuilder sb = new StringBuilder("Hello");
sb.append(" World");
sb.insert(5, ",");
sb.replace(6, 11, "Java");
sb.delete(5, 6);
String finalStr = sb.toString(); // Output: "Hello Java"
```

In the above example, append() adds a string to sb, insert() adds a comma at position 5, replace() replaces " World" with " Java", and delete() removes the comma.

Understanding the intricacies of these operations and manipulations allows handling strings efficiently, becoming critical in building robust Java applications.

3.11 String Searching Algorithms

String searching is a fundamental operation used extensively in text processing, data retrieval, and bioinformatics. This section covers a range of string searching algorithms, from the naive approach to more advanced, efficient algorithms like the Knuth-Morris-Pratt (KMP) and the Boyer-Moore algorithms. Understanding these algorithms provides a robust foundation for solving complex string-matching problems efficiently.

The simplest string searching algorithm is the Naive algorithm. This method checks for a substring presence by iterating through each possible position in the text and comparing the substring with a segment of text. Although this approach is straightforward, it can be inefficient for large inputs.

```
public static int naiveSearch(String text, String pattern) {
    int n = text.length();
    int m = pattern.length();

    for (int i = 0; i <= n - m; i++) {
        int j;
        for (j = 0; j < m; j++) {
            if (text.charAt(i + j) != pattern.charAt(j)) {
                break;
            }
        }
        if (j == m) {
            return i; // Pattern found at index i
        }
    }
    return -1; // Pattern not found
}
```

The Naive algorithm has a time complexity of $O(n \times m)$ in the worst case, where n is the length of the text, and m is the length of the pattern.

A more efficient approach is the Knuth-Morris-Pratt (KMP) algorithm, which preprocesses the pattern to create a longest prefix-suffix array (LPS). This preprocessing allows the algorithm to avoid redundant comparisons, achieving a linear time complexity.

Algorithm 4: KMP String Matching Algorithm

Data: String text, String pattern
Result: Index of the first occurrence of pattern in text, or -1 if pattern is not found

```
begin
    n ← text.length();
    m ← pattern.length();
    lps ← computeLPSArray(pattern);
    i ← 0;
    j ← 0;
    while i < n do
        if pattern[j] == text[i] then
            i++;
            j++;
        if j == m then
            return i - j;
            // Pattern found at index i-j
            j ← lps[j-1];
        else if i < n and pattern[j] != text[i] then
            if j != 0 then
                j ← lps[j-1];
            else
                i++;
    return -1;
    // Pattern not found
```

The LPS array is constructed in a preprocess step:

```
private static void computeLPSArray(String pattern, int lps[]) {
    int length = 0; // length of the previous longest prefix suffix
    int i = 1;
    lps[0] = 0; // lps[0] is always 0

    while (i < pattern.length()) {
        if (pattern.charAt(i) == pattern.charAt(length)) {
            length++;
            lps[i] = length;
            i++;
        } else {
            if (length != 0) {
                length = lps[length - 1];
            } else {
                lps[i] = length;
                i++;
```

```
            }
        }
    }
}
```

The Boyer-Moore algorithm, known for its efficient performance in practice, especially for large alphabets, makes use of two key heuristics: the bad character heuristic and the good suffix heuristic. It preprocesses the pattern to allow potentially larger jumps along the text, reducing the number of comparisons.

The bad character heuristic involves building a table that maps each character in the pattern to its rightmost position. If a mismatch occurs, the pattern is aligned with the next occurrence of the mismatching character in the pattern.

```
private static int[] buildBadCharacterTable(String pattern) {
    final int ALPHABET_SIZE = 256; // Assuming extended ASCII character set
    int[] badChar = new int[ALPHABET_SIZE];

    for (int i = 0; i < badChar.length; i++) {
        badChar[i] = -1;
    }

    for (int i = 0; i < pattern.length(); i++) {
        badChar[pattern.charAt(i)] = i;
    }

    return badChar;
}
```

```
public static int boyerMooreSearch(String text, String pattern) {
    int[] badChar = buildBadCharacterTable(pattern);
    int m = pattern.length();
    int n = text.length();
    int s = 0; // s is the shift of the pattern with respect to text

    while (s <= (n - m)) {
        int j = m - 1;

        while (j >= 0 && pattern.charAt(j) == text.charAt(s + j)) {
            j--;
        }

        if (j < 0) {
            return s; // Pattern found at index s
            if (s + m < n) {
                s += m - badChar[text.charAt(s + m)];
            } else {
                s += 1;
            }
        } else {
            s += Math.max(1, j - badChar[text.charAt(s + j)]);
        }
    }

    return -1; // Pattern not found
```

```
}
```

Both KMP and Boyer-Moore algorithm optimizations are highly recommended over the Naive approach, especially for large datasets. Users are encouraged to select the algorithm based on the specific characteristics of their input data and computational constraints.

3.12 String Comparison and Palindromes

String comparison is a fundamental operation that allows us to determine the lexicographical order of strings or establish whether two strings are identical. The primary mechanism for string comparison in Java is the compareTo() method from the String class, which conforms to the contract specified in the Comparable interface. Understanding how to effectively compare strings and identify palindromic sequences is critical for numerous applications in computer science, including sorting algorithms and text processing.

The compareTo() method compares two strings lexicographically, based on the Unicode value of each character. The following Java code snippet demonstrates the use of compareTo():

```
public class StringComparison {
    public static void main(String[] args) {
        String str1 = "apple";
        String str2 = "banana";
        int result = str1.compareTo(str2);

        System.out.println("Comparison Result: " + result);

        if (result < 0) {
            System.out.println(str1 + " comes before " + str2);
        } else if (result > 0) {
            System.out.println(str1 + " comes after " + str2);
        } else {
            System.out.println(str1 + " is equal to " + str2);
        }
    }
}
```

In this example, the compareTo() method returns a negative integer, zero, or a positive integer if str1 is lexicographically less than, equal to, or greater than str2, respectively. The comparison is case-sensitive; hence, "apple" is treated as different from "Apple". Additionally, using the compareToIgnoreCase() method can be beneficial when the case should be ignored:

```
public class StringComparison {
```

```
    public static void main(String[] args) {
        String str1 = "Apple";
        String str2 = "apple";
        int result = str1.compareToIgnoreCase(str2);

        System.out.println("Comparison Result (Ignore Case): " + result);

        if (result < 0) {
            System.out.println(str1 + " comes before " + str2);
        } else if (result > 0) {
            System.out.println(str1 + " comes after " + str2);
        } else {
            System.out.println(str1 + " is equal to " + str2);
        }
    }
}
```

The equality of two strings can be checked using the equals() and equalsIgnoreCase() methods, which provide a straightforward way to verify string identity. Below is a code example:

```
public class StringEquality {
    public static void main(String[] args) {
        String str1 = "Hello";
        String str2 = "hello";

        boolean areEqual = str1.equals(str2);
        boolean areEqualIgnoreCase = str1.equalsIgnoreCase(str2);

        System.out.println("Equals (case-sensitive): " + areEqual);
        System.out.println("Equals (ignore case): " + areEqualIgnoreCase);
    }
}
```

A palindrome is a string that reads the same forwards and backwards, ignoring spaces, punctuation, and capitalization. To verify if a string is a palindrome, one efficient approach is to compare characters from the beginning and the end moving towards the center. Here's an algorithmic approach to determine if a string is a palindrome:

Algorithm 5: Palindrome Check

Data: A string s

Result: A boolean value indicating if s is a palindrome

```
begin
    left := 0;
    right := length(s) − 1;
    while left < right do
        if s[left] is not equal to s[right] then
            return false;
        left := left + 1;
        right := right - 1;
    return true;
```

Here's the corresponding Java implementation for the above algorithm:

```
public class PalindromeChecker {
    public static boolean isPalindrome(String s) {
        int left = 0;
        int right = s.length() - 1;

        while (left < right) {
            if (s.charAt(left) != s.charAt(right)) {
                return false;
            }
            left++;
            right--;
        }

        return true;
    }

    public static void main(String[] args) {
        String candidate = "racecar";
        boolean result = isPalindrome(candidate);
        System.out.println("Is the string \"" + candidate + "\" a palindrome? " +
                result);
    }
}
```

It is important to handle string normalization when checking for palindromes, particularly in real-world scenarios where strings may contain spaces, punctuation, or capitalization differences. Normalizing a string involves removing non-alphanumeric characters and converting it to lower case. The following Java code snippet demonstrates string normalization before palindrome checking:

```
public class PalindromeChecker {
    public static boolean isPalindrome(String s) {
        String normalized = s.replaceAll("[^A-Za-z0-9]", "").toLowerCase();
        int left = 0;
        int right = normalized.length() - 1;
```

```
        while (left < right) {
            if (normalized.charAt(left) != normalized.charAt(right)) {
                return false;
            }
            left++;
            right--;
        }

        return true;
    }

    public static void main(String[] args) {
        String candidate = "A man, a plan, a canal: Panama";
        boolean result = isPalindrome(candidate);
        System.out.println("Is the string \"" + candidate + "\" a palindrome? " +
              result);
    }
}
```

The replaceAll() method utilizes a regular expression to remove all non-alphanumeric characters, and toLowerCase() ensures that the comparison is case-insensitive. This approach allows us to accurately assess complex strings for palindromic properties.

String comparison and palindrome validation are essential techniques in string manipulation. Utilizing Java's built-in methods and understanding algorithmic principles enables efficient implementation of these operations.

Chapter 4

Linked Lists

This chapter provides a comprehensive introduction to linked lists as a fundamental data structure. It covers various types of linked lists, including singly, doubly, and circular linked lists. The chapter details essential operations such as insertion, deletion, traversal, and searching within linked lists. Additionally, it explores advanced topics like reversing linked lists and detecting and removing loops. Practical applications and implementation details in Java are provided to ensure a solid understanding of linked lists and their real-world uses.

4.1 Introduction to Linked Lists

A linked list is a linear data structure where elements, called nodes, are not stored in contiguous memory locations. Instead, each node contains two components: the data and a reference (or link) to the next node in the sequence. This structure contrasts with arrays, where elements are indexed and stored in adjacent memory locations.

Linked lists come in various forms, with three primary types discussed in this chapter: singly linked lists, doubly linked lists, and circular linked lists. Each type has unique characteristics and use cases, making them suitable for different scenarios in programming and algorithm design.

Singly linked lists (SLL) are the most basic type, where each node contains a single link pointing to the next node. The initial node is called the head, and the final node in a singly linked list points to null, indicating the end of the list.

```
class Node {
    int data;
    Node next;

    public Node(int data) {
        this.data = data;
        this.next = null;
    }
}
```

Doubly linked lists (DLL) enhance the structure by adding an additional link to each node, pointing to the previous node. This bidirectional referencing allows traversal in both forward and backward directions, providing greater flexibility and certain performance benefits for specific operations.

```
class Node {
    int data;
    Node next;
    Node prev;

    public Node(int data) {
        this.data = data;
        this.next = null;
        this.prev = null;
    }
}
```

Circular linked lists (CLL) modify the design such that the last node's link points back to the first node, forming a circular structure. This type can be implemented as either singly or doubly circular linked lists and is particularly useful for applications requiring a cyclic iteration over elements.

```
class Node {
    int data;
    Node next;

    public Node(int data) {
        this.data = data;
        this.next = null;
    }
}
```

Advantages of Linked Lists:

- Dynamic Size: Linked lists can grow and shrink at runtime by allocating and deallocating memory, unlike arrays where the size must be defined at compile time.

- Ease of Insertions/Deletions: Unlike arrays where elements need to be shifted, linked lists allow for O(1) insertion and deletion if the node reference is known.

Disadvantages of Linked Lists:

- Memory Overhead: Each node requires extra memory for storing references.
- Lack of Direct Access: To access an element, the list must be traversed sequentially from the head, resulting in O(n) access time.

Applications of Linked Lists:

- Implementation of Data Structures: Linked lists are foundational for implementing advanced data structures such as stacks, queues, and graphs.
- Graph Adjacency Representations: Particularly in adjacency lists for representing sparse graphs.
- Memory Management: Useful in dynamic memory allocation algorithms and garbage collection schemes.

Understanding the underlying principles of linked lists is essential. They offer insights into more complex data structures and algorithms, serving as building blocks for higher-level system design. Recognizing their characteristics and knowing when to apply each type is crucial in optimizing performance and resource management in software development.

The following sections will delve deeper into the implementation details and operations associated with singly, doubly, and circular linked lists. This will provide a comprehensive foundation for leveraging linked lists effectively in various programming challenges.

4.2 Singly Linked Lists

A singly linked list is a collection of elements called nodes, where each node contains data and a reference or pointer to the next node in the sequence. This structure forms a linear sequence, allowing traversal from the head node to the last node. The primary components of a singly linked list are:

- Node: The basic building block of the linked list containing data and a reference to the next node.
- Head: A reference to the first node in the linked list.
- Null (or None): A reference indicating the end of the list by pointing to nothing.

Structure of a Singly Linked List Node:

Each node in a singly linked list typically contains two fields: the data field and the next field. The data field stores the node's data, and the next field stores a reference to the next node.

Here is the structure of a simplified node class in Java:

```
public class Node {
    int data;
    Node next;

    // Constructor
    public Node(int data) {
        this.data = data;
        this.next = null;
    }
}
```

In the above example, Node is the class representing individual nodes in the linked list. The data variable stores the value of the node, and the next variable points to the next node in the list.

Creating a Singly Linked List:

To create a singly linked list, we need to maintain a reference to the head node and manage the list's size.

```
public class SinglyLinkedList {
    private Node head;
    private int size;

    // Constructor initializes the head to null and size to 0
    public SinglyLinkedList() {
        this.head = null;
        this.size = 0;
    }

    // Method to get the size of the linked list
    public int getSize() {
        return size;
    }

    // Method to check if the linked list is empty
    public boolean isEmpty() {
        return head == null;
    }
}
```

In this class, we have a private head that points to the first node in the list and a private size variable to keep track of the list length. The getSize() and isEmpty() methods provide utility functions for basic operations.

Insertion in a Singly Linked List:

Insertion operations in a singly linked list can be categorized based on where the new node is added. The common insertions are at the beginning, at the end, and at a specific position in the list.

Insertion at the Beginning

To insert a node at the beginning of the linked list, we need to update the new node's next reference to point to the current head and then update the head to the new node.

```
public void insertAtBeginning(int data) {
    Node newNode = new Node(data);
    newNode.next = head;
    head = newNode;
    size++;
}
```

Insertion at the End

To insert a node at the end of the linked list, we need to traverse the list to find the last node and then update the last node's next reference to the new node.

```
public void insertAtEnd(int data) {
    Node newNode = new Node(data);
    if (head == null) {
        head = newNode;
    } else {
        Node temp = head;
        while (temp.next != null) {
            temp = temp.next;
        }
        temp.next = newNode;
    }
    size++;
}
```

Insertion at a Specific Position

To insert a node at a specific position, we need to traverse to the node just before the desired position, update the new node's next reference to point to the next node, and update the previous node's next reference to the new node.

```
public void insertAtPosition(int data, int position) {
    if (position < 0 || position > size) {
        throw new IndexOutOfBoundsException("Invalid position");
    }
    Node newNode = new Node(data);
```

```
    if (position == 0) {
        newNode.next = head;
        head = newNode;
    } else {
        Node temp = head;
        for (int i = 0; i < position - 1; i++) {
            temp = temp.next;
        }
        newNode.next = temp.next;
        temp.next = newNode;
    }
    size++;
}
```

Traversal of a Singly Linked List:

To traverse a singly linked list, we start from the head and follow the next references until we reach the end of the list (where the next reference is null).

```
public void traverse() {
    Node temp = head;
    while (temp != null) {
        System.out.print(temp.data + " ");
        temp = temp.next;
    }
    System.out.println();
}
```

Searching in a Singly Linked List:

Searching for an element involves traversing through the list and comparing the data field of each node with the target value.

```
public boolean search(int target) {
    Node temp = head;
    while (temp != null) {
        if (temp.data == target) {
            return true;
        }
        temp = temp.next;
    }
    return false;
}
```

The traversal continues until the target element is found or the end of the list is reached.

Deletion in a Singly Linked List:

Deletion operations involve removing nodes from the linked list. Similar to insertion, deletion can be performed at the beginning, at the end, or at a specific position.

Deletion at the Beginning

To delete a node from the beginning, we update the head to the next node in the list:

```
public void deleteAtBeginning() {
    if (head != null) {
        head = head.next;
        size--;
    }
}
```

Deletion at the End

To delete the last node, we traverse the list to find the second-last node (the node before the last node) and set its next reference to null:

```
public void deleteAtEnd() {
    if (head == null) {
        return;
    }
    if (head.next == null) {
        head = null;
    } else {
        Node temp = head;
        while (temp.next.next != null) {
            temp = temp.next;
        }
        temp.next = null;
    }
    size--;
}
```

Deletion at a Specific Position

Deleting a node at a specific position involves updating the next reference of the previous node to skip the node to be deleted:

```
public void deleteAtPosition(int position) {
    if (position < 0 || position >= size) {
        throw new IndexOutOfBoundsException("Invalid position");
    }
    if (position == 0) {
        head = head.next;
    } else {
        Node temp = head;
        for (int i = 0; i < position - 1; i++) {
            temp = temp.next;
        }
        temp.next = temp.next.next;
    }
    size--;
}
```

Understanding the basic operations and structure of singly linked lists is fundamental for advanced data structure and algorithm design. The seamless handling of dynamic memory through link manipulation allows the implementation of flexible data management strategies.

4.3 Doubly Linked Lists

A doubly linked list is a type of linked list in which each node maintains two pointers: one to the next node and another to the previous node. This bi-directional reference offers greater flexibility in terms of traversal. This capability makes certain operations more efficient and simplifies others.

Structure of a Doubly Linked List Node

The fundamental building block of a doubly linked list is a node that contains three fields: the data, a reference to the next node, and a reference to the previous node. Below is the Java class definition for a doubly linked list node:

```
class Node {
    int data;
    Node next;
    Node prev;

    Node(int data) {
        this.data = data;
        this.next = null;
        this.prev = null;
    }
}
```

Insertion in a Doubly Linked List

Insertion operations can be performed at different positions within the list: at the beginning, at the end, or at a specific index. The presence of a prev pointer simplifies certain operations compared to a singly linked list.

1. **Insertion at the beginning**

To insert a node at the beginning of a doubly linked list:

1. Create the new node.
2. Set the next pointer of the new node to the current head.
3. If the list is not empty, set the prev pointer of the current head to the new node.
4. Update the head to be the new node.

```
class DoublyLinkedList {
    Node head;

    public void insertAtBeginning(int data) {
```

```
        Node newNode = new Node(data);
        newNode.next = head;
        if (head != null) {
            head.prev = newNode;
        }
        head = newNode;
    }
}
```

2. **Insertion at the end**

To insert a node at the end of the list:

1. Create the new node.
2. Traverse to the last node of the list.
3. Set the next pointer of the last node to the new node.
4. Set the prev pointer of the new node to the last node.

```
public void insertAtEnd(int data) {
    Node newNode = new Node(data);
    if (head == null) {
        head = newNode;
        return;
    }
    Node temp = head;
    while (temp.next != null) {
        temp = temp.next;
    }
    temp.next = newNode;
    newNode.prev = temp;
}
```

3. **Insertion at a specific position**

To insert a node at a specified position:

1. Create the new node.
2. Traverse to the node after which the new node is to be inserted.
3. Adjust the next and prev pointers to insert the new node at the desired position.

```
public void insertAtPosition(int data, int position) {
    if (position < 1) return;

    Node newNode = new Node(data);
    if (position == 1) {
        newNode.next = head;
        if (head != null) {
            head.prev = newNode;
```

```
        }
        head = newNode;
        return;
    }

    Node temp = head;
    for (int i = 1; i < position - 1 && temp != null; i++) {
        temp = temp.next;
    }

    if (temp == null) return;

    newNode.next = temp.next;
    if (temp.next != null) {
        temp.next.prev = newNode;
    }
    temp.next = newNode;
    newNode.prev = temp;
}
```

Deletion in a Doubly Linked List

Deletion in a doubly linked list also benefits from the bi-directional links. Nodes can be deleted from the beginning, end, or a specific position.

1. **Deletion at the beginning**

To delete a node from the beginning:

1. Check if the list is empty.
2. Update the head to the next node.
3. If the updated head is not null, set its prev pointer to null.

```
public void deleteAtBeginning() {
    if (head == null) return;

    head = head.next;
    if (head != null) {
        head.prev = null;
    }
}
```

2. **Deletion at the end**

To delete a node from the end:

1. Check if the list is empty.
2. Traverse to the last node.
3. Update the next pointer of the second-last node to null.

```
public void deleteAtEnd() {
    if (head == null) return;

    if (head.next == null) {
        head = null;
        return;
    }

    Node temp = head;
    while (temp.next != null) {
        temp = temp.next;
    }
    temp.prev.next = null;
}
```

3. **Deletion at a specific position**

To delete a node from a specified position:

1. Check if the list is empty.
2. Traverse to the node to be deleted.
3. Adjust the next and prev pointers to remove the node from the list.

```
public void deleteAtPosition(int position) {
    if (position < 1 || head == null) return;

    if (position == 1) {
        head = head.next;
        if (head != null) {
            head.prev = null;
        }
        return;
    }

    Node temp = head;
    for (int i = 1; i < position && temp != null; i++) {
        temp = temp.next;
    }

    if (temp == null) return;

    if (temp.next != null) {
        temp.next.prev = temp.prev;
    }
    if (temp.prev != null) {
        temp.prev.next = temp.next;
    }
}
```

Traversal in a Doubly Linked List

Traversing a doubly linked list can be done in two ways: forward traversal and backward traversal. Forward traversal iterates from the head to the tail, while backward traversal iterates from the tail to the head.

1. **Forward Traversal**

```
public void traverseForward() {
    Node temp = head;
    while (temp != null) {
        System.out.print(temp.data + " ");
        temp = temp.next;
    }
    System.out.println();
}
```

2. **Backward Traversal**

```
public void traverseBackward() {
    if (head == null) return;

    Node temp = head;
    while (temp.next != null) {
        temp = temp.next;
    }
    while (temp != null) {
        System.out.print(temp.data + " ");
        temp = temp.prev;
    }
    System.out.println();
}
```

Understanding the two-way linkage of nodes in a doubly linked list engrosses essential concepts of linked list manipulation, paving the way for more complex data structures and operations. This fosters a comprehensive grasp of data structure fundamentals.

4.4 Circular Linked Lists

A circular linked list is a variation of a linked list where the last node points back to the first node instead of null. This forms a circular structure, allowing the list to be traversed starting from any node, without ever reaching the end of the list since it loops indefinitely. This feature can be particularly useful in applications that require a continuous, cyclic traversal of elements, such as round-robin scheduling, buffering systems, and certain scenarios in multiplayer board games.

The primary types of circular linked lists are:

- Singly Circular Linked List
- Doubly Circular Linked List

Singly Circular Linked List

In a singly circular linked list, each node contains a data part and a reference to the next node in the sequence. The last node holds a reference to the first node, creating the circular link.

```
public class Node {
    int data;
    Node next;

    public Node(int data) {
        this.data = data;
        this.next = null;
    }
}
```

An instance of Node class can be created and linked to form a circular linked list by ensuring the next reference of the last node points back to the head of the list:

```
public class CircularLinkedList {
    private Node head = null;
    private Node tail = null;

    // Adding a node at the end
    public void add(int data) {
        Node newNode = new Node(data);
        if (head == null) {
            head = newNode;
            tail = newNode;
            newNode.next = head;
        } else {
            tail.next = newNode;
            tail = newNode;
            tail.next = head;
        }
    }
}
```

Doubly Circular Linked List

The doubly circular linked list extends the singly circular linked list by adding a previous reference in each node that points to the previous node in the sequence. This allows traversal in both directions, making it more versatile.

```
public class DoublyNode {
    int data;
    DoublyNode next;
    DoublyNode previous;

    public DoublyNode(int data) {
        this.data = data;
        this.next = null;
        this.previous = null;
    }
}
```

In a doubly circular linked list, both the next reference of the last node points to the head and the previous reference of the head points to the last node:

```
public class DoublyCircularLinkedList {
    private DoublyNode head = null;
    private DoublyNode tail = null;

    // Adding a node at the end
    public void add(int data) {
        DoublyNode newNode = new DoublyNode(data);
        if (head == null) {
            head = newNode;
            tail = newNode;
            head.next = head;
            head.previous = head;
        } else {
            tail.next = newNode;
            newNode.previous = tail;
            tail = newNode;
            tail.next = head;
            head.previous = tail;
        }
    }
}
```

Basic Operations in Circular Linked Lists

Insertion Insertion in a circular linked list can be performed at the beginning, end, or at a specific position within the list. Given the circular nature, special care must be taken to adjust the next (and previous in doubly circular linked lists) references accordingly.

```
public void addFirst(int data) {
    Node newNode = new Node(data);
    if (head == null) {
        head = newNode;
        tail = newNode;
        newNode.next = head;
    } else {
        newNode.next = head;
        head = newNode;
        tail.next = head;
    }
}
```

Deletion Deletion of a node also requires managing circular references. Removing a node in a circular linked list involves adjusting the next (and previous) references of the surrounding nodes.

```
public void delete(int key) {
    if (head == null) {
        return;
    }

    Node current = head;
    Node previous = null;
```

```
    boolean found = false;

    do {
        if (current.data == key) {
            found = true;
            break;
        }
        previous = current;
        current = current.next;
    } while (current != head);

    if (found) {
        if (current == head && head == tail) {
            head = null;
            tail = null;
        } else if (current == head) {
            head = head.next;
            tail.next = head;
        } else if (current == tail) {
            tail = previous;
            tail.next = head;
        } else {
            previous.next = current.next;
        }
    }
}
```

Traversal Traversing a circular linked list requires starting from a given node and proceeding through the list, resetting the traversal when the start node is reached again. This ensures every node is visited exactly once.

```
public void traverse() {
    if (head == null) {
        return;
    }

    Node current = head;
    do {
        System.out.print(current.data + " ");
        current = current.next;
    } while (current != head);

    System.out.println();
}
```

Searching Searching in a circular linked list involves checking each node's data until the required element is found or the traversal completes a full cycle.

```
public boolean search(int key) {
    if (head == null) {
        return false;
    }

    Node current = head;
    do {
        if (current.data == key) {
```

```
            return true;
        }
        current = current.next;
    } while (current != head);

    return false;
}
```

Circular linked lists offer unique properties, making them suitable for applications requiring constant traversal without explicit terminating conditions. Understanding their construction and manipulation facilitates solving many practical problems effectively.

4.5 Linked List Operations: Insertion

Insertion operations in linked lists can be classified into three primary types: insertion at the beginning, insertion at the end, and insertion at a specific position within the list. Each method has distinct implementation details and time complexities. It is imperative to handle edge cases, such as an empty list, with precision to maintain the integrity of the data structure.

Insertion at the Beginning:

Inserting a node at the beginning of a linked list involves modifying the head pointer to point to the new node, and subsequently linking the new node to the former head of the list. The following Java code snippet illustrates the procedure for a singly linked list:

```
class Node {
    int data;
    Node next;

    Node(int data) {
        this.data = data;
        this.next = null;
    }
}

class SinglyLinkedList {
    Node head;

    public void insertAtBeginning(int data) {
        Node newNode = new Node(data);
        newNode.next = head;
        head = newNode;
    }
}
```

When the above method, insertAtBeginning, is invoked, the newly created node becomes the first node in the list. Time complexity for this operation is $O(1)$, as it involves a constant number of steps, irrespective of the list size.

Insertion at the End:

Insertion at the end of the linked list requires traversing the list to find the last node and then appending the new node after it. This operation has a time complexity of $O(n)$, where n is the number of nodes in the list. Below is the Java implementation for this type of insertion:

```
class SinglyLinkedList {
    Node head;

    public void insertAtEnd(int data) {
        Node newNode = new Node(data);
        if (head == null) {
            head = newNode;
        } else {
            Node current = head;
            while (current.next != null) {
                current = current.next;
            }
            current.next = newNode;
        }
    }
}
```

The above method checks whether the list is empty. If it is, the new node is set as the head. Otherwise, the method iterates through the list until reaching the last node and assigns its next pointer to the new node.

Insertion at a Specific Position:

Inserting a node at a specific position within the list requires locating the node currently at that position or the node immediately preceding it. The details of this operation's time complexity again reach $O(n)$ in the worst case, as it necessitates traversal to the desired location. The following example demonstrates the insertion at a given position in the list:

```
public void insertAtPosition(int data, int position) {
    Node newNode = new Node(data);
    if (position == 0) {
        newNode.next = head;
        head = newNode;
    } else {
        Node current = head;
        for (int i = 0; i < position - 1 && current != null; i++) {
            current = current.next;
        }
        if (current != null) {
            newNode.next = current.next;
            current.next = newNode;
```

```
        }
    }
}
```

The insertAtPosition method handles both inserting at the head (position 0) and inserting at any other valid position. Within the method, a for-loop advances the current pointer to the position immediately preceding the target insertion point, ensuring the new node correctly links into the list without disrupting its structure.

Handling Special Cases:

Special cases such as inserting into an empty list, inserting at the head, and inserting at the end are managed within these methods. It's crucial to handle null references appropriately to avoid runtime errors.

Considering a doubly linked list, similar insertion methods apply, with the addition of handling the prev pointers:

```
class DoublyNode {
    int data;
    DoublyNode next;
    DoublyNode prev;

    DoublyNode(int data) {
        this.data = data;
        this.next = null;
        this.prev = null;
    }
}

class DoublyLinkedList {
    DoublyNode head;

    public void insertAtBeginning(int data) {
        DoublyNode newNode = new DoublyNode(data);
        if (head != null) {
            head.prev = newNode;
        }
        newNode.next = head;
        head = newNode;
    }

    public void insertAtEnd(int data) {
        DoublyNode newNode = new DoublyNode(data);
        if (head == null) {
            head = newNode;
        } else {
            DoublyNode current = head;
            while (current.next != null) {
                current = current.next;
            }
            current.next = newNode;
            newNode.prev = current;
        }
    }

    public void insertAtPosition(int data, int position) {
```

```
        DoublyNode newNode = new DoublyNode(data);
        if (position == 0) {
            if (head != null) {
                head.prev = newNode;
            }
            newNode.next = head;
            head = newNode;
        } else {
            DoublyNode current = head;
            for (int i = 0; i < position - 1 && current != null; i++) {
                current = current.next;
            }
            if (current != null) {
                newNode.next = current.next;
                if (current.next != null) {
                    current.next.prev = newNode;
                }
                current.next = newNode;
                newNode.prev = current;
            }
        }
    }
}
```

These snippets highlight the addition of prev pointer adjustments, ensuring that the doubly linked list maintains bidirectional links between nodes during insertion operations.

Accurate implementation of insertion operations lays the foundation for manipulating more complex linked list structures, further solidifying the understanding of dynamic data structures within computer science.

4.6 Linked List Operations: Deletion

Deletion in a linked list involves removing an element from the data structure while ensuring the integrity of the remaining elements. Depending on the specific type of linked list (singly, doubly, or circular), the deletion operation may require different approaches and considerations.

To efficiently perform a deletion operation, it is crucial to first understand the structure of the linked list and the position of the element to be deleted. The deletion operation can be classified based on the position of the node to be removed, such as:

- Deleting the first node (head node)
- Deleting the last node (tail node)
- Deleting a node at a specific position

- Deleting a node with a specific value

Let us explore each of these scenarios in the context of a singly linked list. The principles can be similarly extended to other types of linked lists, with additional pointers management in the case of doubly and circular linked lists.

Deletion in Singly Linked List

Deleting the First Node

To delete the first node in a singly linked list, update the head reference to point to the second node of the list. The original head node's memory can then be deallocated if required. Here is the implementation in Java:

```
public void deleteFirst() {
    if (head == null) {
        return; // List is empty
    }
    head = head.next;
}
```

After executing this operation, the second node becomes the new head of the list.

Deleting the Last Node

Deleting the last node requires iterating through the list to find the second-to-last node, then updating its next reference to null. The last node's memory can then be deallocated if necessary. The following code demonstrates this process:

```
public void deleteLast() {
    if (head == null) {
        return; // List is empty
    }
    if (head.next == null) {
        head = null; // List has only one element
        return;
    }
    Node current = head;
    while (current.next.next != null) {
        current = current.next;
    }
    current.next = null;
}
```

This ensures that the second-to-last node becomes the new tail of the list.

Deleting a Node at a Specific Position

To delete a node at a specific position, traverse the list to locate the node immediately before the desired position. Update its next reference to bypass the node being deleted. Here is the corresponding Java implementation:

```
public void deleteAtPosition(int position) {
    if (head == null) {
        return; // List is empty
    }
    if (position == 0) {
        head = head.next; // Remove head node
        return;
    }
    Node current = head;
    for (int i = 0; current != null && i < position - 1; i++) {
        current = current.next;
    }
    if (current == null || current.next == null) {
        return; // Position is out of range
    }
    current.next = current.next.next;
}
```

This implementation ensures that the linked list remains intact after the specified node is removed.

Deleting a Node with a Specific Value

To delete a node with a specific value, iterate through the list to find the node. Once located, update the next reference of the preceding node to bypass the node with the matched value. The following Java method achieves this:

```
public void deleteByValue(int value) {
    if (head == null) {
        return; // List is empty
    }
    if (head.data == value) {
        head = head.next; // Remove head node
        return;
    }
    Node current = head;
    while (current.next != null && current.next.data != value) {
        current = current.next;
    }
    if (current.next == null) {
        return; // Value not found
    }
    current.next = current.next.next;
}
```

This method effectively removes the first occurrence of the specified value.

Considerations for Doubly and Circular Linked Lists

In a doubly linked list, deletion operations involve additional pointer adjustments due to the presence of both next and prev pointers. For instance, when removing a node, the prev pointer of the succeeding node must be updated to point to the preceding node, and vice versa.

In a circular linked list, special care must be taken to handle the circular reference properly, especially when deleting the head or tail nodes.

These deletion operations maintain the structural integrity of the linked list, ensuring efficient data management and traversal capabilities. Mastery of deletion processes is essential for leveraging linked lists in real-world applications such as memory management, navigable data structures, and dynamic storage handling.

4.7 Traversing a Linked List

Traversal in a linked list refers to the process of visiting each node exactly once, typically for the purpose of performing some operation such as printing the elements, calculating the sum, or searching for a particular value. Traversal is a fundamental operation that can be efficiently performed in all types of linked lists, with slight variations depending on the specific type of linked list.

To traverse a singly linked list, we start at the head node and follow each next pointer until we reach the end of the list. Here is a Java code snippet to demonstrate traversal in a singly linked list:

```
class Node {
    int data;
    Node next;

    Node(int data) {
        this.data = data;
        this.next = null;
    }
}

public class SinglyLinkedList {
    Node head;

    // Method to traverse and print the linked list
    public void traverse() {
        Node current = head;
        while (current != null) {
            System.out.print(current.data + " ");
```

```
            current = current.next;
        }
    }

    // Main method to test the traversal
    public static void main(String[] args) {
        SinglyLinkedList list = new SinglyLinkedList();

        // Adding elements to the singly linked list
        list.head = new Node(1);
        list.head.next = new Node(2);
        list.head.next.next = new Node(3);

        list.traverse(); // Output: 1 2 3
    }
}
```

This code defines a simple Node class and a SinglyLinkedList class with a traverse method. The traversal starts at the head node and prints each data value until current.next is null.

When dealing with doubly linked lists, traversal can be performed in both forward and backward directions. Here is an example of traversing a doubly linked list in forward direction:

```
class DoublyNode {
    int data;
    DoublyNode next;
    DoublyNode prev;

    DoublyNode(int data) {
        this.data = data;
        this.next = null;
        this.prev = null;
    }
}

public class DoublyLinkedList {
    DoublyNode head;

    // Method to traverse and print the doubly linked list in forward direction
    public void traverseForward() {
        DoublyNode current = head;
        while (current != null) {
            System.out.print(current.data + " ");
            current = current.next;
        }
    }

    // Method to traverse and print the doubly linked list in backward direction
    public void traverseBackward() {
        DoublyNode current = head;
        while (current != null && current.next != null) {
            current = current.next;
        }

        // Traverse backward from the last node
        while (current != null) {
            System.out.print(current.data + " ");
```

```
            current = current.prev;
        }
    }

    // Main method to test both traversals
    public static void main(String[] args) {
        DoublyLinkedList list = new DoublyLinkedList();

        // Adding elements to the doubly linked list
        list.head = new DoublyNode(1);
        list.head.next = new DoublyNode(2);
        list.head.next.prev = list.head;
        list.head.next.next = new DoublyNode(3);
        list.head.next.next.prev = list.head.next;

        list.traverseForward(); // Output: 1 2 3
        System.out.println();
        list.traverseBackward(); // Output: 3 2 1
    }
}
```

This code incorporates both forward and backward traversal methods in a doubly linked list. The traverseForward method is similar to the singly linked list traversal, while the traverseBackward method first moves to the last node and then traverses backward using the prev pointer.

Traversal in circular linked lists is slightly more complex due to the circular nature, but the principle remains the same. Each node points to the next, and the last node points back to the first node. Here is a traversal method for a circular singly linked list:

```
class CircularNode {
    int data;
    CircularNode next;

    CircularNode(int data) {
        this.data = data;
        this.next = null;
    }
}

public class CircularLinkedList {
    CircularNode head;

    // Method to traverse and print the circular linked list
    public void traverse() {
        if (head == null) {
            return;
        }

        CircularNode current = head;
        do {
            System.out.print(current.data + " ");
            current = current.next;
        } while (current != head);
    }

    // Main method to test the traversal
```

```
    public static void main(String[] args) {
        CircularLinkedList list = new CircularLinkedList();

        // Adding elements to the circular singly linked list
        list.head = new CircularNode(1);
        CircularNode second = new CircularNode(2);
        CircularNode third = new CircularNode(3);

        list.head.next = second;
        second.next = third;
        third.next = list.head;

        list.traverse(); // Output: 1 2 3
    }
}
```

In this example, the traverse method utilizes a do-while loop to ensure that the head node is processed and continues to traverse until it encounters the head node again.

The underlying concept of traversal remains consistent across different types of linked lists: starting from a designated node (typically the head or tail) and following pointers while performing a specific operation at each node. The difference lies in how pointers and nodes are managed, whether it is a simple next pointer in singly linked lists, next and prev pointers in doubly linked lists, or the circular references in circular linked lists.

4.8 Searching in a Linked List

Searching in a linked list involves traversing the list to locate a node that contains a specific value. The search operation can be performed on any type of linked list—singly linked, doubly linked, or circular linked lists. The basic concept remains the same, though the implementation details may vary slightly.

To search for an element x in a linked list, we must start from the head of the list and compare the value of each node with x. If a node with the value x is found, the search is successful. If the end of the list is reached without finding x, the search is unsuccessful.

Consider the following Java method to search for an element in a singly linked list:

```
public class Node {
    int data;
    Node next;

    public Node(int data) {
```

```
        this.data = data;
        this.next = null;
    }
}

public class SinglyLinkedList {
    Node head;

    public SinglyLinkedList() {
        this.head = null;
    }

    // Method to search for an element in the linked list
    public boolean search(int x) {
        Node current = head; // Initialize current node to head
        while (current != null) {
            if (current.data == x) {
                return true; // Element found
            }
            current = current.next; // Move to next node
        }
        return false; // Element not found
    }
}
```

In this method, search(int x), we start at the head of the singly linked list and traverse each node. For each node, we check if the node's data matches the value x. If a match is found, the method returns true, indicating a successful search. If we reach the end of the list (i.e., the current node becomes null) without finding the value, the method returns false.

The time complexity of searching in a linked list is $O(n)$, where n is the number of nodes in the list. This is because, in the worst case, we may need to traverse all n nodes to determine whether the element is present.

In a doubly linked list, the search operation is fundamentally the same, albeit with the nodes having an additional pointer to their previous nodes. Here is an analogous search method for a doubly linked list:

```
public class DoublyNode {
    int data;
    DoublyNode next;
    DoublyNode prev;

    public DoublyNode(int data) {
        this.data = data;
        this.next = null;
        this.prev = null;
    }
}

public class DoublyLinkedList {
    DoublyNode head;
```

```
    public DoublyLinkedList() {
        this.head = null;
    }

    // Method to search for an element in the doubly linked list
    public boolean search(int x) {
        DoublyNode current = head; // Initialize current node to head
        while (current != null) {
            if (current.data == x) {
                return true; // Element found
            }
            current = current.next; // Move to next node
        }
        return false; // Element not found
    }
}
```

Searching in a circular linked list also follows a similar pattern. However, special care must be taken to avoid infinite loops. In a circular linked list, the last node points back to the head. Thus, a termination condition is necessary to break the loop and prevent an infinite traversal.

Here is an example of a search operation in a circular singly linked list:

```
public class CircularNode {
    int data;
    CircularNode next;

    public CircularNode(int data) {
        this.data = data;
        this.next = null;
    }
}

public class CircularLinkedList {
    CircularNode head;

    public CircularLinkedList() {
        this.head = null;
    }

    // Method to search for an element in the circular linked list
    public boolean search(int x) {
        if (head == null) {
            return false; // List is empty
        }

        CircularNode current = head;
        do {
            if (current.data == x) {
                return true; // Element found
            }
            current = current.next;
        } while (current != head);

        return false; // Element not found
    }
}
```

In this example, the do-while loop ensures that traversal continues until we either find the element or return to the head node. The loop is essential for the circular linked list to prevent an endless loop.

Implementations of search operations retain the same logical structure across different types of linked lists. However, it's crucial to consider the unique properties of each list—be it the nature of node pointers in doubly linked lists or the circular references in circular lists.

The correctness of these implementations relies on systematically checking each node. Exact equality checking (using '==' for primitives or 'equals' for objects) ensures that the search process is both accurate and efficient.

Linking search operations with real-world applications, such as finding a specific entry (like a contact in an address book or an item in a shopping list), can illustrate their practical utility.

4.9 Reversing a Linked List

Reversing a linked list involves altering the direction of the pointers, such that the last node becomes the head and the previous heads follow in reverse order. This operation is essential for various applications where the data needs to be processed in reverse order or when transforming data structures for specific computational needs. Several algorithms can achieve this, including iterative and recursive methods.

Iterative Method

The iterative method employs a loop to traverse the linked list and reverse the links one by one. Below is the Java implementation of the iterative method:

```
public class LinkedList {
    Node head;

    class Node {
        int data;
        Node next;

        Node(int d) {
            data = d;
            next = null;
        }
    }

    // Function to reverse the linked list iteratively
    public void reverseIterative() {
        Node prev = null;
```

```
        Node current = head;
        Node next = null;

        while (current != null) {
            // Store next node
            next = current.next;
            // Reverse current node's pointer
            current.next = prev;
            // Move pointers one position ahead
            prev = current;
            current = next;
        }
        head = prev;
    }
}
```

In this implementation:

- prev is a pointer to the previous node and is initialized to null.
- current is a pointer initialized to the head of the list.
- next temporarily stores the next node before changing the link.

The loop continues until all pointers are reversed, eventually setting the head to the previous node, thus completing the reversal.

Recursive Method

The recursive method, although slightly complex to grasp initially, provides a cleaner and more elegant approach by breaking down the problem into smaller subproblems. The recursion effectively reverses the rest of the list and then adjusts the pointers accordingly. Below is the Java implementation for reversing a linked list recursively:

```
public class LinkedList {
    Node head;

    class Node {
        int data;
        Node next;

        Node(int d) {
            data = d;
            next = null;
        }
    }

    // Function to reverse the linked list recursively
    public Node reverseRecursive(Node head) {
        // Base case: if head is empty or has reached the list end
        if (head == null || head.next == null) {
            return head;
        }

        // Reverse the rest of the list
```

```
        Node newHead = reverseRecursive(head.next);
        // Adjust the pointers
        head.next.next = head;
        head.next = null;

        // Return the new head of the reversed list
        return newHead;
    }
}
```

In this implementation:

- The base case checks if the list is empty or has a single node.
- It recursively reverses the rest of the list, returning the new head.
- It adjusts the pointers such that the next node's next pointer refers back to the current node, and the current node's next pointer is set to null.
- The final returned value is the new head of the reversed list.

To call this method, you would typically have a wrapper function:

```
public void reverse() {
    head = reverseRecursive(head);
}
```

Analysis and Comparison

Both methods achieve the reversal of a singly linked list, yet their performance and use cases differ.

- **Iterative Method:** This approach uses a constant amount of extra space, $O(1)$, making it highly efficient in terms of space complexity. The time complexity is $O(n)$, where n is the number of nodes in the linked list.
- **Recursive Method:** While elegant, the recursive approach utilizes the call stack to store intermediate states. This results in $O(n)$ space complexity due to the depth of the recursion. The time complexity remains $O(n)$.

Choosing between these two methods depends on the specific requirements of the problem at hand. For scenarios prioritizing minimal space usage, the iterative approach is preferable. However, if code readability and simplicity are paramount, especially with manageable list sizes, the recursive method is an excellent choice.

In Java, managing stack overflow risks is crucial when utilizing recursion on extremely large lists. Thus, understanding the application's constraints and the characteristics of the data being processed is essential when making this decision.

4.10 Detecting and Removing Loops in a Linked List

The presence of loops within a linked list structure can lead to unintended behavior and inefficiency in data processing. Identifying and eliminating these loops is crucial for maintaining the integrity of your linked list operations. This section will cover effective methods to detect and remove loops in a linked list using algorithms and Java code implementations.

Loop Detection: Detecting a loop in a linked list can be efficiently executed using Floyd's Cycle-Finding Algorithm, also known as the tortoise and hare algorithm. This algorithm employs two pointers, slow and fast, which traverse the list at different speeds. The slow pointer moves one step at a time, while the fast pointer moves two steps at a time. If there is a loop, the fast pointer will eventually meet the slow pointer within the loop, confirming its presence.

The Java implementation of Floyd's Cycle-Finding Algorithm is as follows:

```
public class LinkedList {

    class Node {
        int data;
        Node next;
        Node(int data) {
            this.data = data;
            this.next = null;
        }
    }

    Node head;

    // Function to detect a loop in a linked list using Floyd's Cycle-Finding Algorithm
    public boolean hasLoop() {
        Node slow = head;
        Node fast = head;

        while (slow != null && fast != null && fast.next != null) {
            slow = slow.next;
            fast = fast.next.next;

            if (slow == fast) {
```

```
            return true; // Loop detected
        }
    }
    return false; // No loop detected
  }
}
```

Loop Removal: Once a loop is detected, the next task is to remove it. First, detect the loop using the procedure described above. When the slow and fast pointers meet, keep one pointer at the meeting point and move the other pointer to the head of the linked list. Move both pointers one step at a time; they will meet at the beginning of the loop.

To remove the loop, maintain a pointer to the node before the meeting point and set its next reference to null.

The following Java code demonstrates the full process:

```
public class LinkedList {

    class Node {
        int data;
        Node next;
        Node(int data) {
            this.data = data;
            this.next = null;
        }
    }

    Node head;

    // Function to detect and remove a loop in a linked list
    public void detectAndRemoveLoop() {
        Node slow = head;
        Node fast = head;

        // Detecting the loop using Floyd's Cycle-Finding Algorithm
        while (slow != null && fast != null && fast.next != null) {
            slow = slow.next;
            fast = fast.next.next;

            if (slow == fast) {
                removeLoop(slow);
                return;
            }
        }
    }

    // Function to remove the detected loop
    private void removeLoop(Node loopNode) {
        Node ptr1 = head;
        Node ptr2 = loopNode;

        // Finding the starting point of the loop
        while (ptr1 != ptr2) {
            ptr1 = ptr1.next;
            ptr2 = ptr2.next;
        }
```

```
            // Finding the last node in the loop and setting its next to null
            Node prev = null;
            while (ptr2.next != ptr1) {
                prev = ptr2;
                ptr2 = ptr2.next;
            }
            prev.next = null;
        }
}
```

In this implementation, the removeLoop function is tasked with severing the loop. By locating the loop's starting point and then advancing the ptr2 pointer until it reaches the last node in the loop, we can set the next reference to null, effectively removing the loop. This method ensures that the linked list is restored to its intended structure without any cyclic references, thereby preventing infinite traversals during subsequent operations.

Recognizing and addressing loops in a linked list is vital for maintaining accurate and efficient data manipulation. Employing Floyd's Cycle-Finding Algorithm for detection and a precise node traversal for loop removal are effective strategies to ensure linked list reliability.

4.11 Intersection and Merging of Linked Lists

Determining the intersection and merging of linked lists are key operations that are frequently encountered in various applications. Understanding these concepts requires us to delve into the specifics of linked list structures and address how their elements interrelate in memory.

The task of finding the intersection of two linked lists involves identifying a common node that appears in both lists. To efficiently determine if two linked lists intersect, we can use algorithmic approaches leveraging length calculations and pointer manipulations.

Algorithm 6: Finding the Intersection of Two Linked Lists

```
Input: Two singly linked lists: list1 and list2
Output: A common node if an intersection exists, otherwise
        None
len1 ← length(list1);
len2 ← length(list2);
diff ← abs(len1 - len2);
if len1 > len2 then
    advance head of list1 by diff nodes;
end
else
    advance head of list2 by diff nodes;
end
while list1 ≠ NULL and list2 ≠ NULL do
    if list1 == list2 then
        return list1
    end
    list1 ← list1->next;
    list2 ← list2->next;
end
return None;
```

The above algorithm first measures the lengths of list1 and list2. By advancing the head of the longer list by the difference in lengths, the two lists align such that they can be compared node by node. This alignment allows for an efficient determination of whether and where an intersection occurs.

```
public class LinkedListIntersection {
    static class ListNode {
        int data;
        ListNode next;
        ListNode(int x) {
            data = x;
            next = null;
        }
    }

    public static ListNode getIntersectionNode(ListNode headA, ListNode headB) {
        int lenA = getLength(headA);
        int lenB = getLength(headB);
        int diff = Math.abs(lenA - lenB);

        if (lenA > lenB) {
            headA = advanceListByK(headA, diff);
        } else {
            headB = advanceListByK(headB, diff);
        }
```

```
        while (headA != null && headB != null) {
            if (headA == headB) {
                return headA;
            }
            headA = headA.next;
            headB = headB.next;
        }
        return null;
    }

    private static int getLength(ListNode head) {
        int length = 0;
        while (head != null) {
            length++;
            head = head.next;
        }
        return length;
    }

    private static ListNode advanceListByK(ListNode head, int k) {
        while (k > 0 && head != null) {
            head = head.next;
            k--;
        }
        return head;
    }
}
```

The above Java implementation exemplifies the algorithm for finding the intersection of two singly linked lists. The helper methods getLength and advanceListByK facilitate operations by measuring list lengths and aligning their respective pointers.

Merging two linked lists is a slightly different operation, aiming to create a single linked list that combines elements from both lists while maintaining order based on specific criteria. A common approach is merging two sorted linked lists, which requires iterating through both lists and creating a new sorted list.

Algorithm 7: Merging Two Sorted Linked Lists

Input: Two sorted singly linked lists: list1 and list2
Output: A merged sorted linked list

```
dummyNode ← new ListNode(0);
currentNode ← dummyNode;
while list1 ≠ NULL and list2 ≠ NULL do
    if list1->data ≤ list2->data then
        currentNode->next ← list1;
        list1 ← list1->next;
    end
    else
        currentNode->next ← list2;
        list2 ← list2->next;
    end
    currentNode ← currentNode->next;
end
if list1 ≠ NULL then
    currentNode->next ← list1;
end
if list2 ≠ NULL then
    currentNode->next ← list2;
end
return dummyNode->next;
```

This algorithm initializes a dummyNode to assist with building the merged list and maintains a pointer currentNode to track the last node in the new list. Comparisons are made between nodes of list1 and list2 to append the smaller node to currentNode->next. Upon exhaustively traversing either list, remaining nodes from the non-exhausted list are appended directly.

```
public class LinkedListMerge {
    static class ListNode {
        int data;
        ListNode next;
        ListNode(int x) {
            data = x;
            next = null;
        }
    }

    public static ListNode mergeTwoLists(ListNode list1, ListNode list2) {
        ListNode dummyNode = new ListNode(0);
        ListNode currentNode = dummyNode;

        while (list1 != null && list2 != null) {
            if (list1.data <= list2.data) {
```

```
                currentNode.next = list1;
                list1 = list1.next;
            } else {
                currentNode.next = list2;
                list2 = list2.next;
            }
            currentNode = currentNode.next;
        }

        if (list1 != null) {
            currentNode.next = list1;
        }

        if (list2 != null) {
            currentNode.next = list2;
        }

        return dummyNode.next;
    }
}
```

This Java code demonstrates the process of merging two sorted linked lists. It efficiently maintains the order by consistently selecting the smaller current node values from list1 and list2 and linking them via currentNode. The dummy node helps manage the head of the new linked list.

Implementing these operations is paramount for mastering linked list manipulations, yielding deeper insights into more complex data structures and algorithms.

Chapter 5

Stacks and Queues

This chapter explores stacks and queues, key linear data structures in computer science. It introduces the concepts and operations of stacks, including push, pop, and peek, and covers their implementations using arrays and linked lists. The chapter then transitions to queues, detailing operations such as enqueue, dequeue, front, and rear, and their implementations. It also examines circular queues, double-ended queues (deques), and priority queues. Practical applications and real-world examples are provided to illustrate the utility and implementation of these structures.

5.1 Introduction to Stacks

Stacks are a fundamental data structure in computer science, characterized by the Last-In-First-Out (LIFO) principle. This means the last element added (pushed) to the stack will be the first element removed (popped). This behavior models real-world scenarios where access is restricted to the most recently added item, such as a stack of plates or a stack of books.

Stack is essentially a collection of elements with two main operations:

- **Push**: Add an element to the top of the stack.
- **Pop**: Remove the element from the top of the stack.

Additionally, stacks often provide the following auxiliary operations:

- **Peek**: Retrieve, but do not remove, the element at the top of the stack.
- **isEmpty**: Check if the stack is empty.
- **isFull**: Check if the stack has reached its capacity (applicable in cases with fixed stack sizes).

The Stack data structure is widely used due to its simplicity and efficiency. It plays an important role in various algorithms, especially in problems where the most recent data needs to be processed first.

Mathematical Definition of a Stack: Given a stack S with the following initial state,

$$S = \{a_1, a_2, a_3, \ldots, a_n\}$$

a push operation adds an element to the top of S,

$$\text{push}(x) \rightarrow S = \{a_1, a_2, a_3, \ldots, a_n, x\}$$

while a pop operation removes the element from the top,

$$\text{pop}() \rightarrow S = \{a_1, a_2, a_3, \ldots, a_{n-1}\}$$

The stack can be implemented using various underlying data structures such as arrays and linked lists, each offering distinct advantages.

Stack Operations:

1. Push Operation:

```
public void push(int element) {
    if (isFull()) {
        throw new StackOverflowException("Stack is full");
    }
    stackArray[++top] = element;
}
```

In this implementation, stackArray is the array holding the stack elements and top indicates the current index of the top element in the stack. Before adding a new element, we increment the top index to point to the next available position and place the new element there. If the stack is full, an exception is thrown.

2. Pop Operation:

```
public int pop() {
    if (isEmpty()) {
        throw new StackUnderflowException("Stack is empty");
    }
    return stackArray[top--];
}
```

Here, the pop method retrieves and removes the current top element from the stack. This is achieved by returning the element at the top index and then decrementing the top index to reflect the updated stack state. If the stack is empty, an exception is thrown.

3. Peek Operation:

```
public int peek() {
    if (isEmpty()) {
        throw new StackUnderflowException("Stack is empty");
    }
    return stackArray[top];
}
```

The peek method simply returns the element at the top index without modifying the stack, providing an efficient way to examine the top element.

Various practical applications utilize stacks due to their LIFO nature. For instance, stacks are instrumental in:

- Reversing data: Since elements are accessed in reverse order of their insertion, stacks are useful for reversing collections of elements.
- Parsing expressions: Stack structures enable efficient parsing and evaluation of expressions, managing operators and operands in computational tasks.
- Backtracking algorithms: Stacks store states to enable efficient backtracking in algorithms like depth-first search, puzzle solvers, and pathfinding routines.
- Memory management: Stacks are used in managing function calls, local variables, and control flow in programming environments through call stacks.

The next section will delve into the detailed operations of the stack, specifically focusing on the push, pop, and peek methods, along with their respective implementations and performance considerations. The particular emphasis will be on both array-based and linked-list-based implementations to highlight their differences and use-cases.

5.2 Stack Operations: Push, Pop, Peek

The stack data structure primarily supports three fundamental operations: *push*, *pop*, and *peek*, each of which will be examined in detail. These operations are essential for working with stacks and are integral to understanding stack behavior.

Push Operation

The push operation adds an element to the top of the stack. This operation must manage several conditions to ensure proper stack functionality, such as checking if the stack is full when using an array-based implementation.

To illustrate the push operation in a stack implemented using an array in Java, consider the following code:

```
class Stack {
    private int top;
    private int maxSize;
    private int[] stackArray;

    public Stack(int size) {
        maxSize = size;
        stackArray = new int[maxSize];
        top = -1;
    }

    public void push(int value) {
        if (isFull()) {
            System.out.println("Stack is full. Cannot push element: " + value);
            return;
        }
        stackArray[++top] = value;
    }

    public boolean isFull() {
        return (top == maxSize - 1);
    }
}
```

In the above code, the push method first checks if the stack is full using the isFull method. If the stack is not full, it increments the top variable and then places the new value in the array at the position indicated by top.

The push operation can also be represented using a linked list. Here is an example:

```
class Node {
    int data;
    Node next;
}
```

```
class Stack {
    private Node top;

    public Stack() {
        top = null;
    }

    public void push(int value) {
        Node newNode = new Node();
        newNode.data = value;
        newNode.next = top;
        top = newNode;
    }
}
```

In the linked list implementation, a new node is created and assigned the value to be pushed. This new node is then linked to the top node of the stack, and the top pointer is updated to this new node.

Pop Operation

The pop operation removes the element from the top of the stack and returns it. This operation must ensure the stack is not empty before attempting to remove an element, to avoid underflow errors.

Here is the pop operation for an array-based stack:

```
public int pop() {
    if (isEmpty()) {
        System.out.println("Stack is empty. Cannot pop an element.");
        return -1;
    }
    return stackArray[top--];
}

public boolean isEmpty() {
    return (top == -1);
}
```

The pop method checks if the stack is empty. If the stack is not empty, it accesses the top element, decrements the top pointer, and returns the element.

For a linked list implementation, the pop method is shown below:

```
public int pop() {
    if (top == null) {
        System.out.println("Stack is empty. Cannot pop an element.");
        return -1;
    }
    int value = top.data;
    top = top.next;
    return value;
}
```

In this linked list implementation, the pop method first checks if the stack is empty by verifying if top is null. If it is not, the data from the top node is stored, the top pointer is updated to the next node, and the stored data is returned.

Peek Operation

The peek operation returns the element on the top of the stack without removing it. This operation is useful for obtaining the current top element without modifying the stack's structure.

For an array-based implementation, the peek operation can be defined as follows:

```
public int peek() {
    if (isEmpty()) {
        System.out.println("Stack is empty. Cannot perform peek operation.");
        return -1;
    }
    return stackArray[top];
}
```

In this code, the peek method checks if the stack is empty. If not, it returns the element at the top position of the stack array.

In a linked list implementation, the peek method looks like this:

```
public int peek() {
    if (top == null) {
        System.out.println("Stack is empty. Cannot perform peek operation.");
        return -1;
    }
    return top.data;
}
```

Here, the peek method verifies that the top is not null. If it is not, it returns the data from the top node without altering the stack structure.

These fundamental operations (push, pop, and peek) form the core interactions with a stack. Proper understanding and implementation of these operations are critical for utilizing stack-based structures in various computational problems and applications.

5.3 Implementing Stacks using Arrays

The array-based implementation of a stack is one of the fundamental representations of this data structure. In this method, an array is utilized to store the elements of the stack, and a variable known as the top is employed to track the position of the last added element. Initially, the top variable is set to -1 to indicate that the stack is empty. Each element insertion (i.e., push operation) increases the top value, while each element removal (i.e., pop operation) decreases it.

Class Definition and Data Members

To create an array-based stack in Java, we define a class ArrayStack. The class contains an array to hold the stack elements and an integer top to keep track of the stack's current position.

```
public class ArrayStack {
    private int[] stack;
    private int top;
    private int capacity;

    public ArrayStack(int size) {
        stack = new int[size];
        capacity = size;
        top = -1;
    }
}
```

In this class:

- stack is the array used to store stack elements.
- top is the index of the top element in the stack.
- capacity is the maximum number of elements the stack can hold.

Push Operation

The push operation adds a new element to the top of the stack. Before adding an element, it checks if the stack is full. If the stack is full, an error message is displayed; otherwise, the element is added, and the top is incremented.

```
public void push(int x) {
    if (isFull()) {
        System.out.println("Stack Overflow");
        return;
    }
    stack[++top] = x;
    System.out.println("Pushed " + x);
}
```

The key steps in the push method are:

- Check if the stack is full using isFull method.

- Increment the top index.
- Insert the element at the top index of the array.
- Display a message indicating the element pushed onto the stack.

Pop Operation

The pop operation removes the top element of the stack. It first checks if the stack is empty. If the stack is empty, an error message is displayed; otherwise, the element at the top is removed, and the top is decremented.

```
public int pop() {
    if (isEmpty()) {
        System.out.println("Stack Underflow");
        return -1;
    }
    return stack[top--];
}
```

The steps in the pop method are:

- Check if the stack is empty using isEmpty method.
- Retrieve the element at the top index.
- Decrement the top index.
- Return the retrieved element.

Peek Operation

The peek operation returns the top element of the stack without removing it. Like the pop operation, it checks if the stack is empty before proceeding.

```
public int peek() {
    if (isEmpty()) {
        System.out.println("Stack is empty");
        return -1;
    }
    return stack[top];
}
```

In the peek method:

- Check if the stack is empty using isEmpty method.

- Retrieve and return the element at the top index.

Utility Methods

The isFull and isEmpty methods help in checking the status of the stack.

```
public boolean isFull() {
    return top == capacity - 1;
}

public boolean isEmpty() {
    return top == -1;
}
```

isFull returns true if the top is equal to capacity - 1, indicating that no more elements can be added. isEmpty returns true if top is -1, indicating that the stack is empty.

Additional Methods for Debugging and Display

A method for displaying all elements in the stack can be useful for debugging and verification purposes. This method prints each element from the bottom to the top of the stack.

```
public void display() {
    if (isEmpty()) {
        System.out.println("Stack is empty");
        return;
    }
    for (int i = 0; i <= top; i++) {
        System.out.print(stack[i] + " ");
    }
    System.out.println();
}
```

- Check if the stack is empty. If it is, print a message and return.
- Iterate from the bottom (0) to the top of the stack, printing each element.

Using an array to implement a stack is straightforward and efficient when the maximum size of the stack is known in advance. Arrays provide O(1) time complexity for accessing elements. However they require a fixed size, which can lead to inefficiency if the array is not fully utilized, or to a stack overflow if the number of elements exceeds the array's capacity.

5.4 Implementing Stacks using Linked Lists

In this section, we will examine how stacks can be implemented using linked lists. Unlike array-based implementations, linked lists offer dynamic memory allocation, which means the stack's size can grow or shrink as needed without predefining a maximum capacity.

A linked list is a data structure composed of nodes, where each node contains two fields: data and a reference to the next node in the sequence. In a singly linked list, each node points to the next, forming a chain-like structure. This property makes linked lists an ideal choice for implementing a stack, as it allows constant-time insertion and deletion at one end of the sequence.

Node Class Definition: The first step in implementing a stack using linked lists is to define a node structure. In Java, this can be achieved by creating a Node class. Each node will have a data field to store the stack element and a next field to reference the next node in the stack.

```
class Node {
    int data;
    Node next;

    Node(int data) {
        this.data = data;
        this.next = null;
    }
}
```

Stack Class Definition: Next, we define the Stack class. This class will contain a reference to the top node of the linked list, representing the top of the stack. We will implement the primary stack operations: push, pop, and peek, along with utility methods such as isEmpty and size.

```
class Stack {
    private Node top;
    private int size;

    Stack() {
        this.top = null;
        this.size = 0;
    }

    public void push(int data) {
        Node newNode = new Node(data);
        newNode.next = top;
        top = newNode;
        size++;
    }

    public int pop() {
```

```
        if (isEmpty()) {
            throw new RuntimeException("Stack underflow");
        }
        int poppedData = top.data;
        top = top.next;
        size--;
        return poppedData;
    }

    public int peek() {
        if (isEmpty()) {
            throw new RuntimeException("Stack is empty");
        }
        return top.data;
    }

    public boolean isEmpty() {
        return top == null;
    }

    public int size() {
        return size;
    }
}
```

Push Operation: The push method adds a new element to the top of the stack. We create a new Node object, set its next reference to the current top node, and update the top to this new node. This operation has a time complexity of $O(1)$ because it involves a constant amount of work regardless of the stack's current size.

Pop Operation: The pop method removes and returns the element from the top of the stack. If the stack is empty, it throws an exception. Otherwise, it retrieves the data from the top node, updates the top reference to the next node in the stack, and decrements the stack size by one. This operation also has a time complexity of $O(1)$.

Peek Operation: The peek method returns the element at the top of the stack without removing it. If the stack is empty, it throws an exception. This method provides a constant-time $O(1)$ way to inspect the top element.

Utility Methods: The isEmpty method checks if the stack is empty by verifying whether the top is null. The size method returns the number of elements in the stack. Both methods are useful for managing stack operations and ensuring its proper use.

Example Usage: The following example demonstrates how to use the stack implementation:

```
public class Main {
    public static void main(String[] args) {
        Stack stack = new Stack();
        stack.push(10);
```

```
        stack.push(20);
        stack.push(30);

        System.out.println("Top element is: " + stack.peek()); // Output: 30
        System.out.println("Stack size is: " + stack.size()); // Output: 3

        System.out.println("Popped element: " + stack.pop()); // Output: 30
        System.out.println("Top element after pop: " + stack.peek()); // Output: 20
    }
}
```

```
Top element is: 30
Stack size is: 3
Popped element: 30
Top element after pop: 20
```

This example demonstrates the fundamental operations of a stack implemented using linked lists, showcasing their efficiency and ease of use. By leveraging the dynamic nature of linked lists, this implementation provides a robust and flexible alternative to array-based stacks. The constant-time complexity of the primary stack operations ensures optimal performance for various applications.

5.5 Applications of Stacks: Balanced Parentheses

One of the critical applications of stacks is in the validation of balanced parentheses in expressions. The concept of balanced parentheses extends beyond just the simple round brackets (()) and can also encompass other types of brackets, such as square brackets ([]) and curly braces ({}). Properly balanced parentheses are crucial in programming languages, compiler design, and various parsing tasks.

To determine if an expression has balanced parentheses, an algorithm can use a stack data structure effectively. The stack, due to its Last-In-First-Out (LIFO) nature, aligns seamlessly with the requirements for validating nested structures.

Algorithm 8: Check for Balanced Parentheses

Input: A string expr containing parentheses characters
Output: Boolean indicating whether the parentheses are balanced

```
Function CheckBalancedParentheses(expr):
    stack ← new Stack
    for each character ch in expr do
        if ch is in {'(', '[', '{'} then
            stack.push(ch)
        else if ch is in {')', ']', '}'} then
            if stack.isEmpty() then
                return false
            top ← stack.pop()
            if (ch = ')' ∧ top ≠ '(') then
                return false
    return stack.isEmpty()
```

This algorithm processes the input string in a linear scan, applying the following rules:

- When an opening bracket is encountered, it is pushed onto the stack.
- When a closing bracket is encountered, the algorithm checks the top element of the stack. If the top element is a matching opening bracket, it is popped from the stack.
- If a closing bracket is found while the stack is empty, or the top element of the stack does not match the encountered closing bracket, the parentheses are deemed unbalanced.
- After processing all characters, if the stack is empty, the parentheses are balanced.

Below is an example implementation of the algorithm in Java:

```java
import java.util.Stack;

public class BalancedParentheses {

    public static boolean checkBalancedParentheses(String expr) {
        Stack<Character> stack = new Stack<>();

        for (char ch : expr.toCharArray()) {
```

```
            if (ch == '(' || ch == '[' || ch == '{') {
                stack.push(ch);
            } else if (ch == ')' || ch == ']' || ch == '}') {
                if (stack.isEmpty()) {
                    return false;
                }
                char top = stack.pop();
                if ((ch == ')' && top != '(') ||
                    (ch == ']' && top != '[') ||
                    (ch == '}' && top != '{')) {
                    return false;
                }
            }
        }
        return stack.isEmpty();
    }

    public static void main(String[] args) {
        String expression = "{[()]}";
        System.out.println("Expression: " + expression);
        boolean result = checkBalancedParentheses(expression);
        System.out.println("Balanced: " + result);
    }
}
```

Executing the main method with the given example string:

```
Expression: {[()]}
Balanced: true
```

This output confirms that the given expression has balanced parentheses. The pivotal logic of the algorithm resides in effectively managing the stack to reflect the nested structure of the parentheses.

To dissect the behavior of the algorithm:

- **Push Operations:** When encountering an opening bracket, it incrementally builds a context that expects corresponding closing brackets.
- **Pop Operations:** When encountering a closing bracket, it assures that the most recent unmatched opening bracket matches this closing bracket, thereby maintaining structural integrity.
- **Checking Emptiness:** Ensures that no unmatched opening brackets remain post-evaluation.

The complexity of the algorithm is $O(n)$ in time, where n is the length of the expression, and $O(n)$ in space in the worst case, which occurs when all characters in the expression are opening brackets.

By leveraging stacks, this approach efficiently guarantees the well-formedness of parentheses in expressions, serving as a fundamental technique in syntax parsing and validation tasks often required in more extensive computational systems. This ensures expressions are correctly formatted, preventing potential syntax errors that could lead to undefined or erroneous behavior in subsequent processing stages.

5.6 Applications of Stacks: Infix, Prefix, and Postfix Expressions

In computer science, expression evaluation is a common problem, and it is often beneficial to convert expressions from one form to another. The three primary forms of expression notation are infix, prefix, and postfix. Understanding these notations and how to efficiently evaluate and convert these expressions is essential, and stacks play a critical role in these processes.

In infix notation, the operators are placed between the operands, as in the expression $a + b$. This notation is familiar to most people, as it is the standard notation used in arithmetic. However, infix expressions can be ambiguous without parentheses, which necessitates the need for operator precedence and associativity to properly dictate the order of operations.

Prefix notation, also known as Polish notation, places the operator before the operands. For example, the infix expression $a + b$ would be written as $+ab$ in prefix notation. One of the advantages of prefix notation is that it does not require parentheses to enforce precedence rules, which simplifies the parsing of the expression.

Postfix notation, or Reverse Polish notation (RPN), places the operator after the operands. The infix expression $a + b$ would be converted to $ab+$ in postfix notation. Like prefix notation, postfix notation eliminates the need for parentheses and is particularly advantageous in the implementation of stack-based algorithms for expression evaluation.

To convert and evaluate these expressions, we use stacks. The following algorithms detail the process of evaluating postfix expressions, converting infix expressions to postfix, and infix expressions to prefix notation using stacks.

Algorithm 9: Evaluation of Postfix Expression

Input: A postfix expression E with operands and operators
Output: The evaluated result of the postfix expression

Create an empty stack S;
for *each symbol* c *in* E **do**
  if c *is an operand* **then**
    Push c onto stack S;
  else
    Pop the top two elements from stack S;
    Let $\mathrm{op2}$ be the first popped element and $\mathrm{op1}$ be the second;
    Compute $\mathrm{result} = \mathrm{op1} \ \ \mathrm{c} \ \ \mathrm{op2}$;
    Push result onto stack S;
The final result is the top element of stack S;

A worked example of evaluating the postfix expression $23{*}54{*}+$ is as follows:

- Read 2: push it onto stack; Stack: $[2]$
- Read 3: push it onto stack; Stack: $[2, 3]$
- Read $*$: pop 3 and 2; compute $2{*}3 = 6$; push 6; Stack: $[6]$
- Read 5: push it onto stack; Stack: $[6, 5]$
- Read 4: push it onto stack; Stack: $[6, 5, 4]$
- Read $*$: pop 4 and 5; compute $5{*}4 = 20$; push 20; Stack: $[6, 20]$
- Read $+$: pop 20 and 6; compute $6{+}20 = 26$; push 26; Stack: $[26]$

The final result of the expression is 26.

Conversion from infix to postfix can be achieved using the following algorithm:

Algorithm 10: Conversion of Infix to Postfix Expression

```
Input: An infix expression E
Output: A postfix expression
Create an empty stack S and an empty string P for the output
  postfix expression;
for each symbol c in E do
    if c is an operand then
        Append c to P;
    else
        if c is an opening parenthesis then
            Push c onto stack S;
        else
            if c is a closing parenthesis then
                while top of stack S is not an opening
                  parenthesis do
                    Append top of S to P;
                    Pop from stack S;
                Pop the opening parenthesis from stack S;
            else
                while stack S is not empty and precedence of
                  top of S ≥ precedence of c do
                    Append top of S to P;
                    Pop from stack S;
                Push c onto stack S;
while stack S is not empty do
    Append top of S to P;
    Pop from stack S;
The postfix expression P is the output;
```

Using this algorithm, converting the infix expression $(a + b) * c$ would proceed as follows:

- Read (: push onto stack; Stack: [(]
- Read a: append to P; P: a
- Read +: push onto stack; Stack: [(, +]
- Read b: append to P; P: ab
- Read): pop and append until (; P: ab+

- Read *: push onto stack; Stack: [*]
- Read c: append to P; P: ab+c

Final P after emptying the stack: ab+c*.

Lastly, infix to prefix conversion can be achieved by reversing the order of the infix expression, translating it to postfix using the aforementioned algorithm, and reversing the result to obtain the prefix expression. This algorithm is left as an exercise for the reader to implement, providing an opportunity to apply the learned concepts independently.

5.7 Introduction to Queues

A queue is a linear data structure that follows a particular order in which operations are performed. The order is typically *First-In-First-Out* (FIFO). This means that the element added first will be removed first. Queues are widely used in various computing scenarios where tasks need to be managed in a sequential manner.

The primary operations associated with queues are enqueue (insertion of an element into the queue) and dequeue (removal of an element from the queue). Additionally, there are operations to check the item at the front or rear of the queue without removing it, as well as operations to check if the queue is empty or full.

To illustrate the structure of a queue, consider a simple example of a queue containing integers. We can create a queue with a set of initial elements and then perform various operations to observe the effects on the queue's state.

```
Queue<Integer> queue = new LinkedList<>();
queue.add(10); // Enqueue operation
queue.add(20);
queue.add(30);

System.out.println(queue.remove()); // Dequeue operation: outputs 10
System.out.println(queue.peek()); // Peek operation: outputs 20
System.out.println(queue.isEmpty()); // Check if queue is empty: outputs false
```

The expected output of the program is as follows:

```
10
20
false
```

A queue has several real-world applications, such as managing tasks in an operating system's process scheduler or handling the print requests in a printer's queue. Queues are also used in networking, such as managing packets in a router.

Queue Representation Queues can be implemented in various ways, including arrays, linked lists, and dynamic arrays. The choice of implementation can affect the performance characteristics of the queue, such as the time complexity of the different operations.

1. **Array-Based Implementation**: A queue can be implemented using an array by maintaining two indices, one for the front of the queue and one for the rear. However, this simple approach can lead to inefficiencies if not managed correctly (e.g., when the array becomes full but has unused space at the beginning). This inefficiency can be tackled using a circular queue.

2. **Linked List Implementation**: Using a linked list allows for dynamic sizing, which can be more memory efficient than a fixed-size array. This approach uses nodes to represent the queue elements, linking them in a sequence, with pointers to the front and rear of the queue.

Properties of Queues Queues are characterized by the following properties:

- Capacity: The maximum number of elements a queue can hold. In a dynamically sized implementation like a linked list, this can be considered infinite until memory constraints are reached. - Front: The position from where elements are dequeued. - Rear: The position where elements are enqueued. - Size: The current number of elements in the queue.

Basic Queue Operations Let us consider the basic operations in detail:

1. **Enqueue**: Adding an element to the rear of the queue

```
public void enqueue(int item) {
    if (rear == capacity - 1) {
        throw new IllegalStateException("Queue is full");
    } else {
        queueArray[++rear] = item;
        if (front == -1) {
            front = 0;
        }
    }
}
```

2. **Dequeue**: Removing an element from the front of the queue.

```
public int dequeue() {
    if (front == -1 || front > rear) {
        throw new NoSuchElementException("Queue is empty");
```

```
        } else {
            return queueArray[front++];
        }
    }
```

3. **Peek**: Fetching the front element without removing it.

```
public int peek() {
    if (front == -1 || front > rear) {
        throw new NoSuchElementException("Queue is empty");
    } else {
        return queueArray[front];
    }
}
```

4. **IsEmpty**: Checking if the queue is empty.

```
public boolean isEmpty() {
    return front == -1 || front > rear;
}
```

These core operations form the basis for more complex queue structures and functionalities which will be discussed later in the chapter. Practical applications of queues showcase their versatility and importance in both theoretical and applied computer science. The combination of simplicity and efficiency makes the queue an indispensable data structure for various algorithmic strategies and system designs.

5.8 Queue Operations: Enqueue, Dequeue, Front, Rear

Queue operations are fundamental to understanding how queues function as a data structure. The primary operations performed on a queue include enqueue, dequeue, front, and rear. These operations dictate how elements are added, removed, and accessed within the queue. In this section, we will detail these operations, providing a clear and concise understanding of each.

Enqueue operation adds an element to the rear of the queue. It is important to understand the condition that must be checked before performing this operation to avoid overflow in a queue implemented with a fixed-size array. When the queue is full (i.e., the number of elements in the queue equals the maximum capacity), an enqueue operation should not proceed.

```
void enqueue(int[] queue, int element, int rear, int capacity) {
    if (rear == capacity - 1) {
```

```
        System.out.println("Queue is full");
        return;
    }
    rear++;
    queue[rear] = element;
}
```

In this example, the enqueue method adds an element to the queue only if the rear index is less than the capacity - 1.

Dequeue operation removes an element from the front of the queue. Before performing this operation, it is necessary to check if the queue is empty to avoid underflow.

```
int dequeue(int[] queue, int front, int rear) {
    if (front == rear) {
        System.out.println("Queue is empty");
        return -1;
    }
    int element = queue[front];
    front++;
    return element;
}
```

In this example, the dequeue method removes an element from the queue and increments the front index. If the queue is empty (i.e., front equals rear), the method returns -1 indicating the queue is empty.

Front operation returns the front element of the queue without removing it. This operation is particularly useful for accessing the first element in the queue without modifying the queue's state.

```
int front(int[] queue, int front, int rear) {
    if (front == rear) {
        System.out.println("Queue is empty");
        return -1;
    }
    return queue[front];
}
```

In this example, the front method checks if the queue is empty before returning the front element. If the queue is empty, it returns -1.

Rear operation returns the last element of the queue without removing it. This operation allows access to the most recently added element in the queue.

```
int rear(int[] queue, int rear, int front) {
    if (front == rear) {
        System.out.println("Queue is empty");
        return -1;
    }
    return queue[rear];
}
```

In this example, the rear method checks if the queue is empty before returning the last element. If the queue is empty, it also returns -1.

The usage of these operations ensures that the queue maintains its fundamental properties of FIFO (First In, First Out). Proper management of the front and rear indices is essential in maintaining the correct order of elements and ensuring efficient queue operations.

The following code snippet demonstrates a typical use case of performing multiple queue operations:

```
public static void main(String[] args) {
    int capacity = 5;
    int[] queue = new int[capacity];
    int front = 0;
    int rear = -1;

    // Enqueue operations
    enqueue(queue, 1, rear++, capacity);
    enqueue(queue, 2, rear++, capacity);
    enqueue(queue, 3, rear++, capacity);

    // Front operation
    System.out.println("Front element: " + front(queue, front, rear));

    // Dequeue operations
    System.out.println("Dequeued element: " + dequeue(queue, front++, rear));
    System.out.println("Dequeued element: " + dequeue(queue, front++, rear));

    // Rear operation
    System.out.println("Rear element: " + rear(queue, rear, front));
}
```

Executing the above program yields:

```
Front element: 1
Dequeued element: 1
Dequeued element: 2
Rear element: 3
```

The example effectively illustrates how each of the queue operations can be utilized to manage elements in a queue. By understanding and leveraging these operations, one can implement efficient queue-based solutions for various computational problems.

5.9 Implementing Queues using Arrays

In this section, we examine the implementation of queues using arrays. A queue is a linear data structure following the First-In-First-Out (FIFO) principle, where elements are added from one end (rear) and removed from the other (front). Through an array-based approach, we establish an efficient setup for maintaining the queue's operations, i.e., enqueue (adding an element), dequeue (removing an element), front (retrieving the element at the front without removing it), and rear (retrieving the element at the rear).

Class Definition and Member Variables

We begin by defining a queue class in Java, specifying fundamental member variables necessary to represent the queue's state. The array is utilized to store elements, while integers maintain indices for the front and rear and the current size.

```
public class ArrayQueue {
    private int[] queue;
    private int front;
    private int rear;
    private int size;
    private int capacity;

    public ArrayQueue(int capacity) {
        this.capacity = capacity;
        this.queue = new int[capacity];
        this.front = 0;
        this.size = 0;
        this.rear = capacity - 1; // As rear will be incremented later when enqueuing.
    }
}
```

enqueue Operation

The enqueue method ensures elements are added to the rear of the queue. We increment the rear index circularly using the modulus operator to wrap around when it reaches the capacity. The size of the queue is incremented accordingly. A check for queue overflow is performed before enqueuing.

```
public void enqueue(int item) {
    if (isFull()) {
        throw new IllegalStateException("Queue is full");
    }
    this.rear = (this.rear + 1) % this.capacity;
    this.queue[this.rear] = item;
    this.size++;
}
```

dequeue Operation

The dequeue method removes an element from the front. Similar to rear, the front index is incremented circularly using the modulus operator after retrieving the front item. The queue size is decremented subsequently. A check for queue underflow is necessary before dequeuing.

```
public int dequeue() {
    if (isEmpty()) {
```

```
        throw new IllegalStateException("Queue is empty");
    }
    int item = this.queue[this.front];
    this.front = (this.front + 1) % this.capacity;
    this.size--;
    return item;
}
```

front **Operation**

The front method returns the element at the front of the queue without removing it. It is crucial to check that the queue is not empty before accessing the front element.

```
public int front() {
    if (isEmpty()) {
        throw new IllegalStateException("Queue is empty");
    }
    return this.queue[this.front];
}
```

rear **Operation**

Similarly, the rear method retrieves the element at the rear end of the queue without dequeuing it.

```
public int rear() {
    if (isEmpty()) {
        throw new IllegalStateException("Queue is empty");
    }
    return this.queue[this.rear];
}
```

Utility Methods

Two utility methods, isEmpty and isFull, are defined to check the status of the queue.

```
public boolean isEmpty() {
    return this.size == 0;
}

public boolean isFull() {
    return this.size == this.capacity;
}
```

Example Usage

Here is an example demonstrating the usage of ArrayQueue class.

```
public class Main {
    public static void main(String[] args) {
        ArrayQueue queue = new ArrayQueue(5);

        queue.enqueue(10);
        queue.enqueue(20);
```

```
        queue.enqueue(30);
        queue.enqueue(40);
        queue.enqueue(50);

        System.out.println("Front item: " + queue.front()); // 10
        System.out.println("Removing: " + queue.dequeue()); // 10
        System.out.println("Current front item: " + queue.front()); // 20
        System.out.println("Rear item: " + queue.rear()); // 50

        queue.enqueue(60);
        System.out.println("New rear item: " + queue.rear()); // 60
    }
}
```

```
Output:
Front item: 10
Removing: 10
Current front item: 20
Rear item: 50
New rear item: 60
```

Implementing queues using arrays offers a clear and efficient method for maintaining FIFO data structures. By leveraging circular arrays, we can manage the queue within a fixed-size array while maintaining optimal time complexity for core operations.

5.10 Implementing Queues using Linked Lists

Queues are linear data structures that follow the First In, First Out (FIFO) principle, making them particularly useful in scenarios where order of processing is crucial. The operations associated with queues include enqueue, dequeue, front, and rear. While arrays can be used to implement queues, linked lists offer a more dynamic and flexible approach, eliminating the need for contiguous memory allocation and resizing.

A queue implemented using a linked list consists of nodes where each node contains a data element and a pointer to the next node in line. The basic structure of a queue using a singly linked list includes two pointers: front and rear. The front pointer points to the first node (where dequeue operations take place), and the rear pointer points to the last node (where enqueue operations occur).

Below is a detailed implementation of a queue using a singly linked list in Java:

```
public class LinkedListQueue<T> {
```

```
    private class Node {
        T data;
        Node next;

        Node(T data) {
            this.data = data;
            this.next = null;
        }
    }

    private Node front, rear;

    public LinkedListQueue() {
        this.front = this.rear = null;
    }

    public boolean isEmpty() {
        return front == null;
    }

    public void enqueue(T item) {
        Node newNode = new Node(item);
        if (this.rear == null) {
            this.front = this.rear = newNode;
            return;
        }
        this.rear.next = newNode;
        this.rear = newNode;
    }

    public T dequeue() {
        if (this.front == null) {
            throw new RuntimeException("Queue underflow");
        }
        T item = this.front.data;
        this.front = this.front.next;
        if (this.front == null) {
            this.rear = null;
        }
        return item;
    }

    public T peekFront() {
        if (this.front == null) {
            throw new RuntimeException("Queue underflow");
        }
        return this.front.data;
    }

    public T peekRear() {
        if (this.rear == null) {
            throw new RuntimeException("Queue underflow");
        }
        return this.rear.data;
    }

}
```

The Node class represents the individual elements of the queue. Each node contains data of generic type T and a pointer to the next node.

The LinkedListQueue class maintains two pointers: front and rear, which are initially set to null.

The isEmpty method checks if the queue is empty by verifying if the front pointer is null. The enqueue method adds a new item to the end of the queue. If the queue is initially empty (both front and rear are null), both pointers are updated to point to the new node. Otherwise, the next field of the current rear node is set to the new node, and rear is updated to this new node.

The dequeue method removes and returns the item at the front of the queue. If the queue is empty (checked by front being null), an exception is thrown. Otherwise, the data from the front node is saved, front is updated to point to the next node, and if the queue becomes empty after the operation, rear is set to null.

The methods peekFront and peekRear return the data at the front and rear of the queue, respectively, without removing any elements. If the queue is empty, these methods throw an exception indicating a queue underflow.

An example execution of this queue implementation would be as follows:

```
public class Main {
    public static void main(String[] args) {
        LinkedListQueue<Integer> queue = new LinkedListQueue<>();

        queue.enqueue(10);
        queue.enqueue(20);
        queue.enqueue(30);

        System.out.println("Front element: " + queue.peekFront()); // Outputs: Front
            element: 10
        System.out.println("Rear element: " + queue.peekRear()); // Outputs: Rear
            element: 30

        System.out.println("Dequeued: " + queue.dequeue()); // Outputs: Dequeued: 10
        System.out.println("Front element: " + queue.peekFront()); // Outputs: Front
            element: 20
    }
}
```

```
Front element: 10
Rear element: 30
Dequeued: 10
Front element: 20
```

In this example, enqueue operations add elements 10, 20, and 30 to the queue. The peekFront method shows 10 as the front element, and 30 as the rear element. Subsequent dequeue operation removes 10, making 20 the new front.

This implementation ensures that all operations are performed efficiently and dynamically without the need for resizing, thus providing a robust structure for managing ordered data.

5.11 Circular Queues

A circular queue, also known as a circular buffer or ring buffer, is a linear data structure that uses a single, fixed-size buffer as if it were connected end-to-end. This structure allows efficient use of space by reusing the locations in the buffer that have been freed as items are removed. In a circular queue, the positions immediately following the last element are considered to be the positions preceding the first element of the queue.

Advantages of Circular Queues

- Efficient Memory Utilization: Unlike a linear queue, a circular queue does not waste space by leaving behind an unoccupied region. Elements are enqueued and dequeued in a circular fashion, which ensures that memory is efficiently utilized.
- Fixed Size: Circular queues have a fixed size which prevents overflow if careful checks on the queue size are performed. This makes them suitable for systems where resource constraints are significant.
- Ease of Implementation: Implementing a circular queue is straightforward and can be easily achieved with an array.

Operations on Circular Queues

The primary operations in a circular queue are enqueue, dequeue, and inspection operations such as front and rear, just like in a linear queue. However, given the circular nature, these operations require specific handling of the buffer's boundaries.

Enqueue Operation

The enqueue operation adds an element to the queue. If the queue is full, the operation fails. Otherwise, the element is added, and the rear is updated accordingly. If the rear reaches the end of the buffer, it wraps around the buffer to reuse the beginning positions.

```
public class CircularQueue {
```

```
    private int[] queue;
    private int size;
    private int front;
    private int rear;
    private int count;

    public CircularQueue(int size) {
        this.size = size;
        queue = new int[size];
        front = 0;
        rear = -1;
        count = 0;
    }

    public boolean enqueue(int item) {
        if (count == size) {
            System.out.println("Queue is full");
            return false;
        }
        rear = (rear + 1) % size;
        queue[rear] = item;
        count++;
        return true;
    }
}
```

Dequeue Operation

The dequeue operation removes an element from the queue. If the queue is empty, the operation fails. Otherwise, the element at the front is removed, and the front is updated. Once the front reaches the end of the buffer, it wraps around to the beginning.

```
public boolean dequeue() {
    if (count == 0) {
        System.out.println("Queue is empty");
        return false;
    }
    front = (front + 1) % size;
    count--;
    return true;
}
```

Inspection Operations

To inspect elements in the queue, the front and rear operations return the elements at the respective positions without removing them, thus allowing the examination of the queue's state.

```
public int front() {
    if (count == 0) {
        throw new NoSuchElementException("Queue is empty");
    }
    return queue[front];
}

public int rear() {
    if (count == 0) {
```

```
        throw new NoSuchElementException("Queue is empty");
    }
    return queue[rear];
}
```

Key Considerations

When implementing a circular queue, it is pivotal to manage edge cases such as distinguishing between a full and an empty queue. Both cases involve the front and rear pointers potentially pointing to the same index. A common approach to differentiate these cases is through an additional count variable, which keeps track of the number of elements in the queue.

Algorithm 11: Circular Queue Operations

```
Data: Array queue of size n, Integer front, Integer rear, Integer
      count
Function enqueue(item):
    if count == n then
        return false
    rear ← (rear + 1) % n ;
    queue[rear] ← item ;
    count ← count + 1 ;
    return true
Function dequeue():
    if count == 0 then
        return false
    front ← (front + 1) % n ;
    count ← count - 1 ;
    return true
Function front():
    if count == 0 then
        return NoSuchElementException
    return queue[front]
Function rear():
    if count == 0 then
        return NoSuchElementException
    return queue[rear]
```

Implementing circular queues enables efficient and reusable memory utilization, promoting their usage in various applications such as CPU scheduling and buffering in network routers. By applying a fixed-size buffer, they provide a straightforward yet powerful mechanism for managing a continuous stream of data within constrained environments.

5.12 Double-ended Queues (Deques)

A double-ended queue, often abbreviated as deque, is a generalized version of a queue that allows insertion and removal of elements from both ends, head and tail. Deques can be used in various applications where elements need to be added or removed from both ends efficiently.

Properties of Deques

- Deques allow insertion and deletion of elements at both ends - front and rear.
- They are more generalized data structures than stacks and queues.
- Deques do not impose a fixed direction for adding or removing elements.

Operations on Deques

- insertFront: Inserts an element at the front.
- insertRear: Inserts an element at the rear.
- deleteFront: Deletes an element from the front.
- deleteRear: Deletes an element from the rear.
- getFront: Gets the front element.
- getRear: Gets the rear element.
- isEmpty: Checks whether the deque is empty.
- isFull: Checks whether the deque is full.

Implementing Deques using Arrays

To implement a deque using an array, we use a fixed-size array and two pointers, front and rear. The following is a detailed implementation:

```
class DequeArray {
    private int[] arr;
    private int front;
    private int rear;
    private int size;
    private int capacity;

    public DequeArray(int capacity) {
        this.capacity = capacity;
        arr = new int[capacity];
        front = -1;
        rear = 0; // start of the array
        size = 0;
    }

    public boolean isFull() {
        return (size == capacity);
    }

    public boolean isEmpty() {
        return (size == 0);
    }

    public void insertFront(int key) {
        if (isFull()) {
            throw new IllegalStateException("Deque is full");
        }
        if (front == -1) {
            front = 0;
            rear = 0;
        } else if (front == 0) {
            front = capacity - 1;
        } else {
            front = front - 1;
        }
        arr[front] = key;
        size++;
    }

    public void insertRear(int key) {
        if (isFull()) {
            throw new IllegalStateException("Deque is full");
        }
        if (front == -1) {
            front = 0;
            rear = 0;
        } else if (rear == capacity - 1) {
            rear = 0;
        } else {
            rear = rear + 1;
        }
        arr[rear] = key;
        size++;
    }

    public void deleteFront() {
        if (isEmpty()) {
            throw new IllegalStateException("Deque is empty");
        }
        if (front == rear) {
            front = -1;
            rear = -1;
```

```
        } else if (front == capacity - 1) {
            front = 0;
        } else {
            front = front + 1;
        }
        size--;
    }

    public void deleteRear() {
        if (isEmpty()) {
            throw new IllegalStateException("Deque is empty");
        }
        if (front == rear) {
            front = -1;
            rear = -1;
        } else if (rear == 0) {
            rear = capacity - 1;
        } else {
            rear = rear - 1;
        }
        size--;
    }

    public int getFront() {
        if (isEmpty()) {
            throw new IllegalStateException("Deque is empty");
        }
        return arr[front];
    }

    public int getRear() {
        if (isEmpty()) {
            throw new IllegalStateException("Deque is empty");
        }
        return arr[rear];
    }
}
```

Implementing Deques using Linked Lists

Using a doubly linked list is another efficient way to implement a deque. Here's how it can be done:

```
class DequeLinkedList {
    class Node {
        int data;
        Node prev;
        Node next;
        public Node(int data) {
            this.data = data;
        }
    }

    private Node front;
    private Node rear;
    private int size;

    public DequeLinkedList() {
        front = null;
        rear = null;
        size = 0;
```

```
    }

    public boolean isEmpty() {
        return (front == null);
    }

    public void insertFront(int key) {
        Node newNode = new Node(key);
        if (isEmpty()) {
            front = rear = newNode;
        } else {
            newNode.next = front;
            front.prev = newNode;
            front = newNode;
        }
        size++;
    }

    public void insertRear(int key) {
        Node newNode = new Node(key);
        if (isEmpty()) {
            front = rear = newNode;
        } else {
            newNode.prev = rear;
            rear.next = newNode;
            rear = newNode;
        }
        size++;
    }

    public void deleteFront() {
        if (isEmpty()) {
            throw new IllegalStateException("Deque is empty");
        }
        front = front.next;
        if (front != null) {
            front.prev = null;
        } else {
            rear = null;
        }
        size--;
    }

    public void deleteRear() {
        if (isEmpty()) {
            throw new IllegalStateException("Deque is empty");
        }
        rear = rear.prev;
        if (rear != null) {
            rear.next = null;
        } else {
            front = null;
        }
        size--;
    }

    public int getFront() {
        if (isEmpty()) {
            throw new IllegalStateException("Deque is empty");
        }
        return front.data;
    }
```

```
    public int getRear() {
        if (isEmpty()) {
            throw new IllegalStateException("Deque is empty");
        }
        return rear.data;
    }
}
```

Applications of Deques

Deques are versatile data structures used in various scenarios:

- **Task Scheduling**: Deques can manage tasks where the priority of tasks added or removed can vary.
- **Sliding Window Problems**: Deques can efficiently handle problems involving sliding windows, such as finding the maximum or minimum in a given range within an array.
- **Palindrome Checking**: Deques can facilitate checking if a string is a palindrome by comparing elements from both ends simultaneously.

Understanding the implementation and applications of deques enriches our comprehension of linear data structures and their versatility in solving complex problems.

5.13 Priority Queues

Priority queues are an advanced form of queue data structure where each element is associated with a priority. Unlike typical queues which operate on a First-In-First-Out (FIFO) basis, priority queues allow elements to be dequeued in order of their priority, rather than their chronological order of arrival. High priority elements are dequeued before lower priority elements, and elements of the same priority are dequeued following a specific order, typically FIFO.

Priority queues can be effectively utilized in various applications such as scheduling processes in operating systems, managing tasks in a simulation system, and implementing Dijkstra's shortest path algorithm. This section delves into the detailed structure, operations, and implementations of priority queues, with an emphasis on clarity and precision.

Structure of Priority Queues

The fundamental structure of a priority queue may be conceptualized as a collection of elements, each paired with a priority value. Mathematically, a priority queue can be defined as:

$$\text{Priority Queue} = \{(e_i, p_i) \mid e_i \in E,\ p_i \in P \text{ and } i \in \{1, 2, \ldots, n\}\}$$

Here, e_i represents the element and p_i represents the associated priority for the i-th element.

Various implementations of priority queues include:

- Array: A simple but inefficient method where elements are inserted into an array, and the highest priority element is found by scanning the entire array.
- Linked List: A linked list can maintain an order based on priority, allowing the highest priority element to be at the head, though insertion may still require traversal.
- Heap: A more efficient method employing a binary heap where the highest priority element can be found in logarithmic time.

The heap-based implementation is the most optimal for practical uses and will be the primary focus of this section.

Operations in Priority Queues

The primary operations that can be performed on a priority queue include:

- **Insert (enqueue)**: Add an element to the priority queue with an associated priority.
- **Remove (dequeue)**: Remove the element with the highest priority from the priority queue.
- **Peek**: Retrieve, but do not remove, the element with the highest priority.

Insert Operation (Enqueue)

In a heap-based priority queue, the insert operation involves the following steps:

- Add the element to the end of the heap.

- Heapify the heap to maintain the heap property (i.e., every parent node is greater than or equal to its child nodes if it is a max-heap, or less than or equal to its child nodes if it is a min-heap).

An algorithm for the insert operation is given as follows:

Algorithm 12: Insert Operation in a Priority Queue

Input: element to be inserted, priority of the element
Output: Updated priority queue

```
heap.push((element, priority));
current ← heap.size() − 1;
while current > 0 and
  heap[current].priority > heap[parent(current)].priority do
    swap(heap[current], heap[parent(current)]);
    current ← parent(current);
```

Remove Operation (Dequeue)

The remove operation encompasses the following steps:

- Replace the root of the heap (highest priority element) with the last element in the heap.

- Remove the last element.

- Heapify the heap to maintain the heap property.

The algorithm for the remove operation is detailed below:

Algorithm 13: Remove Operation in a Priority Queue

Output: Element with highest priority

$maxElement \leftarrow heap[0]$;
$heap[0] \leftarrow heap[heap.size() - 1]$;
$heap.pop()$;
heapify(0);
return *maxElement*;
Function *heapify(index)*
    $left \leftarrow 2 \times index + 1$;
    $right \leftarrow 2 \times index + 2$;
    $largest \leftarrow index$;
    if $left < heap.size()$ ***and*** $heap[left].priority > heap[largest].priority$ **then**
        $largest \leftarrow left$;
    if $right < heap.size()$ ***and*** $heap[right].priority > heap[largest].priority$ **then**
        $largest \leftarrow right$;
    if $largest \neq index$ **then**
        swap(heap[index], heap[largest]);
        heapify(largest);

Peek Operation

The peek operation is relatively simple as it merely returns the root element of the heap, which represents the highest priority element. This operation can be implemented as follows:

```
public class PriorityQueue {
    private List<Element> heap;

    public Element peek() {
        if (heap.size() > 0) {
            return heap.get(0);
        }
        return null;
    }
}
```

Time Complexity

The efficiency of a priority queue largely hinges on the underlying data structure used for its implementation. For a heap-based priority queue, the time complexity for each operation is as follows:

- Insert (enqueue): $O(\log n)$

- Remove (dequeue): $O(\log n)$
- Peek: $O(1)$

This makes heap-based priority queues highly efficient for scenarios requiring frequent insertion and deletion of elements.

Priority queues serve a critical function in many advanced algorithms and systems. Their ability to dynamically manage and retrieve elements based on priority rather than order of insertion makes them indispensable for a myriad of computational tasks. Employing a heap structure ensures efficiency, maintaining the balance between computational complexity and performance.

Chapter 6

Recursion

This chapter delves into recursion, a powerful technique in computer science for solving problems iteratively. It introduces the fundamental concepts of base cases and recursive cases, and contrasts recursion with iteration. The chapter explores classic recursive algorithms such as calculating factorials, generating Fibonacci sequences, and solving the Towers of Hanoi problem. It also covers backtracking, common pitfalls, optimization strategies, and tail recursion, providing a comprehensive understanding of when and how to effectively use recursion in programming.

6.1 Introduction to Recursion

Recursion is a fundamental concept in computer science where a function calls itself directly or indirectly to solve a problem. This technique allows for elegant solutions to complex problems by breaking them down into simpler sub-problems. In this section, we introduce the basic principles of recursion, emphasizing its utility, structure, and implementation in Java.

A recursive function typically follows a straightforward structure, composed of two main parts:

- **Base Case:** This is the condition under which the recursion terminates. Without a well-defined base case, a recursive function would continue to call itself indefinitely, leading to a stack overflow error.

- **Recursive Case:** This part of the function calls itself with modified parameters, steadily advancing towards the base case.

The concept can be illustrated with a simple example of a recursive function that calculates the factorial of a number n. The factorial of n (denoted as $n!$) is defined as the product of all positive integers up to n. The factorial can be defined recursively as follows:

$$n! = \begin{cases} 1 & \text{if } n = 0 \\ n \times (n-1)! & \text{if } n > 0 \end{cases}$$

Here's how this can be implemented in Java:

```
public class Factorial {
    public static int factorial(int n) {
        if (n == 0) {
            return 1; // Base Case
        } else {
            return n * factorial(n - 1); // Recursive Case
        }
    }

    public static void main(String[] args) {
        int result = factorial(5);
        System.out.println("Factorial of 5 is: " + result);
    }
}
```

When the factorial function is called with an argument of 5, it proceeds as follows:

- factorial(5) calls factorial(4)
- factorial(4) calls factorial(3)
- factorial(3) calls factorial(2)
- factorial(2) calls factorial(1)
- factorial(1) calls factorial(0)
- factorial(0) returns 1 (base case reached)
- factorial(1) returns 1 * factorial(0) = 1
- factorial(2) returns 2 * factorial(1) = 2 * 1 = 2
- factorial(3) returns 3 * factorial(2) = 3 * 2 = 6

- factorial(4) returns 4 * factorial(3) = 4 * 6 = 24
- factorial(5) returns 5 * factorial(4) = 5 * 24 = 120

The output for this execution will be:

```
Factorial of 5 is: 120
```

The above example elucidates how the recursive calls propagate until the base case is reached, followed by unwinding of the recursion with the accumulation of results.

Understanding recursion requires recognizing the underlying principle of self-similarity—solving a problem in terms of smaller instances of itself. This principle is pivotal in various computational algorithms where a complex problem can be broken down recursively. Let's consider another classic example: the Fibonacci sequence.

The Fibonacci sequence is defined as:

$$F(n) = \begin{cases} 0 & \text{if } n = 0 \\ 1 & \text{if } n = 1 \\ F(n-1) + F(n-2) & \text{if } n > 1 \end{cases}$$

A recursive implementation of the Fibonacci sequence in Java is as follows:

```
public class Fibonacci {
    public static int fibonacci(int n) {
        if (n == 0) {
            return 0; // Base Case
        } else if (n == 1) {
            return 1; // Base Case
        } else {
            return fibonacci(n - 1) + fibonacci(n - 2); // Recursive Case
        }
    }

    public static void main(String[] args) {
        int result = fibonacci(6);
        System.out.println("Fibonacci of 6 is: " + result);
    }
}
```

In this implementation:

- fibonacci(6) calls fibonacci(5) and fibonacci(4)
- fibonacci(5) calls fibonacci(4) and fibonacci(3)
- This process continues until the base cases (fibonacci(0) and fibonacci(1)) are reached.

The execution leads to multiple redundant calculations, which is a potential inefficiency of naive recursive implementations that will be addressed later in optimization strategies.

The output for this execution will be:

```
Fibonacci of 6 is: 8
```

Recursion can be beneficial in solving problems where the solution comprises solving smaller instances of the same problem. However, it demands careful handling of base cases to prevent infinite recursion and potential stack overflow.

6.2 Base Case and Recursive Case

Understanding the fundamentals of base case and recursive case is crucial for mastering recursion. These two components form the backbone of any recursive function, ensuring it operates correctly and terminates appropriately.

A recursive function solves a problem by recursively calling itself, each time solving a smaller subproblem. To prevent infinite recursion, it must have at least one base case. The base case is a simple instance of the problem that can be solved directly without further recursion. On the other hand, the recursive case breaks down the complex problem into smaller instances of the same problem, eventually leading to the base case.

Consider the problem of calculating the factorial of a number n. The factorial of a non-negative integer n, denoted as $n!$, is defined as the product of all positive integers less than or equal to n. The recursive definition of the factorial function is:

$$n! = \begin{cases} 1 & \text{if } n = 0 \\ n \times (n-1)! & \text{if } n > 0 \end{cases}$$

In this definition, $n = 0$ is the base case, and $n \times (n-1)!$ represents the recursive case. Implementing this in Java can be done as follows:

```java
public class Factorial {
    public static int factorial(int n) {
        if (n == 0) { // Base Case
            return 1;
        } else { // Recursive Case
            return n * factorial(n - 1);
```

```
        }
    }

    public static void main(String[] args) {
        System.out.println(factorial(5)); // Output: 120
    }
}
```

In this code, the factorial method takes an integer n and returns its factorial. The base case is when n is equal to 0, returning 1. The recursive case handles $n > 0$, calling factorial with $n-1$ and multiplying the result by n.

The base case prevents infinite recursion, ensuring the function eventually stops making recursive calls. Misidentified or missing base cases can lead to infinite loops, causing stack overflow errors. A common mistake is formulating an incorrect or unreachable base case. For example:

```
public class IncorrectFactorial {
    public static int factorial(int n) {
        if (n == -1) { // Incorrect Base Case
            return 1;
        } else {
            return n * factorial(n - 1);
        }
    }

    public static void main(String[] args) {
        System.out.println(factorial(5)); // Output: StackOverflowError
    }
}
```

In the above example, setting the base case condition as $n = -1$ is incorrect because it is never reached during the normal execution for positive integers, resulting in a StackOverflowError.

Another critical aspect is ensuring the progression towards the base case. Each recursive call should gradually reduce the problem size, converging towards the base case. For instance, subtracting 1 from n ensures the problem size decreases, eventually reaching 0.

Consider another example, calculating the sum of the first n natural numbers. The recursive definition is:

$$\text{Sum}(n) = \begin{cases} 0 & \text{if } n = 0 \\ n + \text{Sum}(n-1) & \text{if } n > 0 \end{cases}$$

The Java implementation follows the same principles:

```
public class SumNaturalNumbers {
```

```
    public static int sum(int n) {
        if (n == 0) { // Base Case
            return 0;
        } else { // Recursive Case
            return n + sum(n - 1);
        }
    }

    public static void main(String[] args) {
        System.out.println(sum(5)); // Output: 15
    }
}
```

Here, the base case returns 0 when n is 0. The recursive case adds n to the result of sum(n - 1), reducing n by 1 each time, and converging towards the base case.

Ensuring correct identification of base cases and their reachability, along with proper problem size reduction in recursive cases, forms the foundation of developing efficient recursive solutions. These principles are pivotal across all recursive algorithms and will be further exemplified through subsequent sections focusing on optimization and specific recursive problems.

6.3 Visualizing Recursion with Examples

Understanding recursion can be greatly enhanced by visualizing its execution. In this section, we will explore several illustrative examples in detail, helping to solidify the concepts of base cases and recursive cases. By stepping through these examples, we will demonstrate how recursive calls are made, how the call stack evolves, and how the final results are obtained.

To begin, let's consider the classic example of calculating the factorial of a number n. The factorial of n, denoted as $n!$, is defined as the product of all positive integers less than or equal to n. The recursive definition can be expressed as follows:

$$
\begin{aligned}
n! &= n \times (n-1)! && \text{for } n > 0 \\
0! &= 1 && \text{base case}
\end{aligned}
$$

We can implement this definition in Java using a recursive function. Here is the source code wrapped in the lstlisting environment for clear presentation:

```
public int factorial(int n) {
    if (n == 0) {
        return 1; // base case
    } else {
        return n * factorial(n - 1); // recursive case
    }
}
```

To visualize how this function works, consider calling factorial(3). The execution trace can be broken down as follows:

- Call stack: Initially, the stack is empty. After calling factorial(3), the stack contains factorial(3).
- Base case check: Since $n = 3 \neq 0$, the function proceeds to 3 * factorial(2). The stack now has factorial(3) and factorial(2).
- Recursive call: For factorial(2), since $n = 2 \neq 0$, it proceeds to 2 * factorial(1). The stack now includes factorial(3), factorial(2), and factorial(1).
- Further recursion: For factorial(1), since $n = 1 \neq 0$, it proceeds to 1 * factorial(0). The stack holds factorial(3), factorial(2), factorial(1), and factorial(0).
- Base case reached: For factorial(0), since $n = 0$, it returns 1. The stack now unwinds, starting from factorial(0).
- Unwinding stack:
  - factorial(1) = 1 * 1 = 1
  - factorial(2) = 2 * 1 = 2
  - factorial(3) = 3 * 2 = 6

This step-by-step execution can be visualized as follows:

```
factorial(3)      -> 3 * factorial(2)
  factorial(2)    -> 2 * factorial(1)
    factorial(1)  -> 1 * factorial(0)
      factorial(0) -> 1 (base case)
    factorial(1)  <- 1
  factorial(2)    <- 2
factorial(3)      <- 6
```

Next, we will examine the Fibonacci sequence, where each number is the sum of the two preceding ones. The sequence is defined recursively as:

$$
\begin{aligned}
F(n) &= F(n-1) + F(n-2) && \text{for } n > 1 \\
F(0) &= 0 && \text{base case 1} \\
F(1) &= 1 && \text{base case 2}
\end{aligned}
$$

Here is the corresponding Java implementation:

```
public int fibonacci(int n) {
    if (n == 0) {
        return 0; // base case 1
    } else if (n == 1) {
        return 1; // base case 2
    } else {
        return fibonacci(n - 1) + fibonacci(n - 2); // recursive case
    }
}
```

To visualize $\text{fibonacci}(4)$, consider the recursive calls and the evolution of the call stack:

- Call $\text{fibonacci}(4)$:
  - Computes $\text{fibonacci}(3) + \text{fibonacci}(2)$
- Compute $\text{fibonacci}(3)$:
  - Computes $\text{fibonacci}(2) + \text{fibonacci}(1)$
- Compute $\text{fibonacci}(2)$:
  - Computes $\text{fibonacci}(1) + \text{fibonacci}(0)$
- Base cases:
  - $\text{fibonacci}(1)$ returns 1
  - $\text{fibonacci}(0)$ returns 0
  - $\text{fibonacci}(2)$ returns 1 + 0 = 1
- Compute $\text{fibonacci}(1)$ for $\text{fibonacci}(3)$: (base case)
  - Returns 1
  - $\text{fibonacci}(3)$ returns 1 + 1 = 2
- Compute $\text{fibonacci}(2)$: (from step 1)
  - Repeats steps as above, returns 1

- Final result:
  - fibonacci(4) returns 2 + 1 = 3

The recursive calls and the resulting computation can be visualized as follows:

```
fibonacci(4)        -> fibonacci(3) + fibonacci(2)
  fibonacci(3)      -> fibonacci(2) + fibonacci(1)
    fibonacci(2)    -> fibonacci(1) + fibonacci(0)
      fibonacci(1)  -> 1 (base case)
      fibonacci(0)  -> 0 (base case)
    fibonacci(2)    <- 1
    fibonacci(1)    <- 1 (base case)
  fibonacci(3)      <- 2
  fibonacci(2)      -> fibonacci(1) + fibonacci(0)
    fibonacci(1)    -> 1 (base case)
    fibonacci(0)    -> 0 (base case)
  fibonacci(2)      <- 1
fibonacci(4)        <- 3
```

For clarity, a diagram displaying the execution tree of fibonacci(4) can further enhance visual understanding:

```
                      F(4)
                 /
          F(3)                F(2)
   /                                 /
F(2)           F(1)           F(1)   F(0)
   /
F(1)     F(0)
```

Finally, let us consider the Towers of Hanoi problem. Here, the objective is to move n disks from a source peg to a destination peg using an auxiliary peg, following certain rules. The recursive algorithm follows:

```
Function solveHanoi(n, source, destination, auxiliary):
    if n == 1 then
        Output: Move disk from source to destination
        ;
    solveHanoi(n - 1, source, auxiliary, destination);
    Output: Move disk from source to destination
    ;
    solveHanoi(n - 1, auxiliary, destination, source);
```

Consider solving the Towers of Hanoi for $n = 3$ with pegs A (source), B (auxiliary), and C (destination):

```
public void solveHanoi(int n, char source, char destination, char auxiliary) {
    if (n == 1) {
        System.out.println("Move disk from " + source + " to " + destination);
        return;
    }
    solveHanoi(n - 1, source, auxiliary, destination);
    System.out.println("Move disk from " + source + " to " + destination);
    solveHanoi(n - 1, auxiliary, destination, source);
}
```

Execution trace:

```
solveHanoi(3, 'A', 'C', 'B')
    solveHanoi(2, 'A', 'B', 'C')
        solveHanoi(1, 'A', 'C', 'B') -> Move disk from A to C
        Move disk from A to B
        solveHanoi(1, 'C', 'B', 'A') -> Move disk from C to B
    Move disk from A to C
    solveHanoi(2, 'B', 'C', 'A')
        solveHanoi(1, 'B', 'A', 'C') -> Move disk from B to A
        Move disk from B to C
        solveHanoi(1, 'A', 'C', 'B') -> Move disk from A to C
```

The Towers of Hanoi algorithm visually decomposes the problem into solvable subproblems, illustrating the power and elegance of recursion. Through detailed walk-throughs and visual representations of these examples, recursive thinking becomes more intuitive and clearer.

6.4 Recursion vs Iteration

In computer science, recursion and iteration are two fundamental techniques for solving repetitive problems. While they are conceptually different, both can often be used to achieve the same goal. Understanding the distinctions between these two approaches is invaluable for selecting the most suitable method depending on the problem context.

Recursion is a method where the solution to a problem depends on solutions to smaller instances of the same problem. A recursive function is defined in terms of itself and typically includes:

- A base case, which terminates the recursion.
- A recursive case, which breaks the problem down into simpler or smaller sub-problems and calls the recursive method.

Iteration, on the other hand, is a technique that repeatedly executes a set of instructions until a condition is met. Iterative structures in programming commonly include loops such as for, while, and do-while loops.

Comparison:

1. **Execution Process**: - **Recursion:** A function calls itself within its own definition. Each recursive call requires additional memory to keep track of previous calls, leading to a potentially deeper call stack. - **Iteration:** A loop structure repeats a block of code. No additional memory is required for the call stack, only for the loop control variable and possibly for the loop body variables.

2. **Memory Usage**: - **Recursion:** Each function call adds a new layer to the call stack. This can result in significant memory usage, particularly for deeply nested recursive calls. Recursive programs are susceptible to stack overflow if the recursion depth is too large. - **Iteration:** Generally requires less memory as it doesn't use the call stack in the same way. The memory usage is primarily determined by the variables used within the loop.

3. **Performance Considerations**: - **Recursion:** The overhead of repeated function calls can lead to increased execution time. However, recursion can provide cleaner and more straightforward solutions to problems that naturally fit a recursive structure, such as tree traversals. - **Iteration:** Typically more efficient in terms of execution time because it avoids the overhead associated with function calls. However, iterative solutions can become complex and harder to read for problems that are inherently recursive.

To illustrate the difference, consider the problem of calculating the factorial of a number. Below, we present both the recursive and iterative implementations.

```
public class Factorial {
    public static int recursiveFactorial(int n) {
        if (n <= 1) {
            return 1; // Base case
        } else {
            return n * recursiveFactorial(n - 1); // Recursive case
        }
    }

    public static void main(String[] args) {
        int number = 5;
        System.out.println("Factorial of " + number + " is: " + recursiveFactorial(
            number));
    }
}
```

Factorial of 5 is: 120

```
public class Factorial {
    public static int iterativeFactorial(int n) {
        int result = 1;
        for (int i = 1; i <= n; i++) {
            result *= i;
        }
        return result;
    }

    public static void main(String[] args) {
        int number = 5;
        System.out.println("Factorial of " + number + " is: " + iterativeFactorial(
              number));
    }
}
```

Factorial of 5 is: 120

Both implementations produce the same result, but the choice between recursion and iteration may depend on factors such as readability, problem size, and system constraints (e.g., available memory).

Practical Considerations:

1. **Use Cases**: - **Recursion:** Suitable for problems that can be naturally divided into similar sub-problems, such as tree traversals (e.g., preorder, in-order, post-order), and algorithms like quicksort and mergesort. - **Iteration:** Useful for tasks with a known or predictable number of repetitions, such as summing elements of a list, searching elements, or simple computations.

2. **Optimization Techniques**: - **Improving Recursive Solutions:** Tail recursion optimization can convert certain forms of recursion into efficient iteration, reducing the risk of stack overflow and decreasing memory usage. - **Efficient Iteration:** Loop unrolling and induction variable elimination can improve the performance of loops in some contexts.

By understanding the underlying mechanisms, benefits, and limitations of recursion and iteration, one can make more informed decisions when designing algorithms. Both are pivotal tools in a programmer's toolkit, and their appropriate use can lead to more efficient, readable, and maintainable code.

6.5 Problems Solvable by Recursion

Recursive techniques can be applied to various problem domains where a solution can be constructed incrementally by breaking the problem into smaller, more manageable subproblems. Here are several types of problems that are naturally suited to recursive approaches.

1. Divide and Conquer Algorithms

Divide and conquer is an algorithmic technique that recursively breaks down a problem into subproblems of the same type, solves the subproblems, and combines their solutions to solve the original problem. A classic example is the merge sort algorithm. The merge sort algorithm works as follows:

- Divide the array into two halves.
- Recursively sort each half.
- Merge the two halves to produce the sorted array.

The pseudocode for merge sort can be represented as:

Algorithm 14: Merge Sort

Input: Array A of n elements
Output: Sorted array A

if $n \leq 1$ **then**
  Return A
Divide A into two subarrays A_1 and A_2 of almost equal size;
$L1 =$ mergeSort(A_1);
$L2 =$ mergeSort(A_2);
$A =$ merge($L1, L2$);
Return A;

Here, the merging process involves combining two sorted arrays into a single sorted array. This algorithm exemplifies the power of divide and conquer by simplifying the problem into smaller subproblems that can be solved independently.

2. Dynamic Programming

Dynamic Programming (DP) often involves solving problems recursively but with the key optimization of storing the results of subproblems to avoid redundant computations. This approach is called memoization. A common example is computing the Fibonacci sequence. While a naive recursive implementation can be inefficient due to repeated calculations, using DP significantly improves performance.

Consider the following Java implementation of the Fibonacci function with memoization:

```
import java.util.HashMap;

public class Fibonacci {
    private HashMap<Integer, Integer> memo = new HashMap<>();

    public int fib(int n) {
        if (n <= 1) {
            return n;
        }
        if (memo.containsKey(n)) {
            return memo.get(n);
        }
        int result = fib(n - 1) + fib(n - 2);
        memo.put(n, result);
        return result;
    }
}
```

In this code, the fib method checks if the result for the current n is already computed and stored in the memo map. If so, it returns the stored value to reduce redundant calculations, ensuring efficient computation.

3. Search and Traversal in Data Structures

Recursion is also heavily utilized in tree and graph traversals. For instance, tree traversal algorithms like in-order, pre-order, and post-order traversals rely on recursive calls to navigate through the tree.

Consider a simple binary tree traversal in Java:

```
class Node {
    int value;
    Node left, right;

    Node(int item) {
        value = item;
        left = right = null;
    }
}

public class BinaryTree {
    Node root;

    void inOrderTraversal(Node node) {
        if (node == null) {
            return;
        }
        inOrderTraversal(node.left);
        System.out.print(node.value + " ");
```

```
            inOrderTraversal(node.right);
        }
    }
```

This example demonstrates the elegance of recursion in handling tree structures. The inOrderTraversal method relies on recursion to traverse the left subtree, then processes the node, followed by the right subtree.

4. Backtracking Algorithms

Backtracking is a recursive technique used to solve constraint satisfaction problems. It incrementally builds candidates for the solution and abandons them if they fail to satisfy the constraints. An example is solving a Sudoku puzzle or generating all permutations of a set.

The N-Queens problem is a classic backtracking problem where the objective is to place N queens on an N x N chessboard such that no two queens attack each other.

Here is a simplified version of the algorithm in Java:

```
public class NQueens {
    final int N = 8;
    int board[][] = new int[N][N];

    boolean isSafe(int row, int col) {
        for (int i = 0; i < col; i++)
            if (board[row][i] == 1)
                return false;
        for (int i=row, j=col; i>=0 && j>=0; i--, j--)
            if (board[i][j] == 1)
                return false;
        for (int i=row, j=col; j>=0 && i<N; i++, j--)
            if (board[i][j] == 1)
                return false;
        return true;
    }

    boolean solveNQUtil(int col) {
        if (col >= N)
            return true;

        for (int i = 0; i < N; i++) {
            if (isSafe(i, col)) {
                board[i][col] = 1;

                if (solveNQUtil(col + 1))
                    return true;

                board[i][col] = 0;
            }
        }
        return false;
    }

    boolean solveNQ() {
        if (solveNQUtil(0) == false) {
            System.out.print("Solution does not exist");
```

```
            return false;
        }
        printSolution(board);
        return true;
    }

    void printSolution(int board[][]) {
        for (int i = 0; i < N; i++) {
            for (int j = 0; j < N; j++)
                System.out.print(" " + board[i][j] + " ");
            System.out.println();
        }
    }
}
```

In this solution, the solveNQUtil method recursively attempts to place queens column-by-column, employing the isSafe method to ensure no two queens threaten each other. This systematic exploration and backtrack upon failure represent the backtracking approach.

5. Mathematical Problems

Recursion is apt for various mathematical problems, such as computing the greatest common divisor (GCD), exponentiation, and solving combinatorial problems.

The Euclidean algorithm for finding the GCD of two numbers is inherently recursive:

```
public class EuclideanAlgorithm {
    public int gcd(int a, int b) {
        if (b == 0) {
            return a;
        }
        return gcd(b, a % b);
    }
}
```

Here, the base case is when b equals zero, in which the GCD is a. Otherwise, the method recursively calls itself with b and the remainder of a divided by b.

These examples illustrate the versatility of recursion in solving a broad array of computational problems across different domains. Mastery of recursive techniques enables efficient and elegant solutions for complex problems that might be unwieldy with iterative approaches.

6.6 Recursive Algorithms: Factorial

To understand recursion in depth, it is useful to start with a classic example: the calculation of a factorial. The factorial of a non-negative integer n, denoted by $n!$, is the product of all positive integers less than or equal to n. The mathematical definition of factorial is given by:

$$n! = \begin{cases} 1 & \text{if } n = 0 \\ n \times (n-1)! & \text{if } n > 0 \end{cases}$$

This definition naturally lends itself to a recursive solution since the factorial of n can be defined in terms of the factorial of $n - 1$.

Factorial is a common example in recursion due to its straightforward recursive definition. Let's consider the recursive algorithm in Java:

```
public class Factorial {
    public static long factorial(int n) {
        if (n == 0) {
            return 1;
        } else {
            return n * factorial(n - 1);
        }
    }
}
```

In the factorial method above, the base case is when n equals 0. According to the definition, $0!$ is 1. When n is greater than 0, the method recursively calls itself with $(n - 1)$. This is the recursive case.

Execution of this method involves a sequence of recursive calls. Consider $5!$ as an example. The sequence of calls will be:

```
factorial(5) -> 5 * factorial(4)
factorial(4) -> 4 * factorial(3)
factorial(3) -> 3 * factorial(2)
factorial(2) -> 2 * factorial(1)
factorial(1) -> 1 * factorial(0)
factorial(0) -> 1
```

Once the base case is reached, the recursion starts to unwind as each method call returns its result to the previous call. This can be visualized as follows:

```
factorial(0) returns 1 to factorial(1)
factorial(1) returns 1 * 1 = 1 to factorial(2)
factorial(2) returns 2 * 1 = 2 to factorial(3)
factorial(3) returns 3 * 2 = 6 to factorial(4)
factorial(4) returns 4 * 6 = 24 to factorial(5)
factorial(5) returns 5 * 24 = 120
```

Thus, $5! = 120$.

It's important to note that an improper definition of the base case or missing it entirely can lead to infinite recursion, causing a stack overflow error. For example, if the base case $n == 0$ condition is omitted, the function will keep calling itself indefinitely.

Another key aspect to consider with recursive algorithms is the function call stack. Each recursive call adds a new frame to the stack, storing the state of each call until it can be resolved and removed from the stack. For large values of n, this can quickly lead to high memory usage.

An iterative approach to compute the factorial can avoid the call stack overhead:

```
public class Factorial {
    public static long factorialIterative(int n) {
        long result = 1;
        for (int i = 1; i <= n; i++) {
            result *= i;
        }
        return result;
    }
}
```

The iterative solution keeps a running product and requires only a few additional variables, making it more space-efficient. However, understanding the recursive method is crucial as it lays the foundation for more advanced concepts in algorithms and problem-solving strategies that heavily rely on recursion.

Finally, one must also consider edge cases in the implementation of the factorial function. For example, handling very large values of n can result in overflow errors since the value of factorial grows extremely rapidly. Languages such as Java can mitigate this using data types with larger capacity like BigInteger.

Han import the BigInteger class in Java:

```
import java.math.BigInteger;

public class Factorial {
    public static BigInteger factorialBigInteger(int n) {
        if (n == 0) {
            return BigInteger.ONE;
        } else {
            return BigInteger.valueOf(n).multiply(factorialBigInteger(n - 1));
        }
    }
}
```

The use of BigInteger allows for handling very large results of factorial computations without overflow errors, demonstrating a critical alternative for ensuring robustness in numeric computations.

6.7 Recursive Algorithms: Fibonacci Sequence

The Fibonacci sequence, a series of numbers where each number is the sum of the two preceding ones, usually starting with 0 and 1, is a fundamental example widely used to illustrate recursion. The sequence begins as 0, 1, 1, 2, 3, 5, 8, 13, and so forth. Given its recursive nature, the Fibonacci sequence can be elegantly expressed using a recursive function.

Formally, the Fibonacci sequence $F(n)$ is defined as:

$$F(n) = \begin{cases} 0 & \text{if } n = 0 \\ 1 & \text{if } n = 1 \\ F(n-1) + F(n-2) & \text{if } n > 1 \end{cases}$$

This definition directly translates into a recursive function in Java. Below is an implementation:

```
public class Fibonacci {
    public static int fibonacci(int n) {
        if (n == 0) {
            return 0;
        } else if (n == 1) {
            return 1;
        } else {
            return fibonacci(n - 1) + fibonacci(n - 2);
        }
    }

    public static void main(String[] args) {
        int n = 10; // Example: Calculate the 10th Fibonacci number
        System.out.println("Fibonacci number F(" + n + ") is " + fibonacci(n));
    }
}
```

The output of this program for $n = 10$ would be:

```
Fibonacci number F(10) is 55
```

The recursive function fibonacci contains two base cases: when n is 0, returning 0, and when n is 1, returning 1. For $n > 1$, the function recursively calls itself to compute $F(n-1)$ and $F(n-2)$.

Analysis of Recursive Fibonacci

The recursive algorithm demonstrates how naturally the problem fits into a recursive structure; however, it is essential to analyze its efficiency. The naïve recursive Fibonacci function has significant computational inefficiencies due to redundant calculations. Each call to fibonacci(n) results in two further calls: fibonacci(n-1) and fibonacci(n-2). This results in an exponential number of calls, leading to a time complexity of $O(2^n)$.

Consider calculating $F(5)$:

$$
\begin{aligned}
F(5) &= F(4) + F(3) \\
&= (F(3) + F(2)) + (F(2) + F(1)) \\
&= ((F(2) + F(1)) + (F(1) + F(0))) + ((F(1) + F(0)) + F(1))
\end{aligned}
$$

Notice that $F(3)$ and $F(2)$ are recalculated multiple times — an illustration of exponential growth in the number of function calls.

Optimizing Fibonacci with Memoization

To mitigate the inefficiencies of the naïve recursive approach, memoization (or caching) can be employed. Memoization stores the results of expensive function calls and reuses these results when the same inputs occur again, which effectively reduces the time complexity to $O(n)$.

A Java implementation using memoization:

```
import java.util.HashMap;

public class FibonacciMemoization {
    private static HashMap<Integer, Integer> memo = new HashMap<>();

    public static int fibonacci(int n) {
        if (n == 0) {
            return 0;
        } else if (n == 1) {
            return 1;
        }

        if (memo.containsKey(n)) {
            return memo.get(n);
        }

        int result = fibonacci(n - 1) + fibonacci(n - 2);
        memo.put(n, result);
        return result;
    }

    public static void main(String[] args) {
        int n = 10; // Example: Calculate the 10th Fibonacci number
        System.out.println("Fibonacci number F(" + n + ") is " + fibonacci(n));
    }
}
```

In this optimized version, the HashMap memo caches previously computed values of the Fibonacci sequence. Before recomputing $F(n)$, the algorithm checks whether the value is already present in the cache, thus avoiding redundant recursive calls and significantly improving performance.

Combining recursion with memoization provides a powerful method to enhance the efficiency of recursive algorithms. This technique underscores the importance of optimizing recursive solutions, a theme further explored in subsequent sections of this chapter.

6.8 Recursive Algorithms: Towers of Hanoi

The Towers of Hanoi is a classic problem widely used to illustrate the power and elegance of recursion. The problem consists of three pegs and a set of discs of varying sizes that can slide onto any peg. The objective is to move the entire stack of discs from the source peg to a destination peg, adhering to the following rules:

- Only one disc can be moved at a time.
- Each move consists of taking the upper disc from one of the stacks and placing it on top of another stack or on an empty peg.
- No disc may be placed on top of a smaller disc.

To effectively solve the Towers of Hanoi problem using recursion, it's critical to understand its structure. Let's break down the problem:

Problem Breakdown: 1. Move $n-1$ discs from the source peg to the auxiliary peg. 2. Move the n-th (largest) disc from the source peg to the destination peg. 3. Move the $n-1$ discs from the auxiliary peg to the destination peg.

This recursive breakdown suggests a solution comprising smaller subproblems that are structurally identical to the original problem but involve fewer discs.

The base case occurs when there is only one disc. In this scenario, the solution is straightforward: move the single disc from the source peg to the destination peg.

Algorithm Representation:

Using the "algorithm2e" package in LaTeX, the recursive algorithm can be represented as follows:

Algorithm 15: Towers of Hanoi Solution

Input: n: Number of discs
Input: $source$: The peg holding the initial stack
Input: aux: The auxiliary peg
Input: $destination$: The target peg

```
begin
    if n == 1 then
        Move disc from source to destination;
    end
    else
        solveTowersOfHanoi(n − 1, source, destination, aux);
        Move disc from source to destination;
        solveTowersOfHanoi(n − 1, aux, source, destination);
    end
end
```

Detailed Method Implementation in Java:

To implement this algorithm in Java, follow these steps:

```java
public class TowersOfHanoi {
    public void solveTowersOfHanoi(int n, char source, char aux, char destination) {
        if (n == 1) {
            System.out.println("Move disc 1 from " + source + " to " + destination);
        } else {
            solveTowersOfHanoi(n-1, source, destination, aux);
            System.out.println("Move disc " + n + " from " + source + " to " +
                    destination);
            solveTowersOfHanoi(n-1, aux, source, destination);
        }
    }

    public static void main(String[] args) {
        TowersOfHanoi toh = new TowersOfHanoi();
        int n = 3; // Number of discs
        toh.solveTowersOfHanoi(n, 'A', 'B', 'C'); // A, B, and C are names of the pegs
    }
}
```

Output of the Program:

Given three discs and pegs labeled 'A', 'B', and 'C':

```
Move disc 1 from A to C
Move disc 2 from A to B
Move disc 1 from C to B
Move disc 3 from A to C
Move disc 1 from B to A
Move disc 2 from B to C
Move disc 1 from A to C
```

Explanation:

- Move the top disc from peg ‘A‘ to peg ‘C‘.
- Move the second disc from peg ‘A‘ to peg ‘B‘.
- Move the smallest disc from peg ‘C‘ to peg ‘B‘ (across previously moved discs).
- Move the third (largest) disc from peg ‘A‘ to peg ‘C‘.
- Move the smallest disc from peg ‘B‘ to peg ‘A‘.
- Move the second disc from peg ‘B‘ to peg ‘C‘.
- Finally, move the smallest disc from peg ‘A‘ to peg ‘C‘.

Time Complexity Analysis:

The number of moves required to solve the Towers of Hanoi problem with n discs is $2^n - 1$. The algorithm's time complexity is exponential, denoted $O(2^n)$. This exponential growth rate means the problem becomes computationally expensive as the number of discs increases.

The Towers of Hanoi exemplifies how complex problems can be broken down into simpler tasks using recursion. Despite its simplicity in rules, the recursive solution elegantly demonstrates the methodology to solve repetitive, self-similar problems by addressing smaller instances of the same problem.

6.9 Backtracking: An Introduction

Backtracking is a refined approach for solving computational problems that incrementally build candidates for the solutions and discard those candidates (backtrack) as soon as it determines that the candidate cannot possibly lead to a valid solution. The methodology is akin to depth-first search traversal of a decision tree.

Algorithmic Structure of Backtracking

The backtracking algorithm involves the following key steps:

- Choice: Select a candidate component to be in the solution.
- Constraint: Evaluate whether the candidate remains a viable solution by testing against problem constraints.

- Goal: Determine whether the current candidate satisfies all the constraints sufficient to be accepted as a solution.

Example: N-Queens Problem

Consider the N-Queens problem, where the challenge is to place N queens on an $N \times N$ chessboard so that no two queens threaten each other. We will incrementally construct solutions and apply backtracking when conflicts arise.

Data: An integer N representing the size of the chessboard
Result: All possible ways to place N queens on a $N \times N$ chessboard

```
begin
    solveNQueens(board, col)
    if col ≥ N then
        return true;
    for every row i from 0 to N − 1 do
        if placing queen at board[i][col] is safe then
            place this queen on board[i][col];
            if solveNQueens(board, col+1) then
                return true;
            remove queen from board[i][col];
            // backtrack
    return false;
```

This illustrative N-Queens algorithm demonstrates how backtracking leverages recursion to explore potential solutions and backtrack upon encountering dead-ends.

Code Implementation: N-Queens in Java

A practical Java implementation is provided below to reinforce the concept:

```java
public class NQueens {
    final int N = 8;

    void printSolution(int board[][]) {
        for (int i = 0; i < N; i++) {
            for (int j = 0; j < N; j++) {
                System.out.print(" " + board[i][j] + " ");
            }
            System.out.println();
        }
    }
```

```
    boolean isSafe(int board[][], int row, int col) {
        int i, j;
        for (i = 0; i < col; i++)
            if (board[row][i] == 1)
                return false;

        for (i = row, j = col; i >= 0 && j >= 0; i--, j--)
            if (board[i][j] == 1)
                return false;

        for (i = row, j = col; j >= 0 && i < N; i++, j--)
            if (board[i][j] == 1)
                return false;

        return true;
    }

    boolean solveNQUtil(int board[][], int col) {
        if (col >= N)
            return true;

        for (int i = 0; i < N; i++) {
            if (isSafe(board, i, col)) {
                board[i][col] = 1;
                if (solveNQUtil(board, col + 1))
                    return true;
                board[i][col] = 0;
            }
        }
        return false;
    }

    boolean solveNQ() {
        int board[][] = new int[N][N];
        if (!solveNQUtil(board, 0)) {
            System.out.println("Solution does not exist");
            return false;
        }
        printSolution(board);
        return true;
    }

    public static void main(String args[]) {
        NQueens Queen = new NQueens();
        Queen.solveNQ();
    }
}
```

The solveNQ() method initializes the chessboard and invokes the recursive utility solveNQUtil() method. If a solution exists, it prints the chessboard; otherwise, it announces the absence of a solution.

Performance Considerations

Backtracking efficiently prunes the search space but is still exponential in time complexity in the worst case. Optimizations include:

- Early termination when constraints are violated.

- Using heuristics to decide the most promising candidate.
- Memoization to store previously computed states.

Applications of backtracking extend beyond N-Queens to other problems like Sudoku, Maze solving, and Word search puzzles. Understanding and mastering backtracking imbue the programmer with powerful problem-solving tools for diverse applications.

6.10 Common Pitfalls and How to Avoid Them

When utilizing recursion, a number of common pitfalls can arise that may result in inefficiencies, errors, or unexpected behavior. Understanding these pitfalls and implementing strategies to mitigate them is crucial for effective recursive programming. In this section, we will examine the most frequent pitfalls and provide practical remedies.

One common pitfall is related to incorrect base cases. The base case is the terminating scenario that stops the recursion from continuing indefinitely. An incorrect or missing base case often leads to a stack overflow error due to infinite recursion. The stack overflow error occurs when the call stack pointer exceeds the stack bound. It can be illustrated with an example:

```
// Incorrect base case example
public int incorrectBaseCase(int n) {
    if (n > 0) {
        return incorrectBaseCase(n - 1);
    }
    // Incorrect because n == 0 is not handled
    return n;
}
```

In this incorrect example, n is never checked for equality to zero, causing an infinite recursion for non-positive values. To avoid this, the base case must be explicitly defined:

```
// Correct base case
public int correctBaseCase(int n) {
    if (n <= 0) {
        return n; // Base case: stop recursion
    }
    return correctBaseCase(n - 1);
}
```

Another common pitfall is redundant calculations due to multiple recursive calls with overlapping subproblems. This issue is prevalent in problems like the Fibonacci sequence calculation:

```
// Inefficient Fibonacci calculation
public int naiveFibonacci(int n) {
    if (n <= 1) {
        return n;
    }
    return naiveFibonacci(n - 1) + naiveFibonacci(n - 2);
}
```

This approach recalculates Fibonacci values multiple times, leading to exponential time complexity, O(2^n). A memoization technique, which stores the results of expensive function calls and reuses the cached results, can be implemented to rectify this:

```
// Optimized Fibonacci with memoization
private Map<Integer, Integer> memo = new HashMap<>();

public int memoizedFibonacci(int n) {
    if (n <= 1) {
        return n;
    }
    if (memo.containsKey(n)) {
        return memo.get(n);
    }
    int result = memoizedFibonacci(n - 1) + memoizedFibonacci(n - 2);
    memo.put(n, result);
    return result;
}
```

A significant pitfall is the misuse of global variables, which can cause unintended side effects due to the mutable state being altered across different recursive calls:

```
// Misuse of global state in recursion
private int sum = 0;

public int sumArray(int[] arr, int index) {
    if (index >= arr.length) {
        return sum;
    }
    sum += arr[index];
    return sumArray(arr, index + 1);
}
```

Using global state, as demonstrated, makes the function non-reentrant and non-thread-safe. To avoid this, encapsulate the state within the recursive function:

```
// Proper encapsulation of state
public int sumArray(int[] arr, int index) {
    if (index >= arr.length) {
        return 0;
```

```
    }
    return arr[index] + sumArray(arr, index + 1);
}
```

Additionally, failure to account for stack depth and recursion limits can lead to stack overflow in languages with limited stack sizes. Deep recursion, as in the computation of factorials for large numbers, should be managed properly:

```
// Factorial with potential stack overflow
public int factorial(int n) {
    if (n <= 1) {
        return 1;
    }
    return n * factorial(n - 1);
}

// Tail-recursive version to prevent stack overflow
public int factorialHelper(int n, int accum) {
    if (n <= 1) {
        return accum;
    }
    return factorialHelper(n - 1, n * accum);
}

public int tailRecursiveFactorial(int n) {
    return factorialHelper(n, 1);
}
```

The tail-recursive version, tailRecursiveFactorial, ensures that the recursion can be optimized by the compiler to use constant stack space, thereby avoiding stack overflow.

Awareness of these common pitfalls and the knowledge to avoid them equips you with the necessary tools to write efficient and effective recursive algorithms. Proper base case design, strategic application of memoization, encapsulation of state, and techniques like tail recursion contribute to robust recursive solutions.

6.11 Optimizing Recursive Solutions

Optimizing recursive solutions aims to enhance the performance of recursive algorithms by minimizing redundant computations and improving space efficiency. Several techniques can be employed, including memoization, dynamic programming, and tail recursion optimization. This section explores these strategies in detail.

Memoization

Memoization involves storing results of expensive function calls and reusing these results when the same inputs occur again. By caching previously computed values, we can avoid redundant calculations, thereby reducing the time complexity. Consider the Fibonacci sequence, where naive recursion leads to an exponential time complexity due to repeated calculations.

Implementing memoization in Java involves using a Map to cache results:

```
import java.util.HashMap;
import java.util.Map;

public class FibonacciMemoization {
    private Map<Integer, Integer> cache = new HashMap<>();

    public int fibonacci(int n) {
        if (n <= 1) return n;
        if (cache.containsKey(n)) return cache.get(n);

        int result = fibonacci(n - 1) + fibonacci(n - 2);
        cache.put(n, result);
        return result;
    }

    public static void main(String[] args) {
        FibonacciMemoization fib = new FibonacciMemoization();
        System.out.println(fib.fibonacci(10)); // Output: 55
    }
}
```

In the above code, the cache stores previously computed Fibonacci values. The lookup in cache has an average time complexity of $O(1)$, making the overall algorithm linear $O(n)$.

Dynamic Programming

Dynamic programming is a technique used to solve problems by breaking them down into smaller subproblems and solving each subproblem only once, storing its solution. Unlike memoization, which typically employs recursion, dynamic programming is usually iterative and can lead to simpler, more efficient code.

For the Fibonacci sequence, the iterative dynamic programming approach is as follows:

```
public class FibonacciDynamicProgramming {

    public int fibonacci(int n) {
        if (n <= 1) return n;

        int[] fib = new int[n + 1];
        fib[0] = 0;
        fib[1] = 1;
```

```
        for (int i = 2; i <= n; i++) {
            fib[i] = fib[i - 1] + fib[i - 2];
        }

        return fib[n];
    }

    public static void main(String[] args) {
        FibonacciDynamicProgramming fib = new FibonacciDynamicProgramming();
        System.out.println(fib.fibonacci(10)); // Output: 55
    }
}
```

The iterative approach avoids the overhead of recursive function calls and further reduces the space complexity to $O(n)$.

Tail Recursion Optimization

Tail recursion occurs when a recursive function calls itself as its last operation, allowing the function's stack frame to be reused. Java does not support tail call optimization natively within the language specifications, but understanding and implementing tail-recursive patterns can help prepare code for better optimization under compatible runtimes or conversions.

In tail recursion, the recursive call must be the final action. Consider the factorial function optimized for tail recursion:

```
public class FactorialTailRecursive {

    public int factorial(int n) {
        return factorialHelper(n, 1);
    }

    private int factorialHelper(int n, int accumulator) {
        if (n == 0) return accumulator;
        return factorialHelper(n - 1, n * accumulator);
    }

    public static void main(String[] args) {
        FactorialTailRecursive fact = new FactorialTailRecursive();
        System.out.println(fact.factorial(5)); // Output: 120
    }
}
```

Here, factorialHelper is tail-recursive because the recursive call to factorialHelper is the final action, enabling potential stack frame optimization.

Comparative Analysis

The choice of optimization technique should consider both time and space constraints. Memoization is favorable for problems with overlapping subproblems and where space efficiency can be traded-off for time efficiency. Dynamic programming suits situations where the problem can be iteratively and systematically approached, minimizing both time and space overhead compared to naive recursion. Tail recursion, though less impactful in Java due to the lack of native support, is a pertinent concept for other programming environments and theoretical algorithm design.

These optimization strategies ensure that recursive solutions are viable even for more complex or larger datasets, enabling more efficient and practical applications.

6.12 Tail Recursion

Tail recursion is a subset of recursion where the recursive call is the final operation in the function. This characteristic allows optimizations by the compiler or runtime system, which is often referred to as Tail Call Optimization (TCO). In tail recursion, no further computation is needed once the recursive call returns, making it more memory efficient.

A tail-recursive function can be converted into an iterative function, thereby removing the overhead associated with maintaining multiple stack frames. This can lead to significant performance improvements, especially for algorithms involving deep recursion.

Example of Tail Recursion: Factorial

Consider the conventional recursive implementation of the factorial function:

```
int factorial(int n) {
    if (n == 0) {
        return 1;
    } else {
        return n * factorial(n - 1);
    }
}
```

In this implementation, the multiplication operation n * factorial(n - 1) is performed after the recursive call returns, making it non-tail-recursive. To convert this into a tail-recursive function, we utilize an accumulator to carry the result through recursive calls:

```
int factorialTailRec(int n, int acc) {
    if (n == 0) {
        return acc;
    } else {
        return factorialTailRec(n - 1, n * acc);
    }
```

```
}
```

Here, acc serves as an accumulator, holding the intermediate results. The final call resolves to:

```
int factorial(int n) {
    return factorialTailRec(n, 1);
}
```

Characteristics of Tail Recursion

- The recursive call must be the last action performed in the function.
- Can be optimized by the compiler to improve space efficiency.
- Accumulators are often used to hold intermediate results.

Advantages of Tail Recursion

- **Space Efficiency**: Since a tail-recursive call does not need to maintain previous stack frames, it operates in constant space.
- **Ease of Transformation**: Tail-recursive functions can be more easily transformed into iterative loops.

Example of Tail Recursion: Fibonacci Sequence

The standard recursive implementation of the Fibonacci sequence is:

```
int fibonacci(int n) {
    if (n == 0) {
        return 0;
    } else if (n == 1) {
        return 1;
    } else {
        return fibonacci(n - 1) + fibonacci(n - 2);
    }
}
```

This implementation is not tail-recursive and has exponential time complexity due to redundant calculations.

To create a tail-recursive version, we use two accumulators to store the results of the previous two Fibonacci numbers:

```
int fibonacciTailRec(int n, int a, int b) {
    if (n == 0) {
        return a;
    } else if (n == 1) {
```

```
        return b;
    } else {
        return fibonacciTailRec(n - 1, b, a + b);
    }
}
```

The entry function is defined as:

```
int fibonacci(int n) {
    return fibonacciTailRec(n, 0, 1);
}
```

Transforming Tail-Recursive to Iterative

Given the fundamental similarity between tail recursion and iteration, it is possible to transform a tail-recursive function into an iterative one. This can be demonstrated with the factorial example:

```
int factorialIterative(int n) {
    int result = 1;
    for (int i = n; i > 0; i--) {
        result *= i;
    }
    return result;
}
```

In this iterative version, we maintain a variable result that accumulates the product directly within the loop, eliminating the need for recursive calls.

Tail recursion provides a pathway to optimize recursive solutions, bridging the gap between the conceptual simplicity of recursion and the performance advantages of iteration, especially in languages and environments that support Tail Call Optimization. This makes it a powerful tool in the armory of a proficient Java developer.

Chapter 7

Trees and Binary Search Trees

This chapter provides an in-depth exploration of trees, particularly binary trees and binary search trees (BST). It begins with fundamental tree terminology and introduces various tree traversal methods. The chapter then focuses on binary search trees, covering essential operations such as insertion, deletion, and searching. Additionally, it addresses balancing techniques and self-balancing trees like AVL and Red-Black trees. Real-world applications of trees in computer science are discussed, offering a comprehensive understanding of their significance and functionality.

7.1 Introduction to Trees

Trees are a fundamental data structure in computer science and play a crucial role in a variety of algorithms and applications. A tree is a hierarchical structure consisting of nodes, where each node holds a value and references to its children. The inherent hierarchical nature of trees makes them suitable for representing relationships that naturally form a hierarchy, such as file systems, organizational structures, and XML documents.

A tree T is defined as a collection of nodes, consisting of a distinguished node called the root, and zero or more subtrees, each of which is also a tree. The nodes in the tree represent the entities or values, and the edges (connections between nodes) represent the relationships between these entities.

The main properties of a tree include:

- **Nodes:** The individual elements or entities in the tree.
- **Root:** The top node of the tree, where traversal begins.
- **Edges:** The connections between nodes.
- **Parent:** A node that has one or more child nodes directly connected to it.
- **Child:** A node that is directly connected to another node when moving away from the root.
- **Leaf:** A node with no children.
- **Subtree:** Any node and all of its descendants form a subtree.

A tree with n nodes has exactly $n - 1$ edges, provided there are no cycles or disconnections within the tree. The absence of cycles and the connected nature of the tree ensure that there is a unique path between any two nodes.

Example of a Tree Structure:

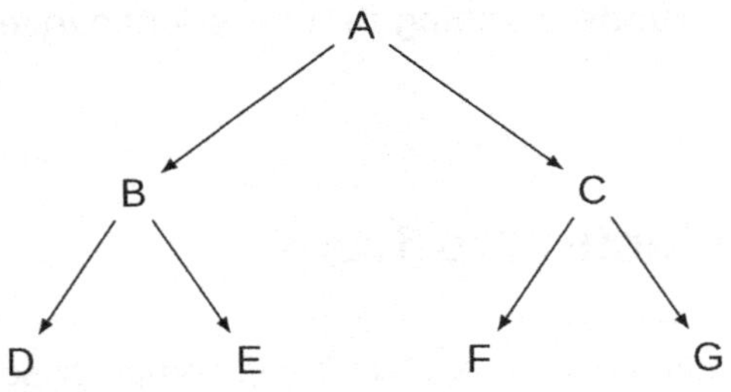

Figure 7.1: An example of a tree with root node A.

In the example diagram (Figure 7.1), node A is the root, nodes B and C are children of A, and nodes D, E, F, and G are leaves.

Trees have many variants including binary trees, AVL trees, and Red-Black trees, each suited to different applications and scenarios. In this chapter, we will start with the basic structures and operation of trees and proceed to more complex forms and algorithms.

Representation of Trees in Java

A tree can be represented using classes where each node contains references to its children. A simple implementation of a tree node in Java can be performed using the class structure as follows:

```
public class TreeNode {
    int value;
    TreeNode left;
    TreeNode right;

    public TreeNode(int value) {
        this.value = value;
        this.left = null;
        this.right = null;
    }
}
```

Here, TreeNode encapsulates the value at the node and references to its left and right children (commonly used in binary trees). To construct a tree, initialize the root node and link children nodes as desired.

Example Construction of a Simple Binary Tree:

```
public class BinaryTree {
    TreeNode root;

    public BinaryTree(int rootValue) {
        root = new TreeNode(rootValue);
    }

    public void addLeftChild(TreeNode parent, int value) {
        parent.left = new TreeNode(value);
    }

    public void addRightChild(TreeNode parent, int value) {
        parent.right = new TreeNode(value);
    }

    public static void main(String[] args) {
        BinaryTree tree = new BinaryTree(1);
        tree.addLeftChild(tree.root, 2);
        tree.addRightChild(tree.root, 3);
        tree.addLeftChild(tree.root.left, 4);
        tree.addRightChild(tree.root.left, 5);
    }
}
```

This representation captures a tree where the root node has the value '1', the left child of root has '2', the right child of root has '3', and so forth, forming a simple binary tree structure.

Traversal of Trees

Traversal is a fundamental operation that involves visiting all the nodes in a tree in a specific order. The three primary methods for tree traversal are:

- **In-Order Traversal:** Visit the left subtree, the root, and the right subtree.
- **Pre-Order Traversal:** Visit the root, the left subtree, and the right subtree.
- **Post-Order Traversal:** Visit the left subtree, the right subtree, and the root.

Implementation examples of these traversal methods in Java are provided below.

```
public void inOrderTraversal(TreeNode node) {
    if (node != null) {
        inOrderTraversal(node.left);
        System.out.print(node.value + " ");
        inOrderTraversal(node.right);
    }
}
```

```
public void preOrderTraversal(TreeNode node) {
    if (node != null) {
        System.out.print(node.value + " ");
        preOrderTraversal(node.left);
        preOrderTraversal(node.right);
    }
}
```

```
public void postOrderTraversal(TreeNode node) {
    if (node != null) {
        postOrderTraversal(node.left);
        postOrderTraversal(node.right);
        System.out.print(node.value + " ");
    }
}
```

Traversing a tree enables various operations, such as searching for a value, validating the structure, and manipulating nodes based on their relationships within the tree.

Understanding trees and their traversal forms the foundation for more advanced topics, such as Binary Search Trees (BST), Self-Balancing Trees, and their applications in optimizing search and sort operations within various domains.

7.2 Tree Terminology

Understanding tree terminology is pivotal in grasping the concepts that underpin tree data structures, especially as we delve into more complex forms like Binary Search Trees (BST) and self-balancing trees. This section will clarify the fundamental terms associated with trees, ensuring a solid foundation for the subsequent algorithms and operations discussed later in this chapter.

Node: A node represents a single element within a tree, containing a value or data, and potentially referencing other nodes (its children). Nodes are the fundamental units from which trees are formed.

Root: The root is the topmost node of a tree. It serves as the starting point for traversing the tree. In a well-defined tree structure, there is exactly one root node.

Parent and Child: A node N is said to be the parent of another node M if there is a direct edge from N to M. Conversely, M is called the child of N. Each node can have zero or more children.

Leaf: A leaf, or terminal node, is a node that does not have any children. Leaves are nodes at the bottom-most level of the tree structure.

Sibling: Nodes that share the same parent are referred to as siblings. For instating, if nodes A and B are both children of node C, then A and B are siblings.

Subtree: A subtree is a portion of a tree that constitutes a tree in itself. A subtree of a node N includes N and all its descendants. Subtrees are useful when considering recursive algorithms.

Path: A path in a tree is a sequence of nodes where each consecutive pair of nodes in the sequence is connected by an edge. For example, a path from the root to a leaf includes every node encountered in moving from the root to that leaf.

Depth: The depth of a node in a tree is the number of edges from the node to the tree's root. Thus, the root node has a depth of 0.

Height: The height of a node is the number of edges on the longest path from that node to a leaf. The height of the tree is the height of the root node.

Level: The level of a node is defined based on its depth, with the root node being at level 0, its children at level 1, its grandchildren at level 2, and so forth.

Degree: The degree of a node is the number of its children. A node with no children (a leaf) has a degree of 0.

To solidify these concepts, consider a basic implementation of a tree node in Java:

```
public class TreeNode {
    int data;
    TreeNode left;
    TreeNode right;

    public TreeNode(int data) {
        this.data = data;
        this.left = null;
        this.right = null;
    }
}
```

In this code snippet, TreeNode represents the structure of a node in a binary tree, containing data and references to its left and right children.

```
TreeNode root = new TreeNode(10);
root.left = new TreeNode(5);
root.right = new TreeNode(15);
```

In the output, the node with value 10 is the root node, 5 is the left child, and 15 is the right child of the root, forming a simple binary tree.

Understanding these terms is crucial as they form the basis for describing trees in both theoretical and practical contexts, particularly when analyzing the efficiency of various tree operations and algorithms.

7.3 Binary Trees

A binary tree is a hierarchical data structure in which each node has at most two children, typically distinguished as the left child and right child. Each node in a binary tree contains three components:

- A data element.
- A reference (or pointer) to the left child.
- A reference (or pointer) to the right child.

The structure of a binary tree allows for efficient operations such as insertion, deletion, and traversal.

Definition and Properties of Binary Trees

A binary tree T is defined recursively as either:

- An empty tree (null), or
- A tree consisting of a root, a left subtree T_{left}, and a right subtree T_{right}, each of which is itself a binary tree.

The maximum number of nodes at level l of a binary tree is 2^l. Therefore, the height h of a binary tree (the number of edges on the longest path from the root to a leaf) determines the maximum number of nodes the tree can hold, expressed as $2^{h+1} - 1$.

Types of Binary Trees

Binary trees can be further classified based on certain properties:

- Full Binary Tree: A binary tree is full if every node has either 0 or 2 children.
- Complete Binary Tree: A binary tree is complete if all levels except possibly the last are fully filled, and all nodes in the last level are as far left as possible.
- Perfect Binary Tree: A binary tree is perfect if all internal nodes have two children and all leaves are at the same level.
- Degenerate (or pathological) Tree: A binary tree is degenerate if each parent node has only one child. In this scenario, the tree effectively behaves as a linked list.

Binary Tree Implementation in Java

Below are the core components for implementing a binary tree in Java:

```
class TreeNode {
  int data;
  TreeNode left;
  TreeNode right;

  TreeNode(int item) {
    data = item;
    left = right = null;
  }
}
```

In this code snippet, TreeNode represents a single node in a binary tree. Each node stores an integer value, data, and pointers to the left and right children, left and right.

BinaryTree defines the binary tree itself:

```
class BinaryTree {
  TreeNode root;

  BinaryTree() {
    root = null;
  }

  void insert(int data) {
    root = insertRec(root, data);
  }

  TreeNode insertRec(TreeNode root, int data) {
    if (root == null) {
      root = new TreeNode(data);
      return root;
    }
    if (data < root.data)
      root.left = insertRec(root.left, data);
    else if (data > root.data)
      root.right = insertRec(root.right, data);

    return root;
  }
}
```

In the BinaryTree class, the insert method initiates insertion by calling the recursive helper method insertRec. This method traverses the tree to find the appropriate location for the new node based on the binary tree property: the left child is smaller than the parent node and the right child is larger.

```
BinaryTree tree = new BinaryTree();
tree.insert(50);
tree.insert(30);
tree.insert(20);
tree.insert(40);
tree.insert(70);
tree.insert(60);
tree.insert(80);
```

This simple sequence of operations constructs a binary tree with the root node having a value of 50, subsequently inserting nodes with values 30, 20, 40, 70, 60, and 80.

Traversing a Binary Tree

Traversal refers to the process of visiting all the nodes in a specified order. The primary traversals for binary trees include:

- In-order Traversal: Visits nodes in ascending order. Algorithmically, it can be expressed as:

Input: root
Output: Traversal of the tree in in-order

```
if root != null then
    inOrderTraversal(root.left);
    processNode(root);
    inOrderTraversal(root.right);
else
```

- Pre-order Traversal: Visits the root node first, followed by the left subtree, and finally the right subtree. Expressed as:

Input: root
Output: Traversal of the tree in pre-order

```
if root != null then
    processNode(root);
    preOrderTraversal(root.left);
    preOrderTraversal(root.right);
else
```

- Post-order Traversal: Visits the left subtree, the right subtree, and finally the root node. Expressed as:

Input: root
Output: Traversal of the tree in post-order

```
if root != null then
    postOrderTraversal(root.left);
    postOrderTraversal(root.right);
    processNode(root);
else
```

These algorithms ensure that each node is visited exactly once, maintaining the defined traversal order. Implementing these traversals in Java would involve creating recursive methods to process nodes as designed in the algorithms above.

```
void inOrderTraversal(TreeNode node) {
  if (node != null) {
    inOrderTraversal(node.left);
    System.out.print(node.data + " ");
    inOrderTraversal(node.right);
  }
}
```

```
void preOrderTraversal(TreeNode node) {
  if (node != null) {
    System.out.print(node.data + " ");
    preOrderTraversal(node.left);
    preOrderTraversal(node.right);
  }
}
```

```
void postOrderTraversal(TreeNode node) {
  if (node != null) {
    postOrderTraversal(node.left);
    postOrderTraversal(node.right);
    System.out.print(node.data + " ");
  }
}
```

These traversal methods provide foundational methods for exploring and manipulating the contents of a binary tree. Understanding and implementing binary trees and their various traversals create a strong base for further exploration of binary search trees and more advanced tree structures.

7.4 Tree Traversal Algorithms: In-order, Pre-order, Post-order

Tree traversal is an essential concept in the study of tree data structures. It refers to the process of visiting each node in a tree data structure systematically. Tree traversals are critical for various tree operations, such as searching, inserting, deleting nodes, and displaying the structure of the tree.

Three primary types of depth-first traversals are commonly used: **In-order**, **Pre-order**, and **Post-order**. Each traversal strategy visits the nodes of the tree in a specific sequence, yielding different outcomes.

In-order Traversal (Left, Root, Right): In this type of traversal, nodes are recursively visited in the following order:

- Traverse the left subtree.
- Visit the root node.
- Traverse the right subtree.

Implementing an in-order traversal in Java can be achieved through the following recursive method:

```
public void inOrderTraversal(TreeNode node) {
    if (node != null) {
        // Traverse the left subtree.
        inOrderTraversal(node.left);

        // Visit the root node.
        System.out.print(node.value + " ");

        // Traverse the right subtree.
        inOrderTraversal(node.right);
    }
}
```

For a binary search tree, an in-order traversal yields nodes in ascending order. Consider the following example binary search tree:

```
    4
   / \
  2   6
 / \ / \
1  3 5  7
```

The in-order traversal of this tree would output:

```
1 2 3 4 5 6 7
```

Pre-order Traversal (Root, Left, Right): In pre-order traversal, the sequence of operations for each node is:

- Visit the root node.
- Traverse the left subtree.
- Traverse the right subtree.

Here is how pre-order traversal can be implemented in Java:

```
public void preOrderTraversal(TreeNode node) {
    if (node != null) {
        // Visit the root node.
        System.out.print(node.value + " ");

        // Traverse the left subtree.
        preOrderTraversal(node.left);

        // Traverse the right subtree.
        preOrderTraversal(node.right);
    }
}
```

Using the same example binary search tree, the pre-order traversal would be:

```
4 2 1 3 6 5 7
```

This traversal method is useful for creating a copy of the tree, as it visits each node before its child nodes.

Post-order Traversal (Left, Right, Root): The post-order traversal method visits nodes in the following order:

- Traverse the left subtree.
- Traverse the right subtree.
- Visit the root node.

The Java implementation for post-order traversal is as follows:

```
public void postOrderTraversal(TreeNode node) {
    if (node != null) {
        // Traverse the left subtree.
        postOrderTraversal(node.left);

        // Traverse the right subtree.
        postOrderTraversal(node.right);

        // Visit the root node.
        System.out.print(node.value + " ");
    }
}
```

Executing a post-order traversal on the same example binary search tree produces the sequence:

```
1 3 2 5 7 6 4
```

This traversal method is particularly useful for deleting binary trees, as it ensures that child nodes are processed before the parent node.

To further deepen our understanding, we can employ iterative methods for these traversals. The iterative approach for in-order traversal, for instance, utilizes a stack data structure to simulate the call stack used in recursion.

An iterative implementation of in-order traversal in Java might look as follows:

```
public void iterativeInOrderTraversal(TreeNode root) {
    Stack<TreeNode> stack = new Stack<>();
    TreeNode current = root;

    while (current != null || !stack.isEmpty()) {
        // Reach the leftmost TreeNode.
        while (current != null) {
            stack.push(current);
            current = current.left;
        }
```

```
        // Current must be null at this point.
        current = stack.pop();
        System.out.print(current.value + " ");

        // Visit the right subtree.
        current = current.right;
    }
}
```

For completeness, let's examine the outputs of iterative methods by running the above iterative in-order traversal on our example binary search tree:

```
1 2 3 4 5 6 7
```

Iterative methods offer advantages in environments with constrained stack sizes or when recursion depth might lead to stack overflow.

Understanding these traversal methods - in-order, pre-order, and post-order - is fundamental to mastering tree-related algorithms and their applications. These methods form the basis for many complex tree operations, making it imperative to understand and implement them well.

7.5 Binary Search Trees (BST)

A Binary Search Tree (BST) is a specialized form of a binary tree, distinguished by the properties that enable efficient search operations. In a BST, each node contains a key, and for any given node, its key is greater than the keys of all nodes in its left subtree and less than the keys of all nodes in its right subtree. This property facilitates logarithmic time complexity for search, insertion, and deletion operations in a balanced BST.

Structure of a BST Node

A typical BST node in Java can be defined as follows:

```
class TreeNode {
    int key;
    TreeNode left, right;

    public TreeNode(int item) {
        key = item;
        left = right = null;
    }
}
```

Properties of Binary Search Trees

The key properties of a BST include:

- **Binary Tree Form**: Each node has at most two children.
- **Binary Search Property**: For any node n, all keys in its left subtree are less than n.key, and all keys in its right subtree are greater than n.key.
- **Balanced BST**: For optimal performance, the tree should be balanced, minimizing the height to ensure logarithmic operation times.

Traversal of Binary Search Trees

The traversal methods for BSTs are similar to those for binary trees and include in-order, pre-order, and post-order traversals.

```
// In-order traversal
void inorderTraversal(TreeNode node) {
    if (node != null) {
        inorderTraversal(node.left);
        System.out.print(node.key + " ");
        inorderTraversal(node.right);
    }
}

// Pre-order traversal
void preorderTraversal(TreeNode node) {
    if (node != null) {
        System.out.print(node.key + " ");
        preorderTraversal(node.left);
        preorderTraversal(node.right);
    }
}

// Post-order traversal
void postorderTraversal(TreeNode node) {
    if (node != null) {
        postorderTraversal(node.left);
        postorderTraversal(node.right);
        System.out.print(node.key + " ");
    }
}
```

Insertion in Binary Search Trees

Insertion involves adding a new node to the BST while maintaining the binary search property. Starting from the root, traverse the tree to find the appropriate position for the new node.

```
TreeNode insert(TreeNode root, int key) {
    if (root == null) {
        root = new TreeNode(key);
        return root;
    }

    if (key < root.key) {
        root.left = insert(root.left, key);
    } else if (key > root.key) {
        root.right = insert(root.right, key);
    }

    return root;
}
```

Searching in Binary Search Trees

Searching in a BST involves comparing the target key with the current node's key and recursively traversing left or right depending on the comparison result.

```
TreeNode search(TreeNode root, int key) {
    if (root == null || root.key == key) {
        return root;
    }

    if (key < root.key) {
        return search(root.left, key);
    }

    return search(root.right, key);
}
```

Deletion in Binary Search Trees

Deletion in a BST is more complex than insertion or searching, as it involves rearranging the tree to maintain the binary search property. There are three main cases to consider:

- **Node to be deleted is a leaf**: Simply remove the node.
- **Node to be deleted has one child**: Copy the child to the node and delete the child.
- **Node to be deleted has two children**: Find the in-order successor (smallest in the right subtree) or in-order predecessor

(largest in the left subtree), replace the node's key with the successor's/predecessor's key, and delete the successor/predecessor.

```
TreeNode delete(TreeNode root, int key) {
    if (root == null) return root;

    if (key < root.key)
        root.left = delete(root.left, key);
    else if (key > root.key)
        root.right = delete(root.right, key);
    else {
        if (root.left == null)
            return root.right;
        else if (root.right == null)
            return root.left;

        root.key = minValue(root.right);
        root.right = delete(root.right, root.key);
    }

    return root;
}

int minValue(TreeNode root) {
    int minv = root.key;
    while (root.left != null) {
        minv = root.left.key;
        root = root.left;
    }
    return minv;
}
```

Understanding the fundamental operations and properties of BSTs is crucial for further exploration of more advanced data structures such as AVL trees and Red-Black trees, which extend the basic principles of BSTs to ensure balanced structures and improved performance.

7.6 Operations on BST: Insertion

Insertion into a Binary Search Tree (BST) is a fundamental operation that maintains the delicate structure of the tree, ensuring that it operates efficiently under the BST properties. The BST property dictates that for any given node, the left subtree contains values less than the node, and the right subtree contains values greater than the node. This invariant allows efficient searching, insertion, and deletion operations.

When inserting a value into a BST, we must locate the proper position to maintain the BST property. This is achieved recursively or iteratively as we traverse the tree from the root to the appropriate null link where the new node will be inserted.

Algorithm for Insertion: We use a key, denoted as key, which we need to insert into the BST. The operation is aimed at finding the correct position for key by comparing it with existing node values, starting from the root and proceeding downward to a leaf node.

Algorithm 16: BST Insertion Algorithm

Data: A binary search tree root and a value key to be inserted.
Result: A BST with the node containing key inserted while maintaining the BST property.

```
Function recursive_insert(node, key):
    if node = NULL then
        return create_node(key)
    else if key < node.key then
        node.left ← recursive_insert(node.left, key)
    else
        node.right ← recursive_insert(node.right, key)
    end
    return node
Function insert_BST(root, key):
    return recursive_insert(root, key)
```

Explanation: The insert_BST function initiates the insertion by calling recursive_insert. The recursive_insert function traverses the tree. If a null reference (i.e., the end of a traversal path) is found, it creates a new node containing key. Otherwise, it continues to traverse the appropriate subtree (left if key is less, right if key is greater) until the leaf node is reached. When the function returns from recursion, each ancestor node is linked properly to the new node, maintaining the BST properties.

Java Implementation: The described algorithm can be directly translated into Java. Below is the implementation of the BST insertion operation in Java.

```
class TreeNode {
    int key;
    TreeNode left, right;

    public TreeNode(int item) {
        key = item;
        left = right = null;
    }
}

class BinarySearchTree {
```

```
    TreeNode root;

    BinarySearchTree() {
        root = null;
    }

    void insert(int key) {
        root = insertRec(root, key);
    }

    TreeNode insertRec(TreeNode root, int key) {
        if (root == null) {
            root = new TreeNode(key);
            return root;
        }

        if (key < root.key)
            root.left = insertRec(root.left, key);
        else if (key > root.key)
            root.right = insertRec(root.right, key);

        return root;
    }
}

public class Main {
    public static void main(String[] args) {
        BinarySearchTree bst = new BinarySearchTree();
        bst.insert(50);
        bst.insert(30);
        bst.insert(20);
        bst.insert(40);
        bst.insert(70);
        bst.insert(60);
        bst.insert(80);
    }
}
```

In this implementation, the BinarySearchTree class encapsulates the tree's root and provides an insert method for public use. The actual insertion logic is handled by the insertRec method, analogous to the recursive_insert function described earlier. Each invocation of insertRec traverses down the tree according to the key value until it finds the null link where a new TreeNode is created and inserted.

The main method demonstrates inserting nodes into the BST with specific key values. You can observe the hierarchical structure which adheres to the binary search tree properties.

Proper understanding and implementation of the insertion operation ensure the BST remains efficient for search operations, typically O(log n) in time complexity for balanced trees. It is crucial for readers to grasp the recursive nature and the maintenance of BST properties during insertion to effectively manage more complex tree manipulations and optimizations.

```
BinarySearchTree bst = new BinarySearchTree();
bst.insert(50);
bst.insert(30);
bst.insert(20);
bst.insert(40);
bst.insert(70);
bst.insert(60);
bst.insert(80);
```

The sample output would range from the tree being empty to the tree containing nodes in a hierarchical binary search format, where each insertion places the node in the correct position according to the BST rules. Thus, the implemented recursive insertion ensures an ordered binary search tree structure.

7.7 Operations on BST: Deletion

Deletion in a Binary Search Tree (BST) is a fundamental operation that maintains the BST properties after a node is removed. The deletion process is intricate as it requires careful handling of three primary scenarios: deleting a leaf node, deleting a node with one child, and deleting a node with two children. Understanding these scenarios ensures the tree's structure remains valid.

Deleting a Leaf Node: A leaf node is a node with no children. Deleting a leaf node is straightforward because it does not affect other nodes.

```
public TreeNode delete(TreeNode root, int key) {
    if (root == null) return root;
    if (key < root.val) {
        root.left = delete(root.left, key);
    } else if (key > root.val) {
        root.right = delete(root.right, key);
    } else {
        // Node to be deleted found and it is a leaf node
        if (root.left == null && root.right == null) {
            root = null;
        }
    }
    return root;
}
```

Deleting a Node with One Child: When a node with one child is deleted, the parent node must connect directly to the single child, effectively bypassing the deleted node. This bypass ensures that the BST properties are maintained.

```
public TreeNode delete(TreeNode root, int key) {
    if (root == null) return root;
    if (key < root.val) {
        root.left = delete(root.left, key);
```

```
    } else if (key > root.val) {
        root.right = delete(root.right, key);
    } else {
        // Node to be deleted found and it has only one child
        if (root.left == null) return root.right;
        else if (root.right == null) return root.left;
        // Node with two children will be handled later
    }
    return root;
}
```

Deleting a Node with Two Children: When dealing with nodes that have two children, finding a suitable replacement for the deleted node is imperative. Typically, this involves either the in-order predecessor (maximum value node in the left subtree) or the in-order successor (minimum value node in the right subtree).

```
private TreeNode findMin(TreeNode root) {
    while (root.left != null) {
        root = root.left;
    }
    return root;
}

public TreeNode delete(TreeNode root, int key) {
    if (root == null) return root;
    if (key < root.val) {
        root.left = delete(root.left, key);
    } else if (key > root.val) {
        root.right = delete(root.right, key);
    } else {
        // Node to be deleted found, it has two children
        if (root.left != null && root.right != null) {
            TreeNode temp = findMin(root.right); // Find in-order successor
            root.val = temp.val; // Replace root value with successor's value
            root.right = delete(root.right, temp.val); // Delete successor node
        } else if (root.left == null) return root.right; // One child cases
        else if (root.right == null) return root.left;
    }
    return root;
}
```

In the delete function, the findMin helper function identifies the in-order successor by traversing to the leftmost node of the right child subtree. The successor's value replaces the value of the node to be deleted, and then the successor node is deleted from its original position.

```
Example:

Initial Tree                Tree after deleting 50
     50                          60
    /  \                        /  \
  30    70                    30    70
 /  \  /  \                  /  \     \
20  40 60  80               20  40     80
```

Attempting to delete a node with two children necessitates replacing it with the in-order successor to maintain the BST order properties. After substituting the node's value with the successor's value, the successor node is deleted as it either has no children or has only one right child (since it's the minimum node of that subtree).

Edge cases such as deleting the root node or nodes in a skewed BST are handled by the same logic, ensuring a uniform strategy regardless of tree structure. Efficient deletion ensures that further operations like insertions and searches continue to respect the logarithmic time complexity attribute of BSTs.

In practical scenarios, maintaining the balance of the tree post-deletion is critical, which is subsequently achieved through self-balancing mechanisms. Deletion directly influences tree height, necessitating careful balancing for optimal performance.

7.8 Operations on BST: Searching

In a Binary Search Tree (BST), the search operation exploits the property that for any given node, all elements in the left subtree are less than the node's key, and all elements in the right subtree are greater. This section provides a thorough explanation of the search operation, demonstrating how to efficiently locate an element within a BST by leveraging its ordered structure.

To search for a particular element, denoted by key, in a BST, we start at the root and recursively traverse the tree. At each node, we compare key with the node's key. There are three possible outcomes:

- If key is equal to the node's key, the search is successful, and the node is returned.
- If key is less than the node's key, the search continues in the left subtree.
- If key is greater than the node's key, the search continues in the right subtree.

The algorithm for searching a key in a BST can be formally described as follows:

Algorithm 17: BST Search Operation

```
Data: root: Node, key: Integer
Result: Node containing the key if found, otherwise null
Function SearchBST(root, key):
    if root = null then
        return null
    if key = root.key then
        return root
    else if key < root.key then
        return SearchBST(root.left, key)
    else
        return SearchBST(root.right, key)
```

In a practical implementation, a method search defined within a BST class is used to invoke the recursive function. Below is an example implementation in Java:

```java
public class BinarySearchTree {
    class Node {
        int key;
        Node left, right;

        public Node(int item) {
            key = item;
            left = right = null;
        }
    }

    Node root;

    public BinarySearchTree() {
        root = null;
    }

    // Method to search a key in BST
    public Node search(int key) {
        return searchRec(root, key);
    }

    // A recursive function to search a key in BST
    private Node searchRec(Node root, int key) {
        // Base Cases: root is null or key is present at root
        if (root == null || root.key == key)
            return root;

        // Key is smaller than root's key
        if (key < root.key)
            return searchRec(root.left, key);

        // Key is larger than root's key
        return searchRec(root.right, key)
    }
}
```

Consider the following BST:

```
      50
     /  \
   30    70
  / \   / \
20 40 60 80
```

To search for the key 60, the search operation proceeds as follows:

1. Start at the root (node with key 50).
2. Since 60 is greater than 50, go to the right subtree.
3. The next node is 70. Since 60 is less than 70, go to the left subtree.
4. The next node is 60. The key matches, so the search stops, returning the node with key 60.

The time complexity of the search operation in a BST is $O(h)$, where h is the height of the tree. In the worst case, h could be equal to $n-1$ (in a totally unbalanced tree), making the time complexity $O(n)$. In the average case, for a balanced tree, the height is $\log n$, making the search operation $O(\log n)$.

It is important to note that the performance of a BST and efficiency of its operations are closely tied to its height. Balancing techniques, such as those discussed in later sections, are employed to ensure that the height of the tree remains logarithmic with respect to the number of nodes, which maintains the efficiency of search operations.

7.9 Balancing Binary Search Trees

Balancing binary search trees is critical for maintaining efficient performance. A balanced binary search tree ensures that the height of the tree is logarithmic in the number of nodes, denoted as $O(\log n)$. This characteristic is essential for achieving optimal time complexity for search, insertion, and deletion operations. Unbalanced trees may degenerate into linear structures, such as linked lists, with $O(n)$ time complexity, negating the primary advantages of binary search trees.

A key property of a balanced binary search tree is that the depths of the two subtrees of any node differ by at most one. This balance condition minimizes the height of the tree, thereby optimizing the worst-case performance of basic operations. The following sections detail commonly used techniques to achieve balancing in binary search trees.

1. Rotations

Tree rotations are fundamental operations used to balance binary search trees. A rotation involves changing the structure without violating the binary search tree properties, i.e., for any node in the tree:

- Nodes in the left subtree have keys less than the node's key.
- Nodes in the right subtree have keys greater than the node's key.

There are two primary types of rotations:

- Right Rotation (R): Converts a left-heavy subtree into a right-leaning subtree.
- Left Rotation (L): Converts a right-heavy subtree into a left-leaning subtree.

```
void rightRotate(Node root) {
    Node newRoot = root.left;
    root.left = newRoot.right;
    newRoot.right = root;
    return newRoot;
}
```

```
void leftRotate(Node root) {
    Node newRoot = root.right;
    root.right = newRoot.left;
    newRoot.left = root;
    return newRoot;
}
```

2. AVL Trees

AVL (Adelson-Velsky and Landis) trees are self-balancing binary search trees where the balance factor (the difference between the heights of the left and right subtrees) of any node is bounded to be in the set {-1, 0, 1}. Upon any insertion or deletion that unbalances the tree, rotations are performed to restore balance. The following examples illustrate the balancing actions for AVL trees.

Consider inserting the value 15 into the following AVL tree:

```
    10
   /  \
  5    20
 /       \
3         30
```

After insertion and balancing using rotations:

```
      10
     /  \
    5    20
   / \     \
  3   7    30
           /
         15
```

3. Rotational Cases in AVL Trees

Balancing AVL trees involves handling four types of imbalances:

- Left-Left (LL): Right Rotation
- Right-Right (RR): Left Rotation
- Left-Right (LR): Left Rotation followed by Right Rotation
- Right-Left (RL): Right Rotation followed by Left Rotation

Algorithm 18: Balancing an Imbalanced AVL Tree

```
Input: Node root
Output: Balanced Node root
if root == null then
    return null;
end
if balanceFactor(root) > 1 then
    if balanceFactor(root.left) < 0 then
        root.left = leftRotate(root.left);
    end
    root = rightRotate(root);
end
if balanceFactor(root) < -1 then
    if balanceFactor(root.right) > 0 then
        root.right = rightRotate(root.right);
    end
    root = leftRotate(root);
end
return root;
```

4. Red-Black Trees

Red-Black trees are a type of self-balancing binary search tree where nodes have one of two colors: red or black. The tree ensures balance through the following properties:

- Every node is either red or black.
- The root is always black.
- Red nodes cannot have red children (no two consecutive red nodes).
- Every path from a node to its descendant NULL nodes must have the same number of black nodes.

Balancing in Red-Black trees is achieved through rotations and recoloring during insertion and deletion operations. The specific rules for maintaining these properties lead to an efficient height logarithmic to the number of elements, maintaining the desired performance characteristics.

Consider insertion and rebalancing in a Red-Black tree:

```
Node insert(Node root, int key) {
    root = bstInsert(root, key);
    root.color = 'B';
    return balanceRedBlackTree(root);
}
```

5. Balancing Operations Recap

Maintaining a balanced binary search tree structure is essential for performance efficiency. Rotations and specific balancing strategies like those used in AVL and Red-Black trees ensure that basic operations remain within logarithmic time complexity, thereby making these trees highly efficient for various applications in computer science.

7.10 Self-Balancing BST: AVL Trees

An AVL (Adelson-Velsky and Landis) tree is a self-balancing binary search tree where the difference between heights of left and right subtrees cannot be more than one for all nodes. This property ensures that the tree remains approximately balanced, thereby providing O(\log n) time complexity for the basic operations of insertion, deletion, and searching.

AVL Tree Properties:

- Height Balance: For each node in the AVL tree, the height of the left and right subtrees can differ by at most one.

- *Rotation Operations*: To maintain the height balance, AVL trees employ rotations when nodes are inserted or deleted. There are four types of rotations: Left-Left (LL), Right-Right (RR), Left-Right (LR), and Right-Left (RL).

Balance Factor: Each node in an AVL tree has a balance factor calculated as:

$$\text{Balance Factor} = \text{height(left subtree)} - \text{height(right subtree)}$$

For a node to be balanced, its balance factor must be -1, 0, or 1.

Tree Rotations:

- Left-Left (LL) Rotation: Applied when a node is inserted into the left subtree of the left child of a node, causing it to become unbalanced.

- Right-Right (RR) Rotation: Applied when a node is inserted into the right subtree of the right child of a node, causing it to become unbalanced.

- Left-Right (LR) Rotation: Applied when a node is inserted into the right subtree of the left child of a node, causing it to become unbalanced.

- Right-Left (RL) Rotation: Applied when a node is inserted into the left subtree of the right child of a node, causing it to become unbalanced.

Insertion in AVL Tree:

Insertion in an AVL tree is a multi-step process involving standard BST insertion followed by checking the balance factors and applying necessary rotations.

Algorithm 19: Insert a node into an AVL tree

```
Input: Node root, Key key
Output: Updated AVL tree
if root is NULL then
    return new node(key);
end
if key < root.key then
    root.left = insert(root.left, key);
end
else if key > root.key then
    root.right = insert(root.right, key);
end
else
    return root; // No duplicates allowed
end
root.height = 1 + max(height(root.left), height(root.right));
balance = getBalance(root); if balance > 1 then
    if key < root.left.key then
        return rightRotate(root); // Left-Left Case
    end
    else
        root.left = leftRotate(root.left); return
          rightRotate(root); // Left-Right Case
    end
else
end
return root;
```

This algorithm ensures the balanced property of the AVL tree is maintained after every insertion.

Deletion in AVL Tree:

The deletion process in an AVL tree requires reducing it to a standard BST deletion followed by checking and balancing the tree.

Algorithm 20: Delete a node from an AVL tree

```
Input: Node root, Key key
Output: Updated AVL tree
if root is NULL then
    return root;
end
if key < root.key then
    root.left = delete(root.left, key);
else
end
else
    if root.left is NULL or root.right is NULL then
        temp = root.left ? root.left : root.right;
        if temp is NULL then
            root = NULL;
        end
        else
            root = temp;
        end
    end
    else
        temp = getMinValueNode(root.right);
        root.key = temp.key;
        root.right = delete(root.right, temp.key);
    end
end
if root is NULL then
    return root;
end
root.height = 1 + max(height(root.left), height(root.right));
balance = getBalance(root);
if balance > 1 then
    if getBalance(root.left) >= 0 then
        return rightRotate(root);
        // Left-Left Case
    end
    else
        root.left = leftRotate(root.left);
        return rightRotate(root);
        // Left-Right Case
    end
else
end
return root;
```

Rotation Functions:

The *leftRotate* and *rightRotate* functions are critical for rebalancing the AVL tree during insertions and deletions.

```
// Function to perform a right rotation
Node rightRotate(Node y) {
    Node x = y.left;
    Node T2 = x.right;

    // Perform rotation
    x.right = y;
    y.left = T2;

    // Update heights
    y.height = Math.max(height(y.left), height(y.right)) + 1;
    x.height = Math.max(height(x.left), height(x.right)) + 1;

    // Return new root
    return x;
}

// Function to perform a left rotation
Node leftRotate(Node x) {
    Node y = x.right;
    Node T2 = y.left;

    // Perform rotation
    y.left = x;
    x.right = T2;

    // Update heights
    x.height = Math.max(height(x.left), height(x.right)) + 1;
    y.height = Math.max(height(y.left), height(y.right)) + 1;

    // Return new root
    return y;
}

// Get the height of the node
int height(Node N) {
    if (N == null)
        return 0;
    return N.height;
}

// Get Balance factor of node N
int getBalance(Node N) {
    if (N == null)
        return 0;
    return height(N.left) - height(N.right);
}

// Find the node with the minimum value
Node getMinValueNode(Node node) {
    Node current = node;
    while (current.left != null)
        current = current.left;
    return current;
}
```

Understanding and implementing these rotations are key to maintaining the AVL tree's balance during insertion and deletion operations. By adhering to strict balancing criteria and utilizing rotations judiciously, the AVL tree ensures efficient and predictable performance for fundamental tree operations.

7.11 Self-Balancing BST: Red-Black Trees

Red-Black Trees are a specific kind of self-balancing binary search tree (BST) that maintain balance through the enforcement of specific properties, ensuring efficient performance in terms of insertion, deletion, and searching operations.

A Red-Black Tree is a BST where each node contains an extra bit that identifies the color of the node, either red or black. To maintain balance, the tree follows these essential properties:

- **Property 1: Node Color** – Each node is either red or black.
- **Property 2: Root Property** – The root of the tree is always black.
- **Property 3: Leaf Property** – Every leaf (NIL nodes) is black.
- **Property 4: Red Property** – If a red node has children, then the children are always black (no two red nodes can be adjacent).
- **Property 5: Black Property** – Every path from a given node to its descendant NIL nodes contains the same number of black nodes.

These properties ensure that the tree remains approximately balanced, offering $O(\log n)$ complexity for search, insert, and delete operations. Here is a detailed implementation of operations in a Red-Black Tree using Java:

```
public class TreeNode {
    int data;
    TreeNode left, right, parent;
    boolean color; // true for red, false for black

    public TreeNode(int data) {
        this.data = data;
        left = right = parent = null;
        this.color = true; // New node must be red
    }
}
```

```
public class RedBlackTree {
    private TreeNode root;
    private TreeNode TNULL;

    public RedBlackTree() {
        TNULL = new TreeNode(0);
        TNULL.color = false;
        root = TNULL;
    }

    public void insert(int key) {
        TreeNode node = new TreeNode(key);
        node.parent = null;
        node.data = key;
        node.left = TNULL;
        node.right = TNULL;
        node.color = true; // New node must be red

        TreeNode y = null;
        TreeNode x = this.root;

        while (x != TNULL) {
            y = x;
            if (node.data < x.data) {
                x = x.left;
            } else {
                x = x.right;
            }
        }

        node.parent = y;
        if (y == null) {
            root = node;
        } else if (node.data < y.data) {
            y.left = node;
        } else {
            y.right = node;
        }

        if (node.parent == null){
            node.color = false;
            return;
        }

        if (node.parent.parent == null) {
            return;
        }

        fixInsert(node);
    }

    private void fixInsert(TreeNode k){
        TreeNode u;
        while (k.parent.color == true) {
            if (k.parent == k.parent.parent.right) {
                u = k.parent.parent.left; // uncle
                if (u.color == true) {
                    u.color = false;
                    k.parent.color = false;
                    k.parent.parent.color = true;
                    k = k.parent.parent;
                } else {
```

```
                if (k == k.parent.left) {
                    k = k.parent;
                    rightRotate(k);
                }
                k.parent.color = false;
                k.parent.parent.color = true;
                leftRotate(k.parent.parent);
            }
        } else {
            u = k.parent.parent.right; // uncle

            if (u.color == true) {
                u.color = false;
                k.parent.color = false;
                k.parent.parent.color = true;
                k = k.parent.parent;
            } else {
                if (k == k.parent.right) {
                    k = k.parent;
                    leftRotate(k);
                }
                k.parent.color = false;
                k.parent.parent.color = true;
                rightRotate(k.parent.parent);
            }
        }
        if (k == root) {
            break;
        }
    }
    root.color = false;
}

private void leftRotate(TreeNode x) {
    TreeNode y = x.right;
    x.right = y.left;
    if (y.left != TNULL) {
        y.left.parent = x;
    }
    y.parent = x.parent;
    if (x.parent == null) {
        this.root = y;
    } else if (x == x.parent.left) {
        x.parent.left = y;
    } else {
        x.parent.right = y;
    }
    y.left = x;
    x.parent = y;
}

private void rightRotate(TreeNode x) {
    TreeNode y = x.left;
    x.left = y.right;
    if (y.right != TNULL) {
        y.right.parent = x;
    }
    y.parent = x.parent;
    if (x.parent == null) {
        this.root = y;
    } else if (x == x.parent.right) {
        x.parent.right = y;
```

```
        } else {
            x.parent.left = y;
        }
        y.right = x;
        x.parent = y;
    }
}
```

The fix-up function fixInsert(TreeNode k) ensures that the tree remains balanced after inserting a new node. It handles the following cases to maintain the Red-Black Tree properties:

- **Case 1** – Recolours and moves the node up the tree.
- **Case 2** – Rotates the tree to maintain balance.

A Red-Black Tree ensures height balance through rotations. These rotations are transformations that maintain the binary search tree property while altering the structure in order to comply with the Red-Black property constraints.

The right rotation is as follows:

Algorithm 21: Right Rotate(x)

Input: x

$y \leftarrow x.left$;
$x.left \leftarrow y.right$;
if $y.right \neq$ *TNULL* **then**
  $y.right.parent \leftarrow x$;
end
$y.parent \leftarrow x.parent$;
if $x.parent ==$ *null* **then**
  root $\leftarrow y$;
end
else if $x == x.parent.right$ **then**
  $x.parent.right \leftarrow y$;
end
else
  $x.parent.left \leftarrow y$;
end
$y.right \leftarrow x$;
$x.parent \leftarrow y$;

Similarly, the left rotation is:

Algorithm 22: Left Rotate(x)

```
Input: x
y ← x.right;
x.right ← y.left;
if y.left ≠ TNULL then
|  y.left.parent ← x;
end
y.parent ← x.parent;
if x.parent == null then
|  root ← y;
end
else if x == x.parent.left then
|  x.parent.left ← y;
end
else
|  x.parent.right ← y;
end
y.left ← x;
x.parent ← y;
```

By enforcing these rotations and color properties, a Red-Black Tree ensures that the tree remains balanced, leading to guaranteed logarithmic height. This ensures efficient execution of basic operations such as insert, delete, and search.

7.12 Applications of Trees in Computer Science

Trees, particularly binary trees and their variations, have a multitude of applications in computer science. These structures are instrumental in organizing and managing data efficiently, enabling faster access, insertion, and deletion operations. Below we discuss several key applications where trees play a critical role.

- **Binary Search Trees in Databases:** Binary Search Trees (BSTs) are widely used in database indexing. They allow for efficient querying of records based on comparison, leveraging the BST properties to perform search operations in $O(\log n)$ time on average. This efficiency is crucial for databases involving large number of records, ensuring quick retrievals.

- **Heaps in Priority Queues:** A heap is a specialized binary tree used to implement priority queues. Heaps ensure that the parent node is always greater than its children (max-heap) or smaller (min-heap). This property enables priority queues to efficiently extract the highest or lowest priority element, making operations such as scheduling and event simulation computationally feasible.

- **Syntax Trees in Compilers:** Abstract syntax trees (ASTs) are used in compilers to represent the structure of program code. Each node in the tree corresponds to a construct occurring in the source code. This hierarchical representation is crucial for semantic analysis and code generation, allowing compilers to efficiently transform source code into executable code.

- **File Systems:** Many file systems utilize tree structures, specifically binary and n-ary trees, for managing directories and files. This hierarchical organization enables efficient navigation, searching, and management of files and directories. For example, the B-tree and its variants are commonly used in databases and file systems to manage balanced, sorted data, ensuring logarithmic time complexity for insertions, deletions, and lookups.

- **Networking:** In networking, trees are used to model and manage hierarchical routing protocols. For instance, spanning trees are utilized to prevent loops in network topologies, ensuring an optimal path between nodes. Protocols such as the Spanning Tree Protocol (STP) in Ethernet networks rely on tree algorithms to maintain network redundancy effectively while avoiding cycles.

Tree data structures go beyond these applications, finding use in more specialized and advanced areas:

- **AI and Machine Learning:** Decision trees are fundamental in various machine learning algorithms. They serve as predictive models mapping observations to conclusions about target values. Decision trees are used in classification and regression tasks, owing to their interpretability and simplicity.

- **XML/HTML Data:** Document Object Model (DOM) trees are used to represent the structure of XML and HTML documents. These trees allow programs to dynamically access and update content, structure, and style, facilitating web development and manipulation of document data.

- **Cryptographic Algorithms:** Balanced tree structures, such as Merkel Trees, are employed in cryptographic algorithms to ensure data integrity and consistency. By hashing a tree of blocks of data, these structures provide efficient and secure ways to verify the content.

- **Spatial Data Indexing:** Trees like R-trees and KD-trees are used in spatial databases to index multi-dimensional information such as geographical coordinates, making queries like nearest neighbor search efficient.

Consider the example of a syntax tree. Suppose we need to parse the mathematical expression $3 + 5 * (2 - 4)$. The abstract syntax tree for this expression is constructed as follows:

```
class Node {
    String value;
    Node left, right;

    Node(String item) {
        value = item;
        left = right = null;
    }
}

// Example syntax tree creation
Node root = new Node("+");
root.left = new Node("3");
root.right = new Node("*");
root.right.left = new Node("5");
root.right.right = new Node("-");
root.right.right.left = new Node("2");
root.right.right.right = new Node("4");
```

The resultant tree facilitates the compiler's task by representing the hierarchical structure of the expression clearly. Evaluation of the expression can be done efficiently by traversing this tree in a post-order manner.

Applications of trees in computer science thus span a wide array of domains, from fundamental data structures in databases to complex algorithms in machine learning. Their versatility and efficiency in organizing hierarchies and ensuring effective data operations underscore their significance in computational tasks.

Chapter 8

Heaps and Priority Queues

This chapter covers heaps and priority queues, essential data structures for efficiently managing prioritized data. It begins with an introduction to heap properties and types, focusing primarily on binary heaps. The chapter details heap operations such as insertion, deletion, and heap construction, followed by an explanation of the heap sort algorithm. It then transitions to priority queues, explaining their implementation using heaps and exploring applications. Additionally, advanced topics like D-ary heaps and Fibonacci heaps are discussed to provide a comprehensive understanding of these powerful structures.

8.1 Introduction to Heaps

Heaps are specialized tree-based data structures that satisfy the heap property. Typically realized as binary trees, heaps serve as the foundation for constructing priority queues and implementing efficient sorting algorithms, such as heapsort.

A heap is a complete binary tree, meaning all levels are fully filled except possibly for the last level, which is filled from left to right. The binary tree must satisfy one of the two conditions:

- **Max-Heap Property:** In a max-heap, for any node i other than the root, the key of i is less than or equal to the key of its parent. Thus, the largest key is stored at the root.
- **Min-Heap Property:** In a min-heap, for any node i other than the root, the key of i is greater than or equal to the key of its parent. Thus, the smallest key is stored at the root.

In both max-heaps and min-heaps, the parent node's key is always larger (or smaller) than the keys of its children, maintaining a hierarchy based on value which facilitates priority.

BinaryHeap is generally preferred due to simplicity and efficiency. The binary heap is often implemented using an array, where the root element is at index 0. For any element at index i, its children can be found at indices $2i+1$ and $2i+2$, and its parent can be found at index $\left\lfloor \frac{(i-1)}{2} \right\rfloor$.

```
public class BinaryHeap {
    private int[] heap;
    private int size;

    public BinaryHeap(int capacity) {
        heap = new int[capacity];
        size = 0;
    }

    private int getParentIndex(int index) {
        return (index - 1) / 2;
    }

    private int getLeftChildIndex(int index) {
        return 2 * index + 1;
    }

    private int getRightChildIndex(int index) {
        return 2 * index + 2;
    }

    public void insert(int value) {
        if (size == heap.length) {
            throw new IllegalStateException("Heap is full");
        }
        heap[size] = value;
        size++;
        heapifyUp(size - 1);
    }

    private void heapifyUp(int index) {
        int newValue = heap[index];
        while (index > 0 && newValue > heap[getParentIndex(index)]) {
            heap[index] = heap[getParentIndex(index)];
            index = getParentIndex(index);
        }
        heap[index] = newValue;
    }
}
```

The insert operation appends the new value to the end of the array and then calls the heapifyUp method to restore the heap property. The heapifyUp method ensures that the newly added value is bubbled up until it is correctly placed according to the heap property.

Heaps are powerfully characterized by their logarithmic height, ensuring that operations such as insertions and deletions maintain $O(\log n)$ time complexity, where n is the number of elements. This efficiency is due to the balanced nature and complete tree structure inherent in heaps.

When working with heaps, understanding array-based implementation is crucial, given its use in practical applications and efficiency in terms of space and operations. It is worthwhile noting that alternative heap structures, such as Fibonacci and D-ary heaps, offer further optimizations for specific use cases.

Heaps serve as the backbone for priority queues, enabling fast retrieval of the highest (or lowest) priority element. This is particularly useful in scenarios such as task scheduling, event simulation, and algorithms like Dijkstra's shortest path and Prim's Minimum Spanning Tree.

8.2 Heap Properties and Types

A heap is a specialized tree-based data structure that satisfies the heap property. In this section, we will examine the properties that define a heap and explore various types of heaps that are commonly used in practice.

Heap Property: The heap property is a critical characteristic that differentiates heaps from other binary trees. There are two main types of heap properties:

- **Max-Heap Property:** In a max-heap, for any given node i, the value of i is greater than or equal to the values of its children. Mathematically, for any node i,

  $$A[\text{Parent}(i)] \geq A[i]$$

  where $A[i]$ represents the value of the node i. Hence, the largest element is always at the root.

- **Min-Heap Property:** Conversely, in a min-heap, for any given node i, the value of i is less than or equal to the values of its children. Mathematically, for any node i,

  $$A[\text{Parent}(i)] \leq A[i]$$

  Consequently, the smallest element resides at the root.

Binary Heaps: A binary heap is a common implementation of the heap data structure, specifically designed to maintain a complete binary tree. In a complete binary tree, all levels, except possibly the last, are fully filled, and all nodes are as left as possible.

```
class BinaryHeap {
    private int[] heap;
    private int size;
    private int capacity;

    public BinaryHeap(int capacity) {
        this.capacity = capacity;
        this.size = 0;
        this.heap = new int[capacity];
    }

    // Helper methods such as insert, delete, heapify, etc.
}
```

The BinaryHeap class encapsulates the properties of a binary heap, including its array representation, current size, and capacity.

Heap Operations and Maintenance: To maintain the heap property, various operations like inserting elements, extracting the root, and heapifying subtrees are crucial. These operations ensure that the binary heap retains its complete tree structure and the heap property is preserved.

```
Function heapify(A, i, n):
    l ← 2i + 1;
    r ← 2i + 2;
    largest ← i;
    if l < n and A[l] > A[largest] then
        largest ← l;
    if r < n and A[r] > A[largest] then
        largest ← r;
    if largest ≠ i then
        swap A[i] and A[largest];
        heapify(A, largest, n);
```

In this algorithm, the heapify function ensures the max-heap property by comparing the node with its children and swapping them if necessary. This recursive process continues until the node satisfies the heap property relative to its children.

Types of Heaps: Beyond binary heaps, there are several other types of heaps, each optimized for specific use cases.

- **D-ary Heaps:** A generalization of binary heaps, D-ary heaps allow each node to have D children. This can lead to shallower trees and potentially faster decrease-key or insertion operations. However, heapify operations may become more complex.

- **Fibonacci Heaps:** Fibonacci heaps offer better amortized time complexities for common operations. They are particularly useful in algorithms like Dijkstra's shortest path and Prim's minimum spanning tree. Fibonacci heaps support insert, extract-min, decrease-key, and merge operations in very efficient amortized time.

- **Binomial Heaps:** Binomial heaps are a collection of binomial trees that are linked together. They support efficient merging of two heaps, which makes them suitable for meldable heaps in specific applications.

Each of these heap types presents unique advantages and trade-offs. For instance, while binary heaps are simple and effective for priority queues, Fibonacci heaps excel in scenarios requiring frequent key decreases and merges. Understanding the strengths and appropriate use cases of each is essential for implementing efficient algorithms.

Complexity of Heap Operations: The efficiency of heap operations is a decisive factor in selecting the appropriate heap type. Binary heaps typically offer logarithmic time complexity for both insertion and deletion operations:

Insert: O(log n)
Delete: O(log n)
Heapify: O(log n)
Build-Heap: O(n)

D-ary heaps, depending on D, may provide varying time complexities, usually balancing the depth of the tree with the number of comparisons per node. Fibonacci heaps, while more complex, provide constant-time insertions and optimistically fast decrease-key and delete operations:

Insert: O(1) amortized
Delete: O(log n) amortized
Decrease-key: O(1) amortized

These operations make Fibonacci heaps particularly advantageous for specific graph algorithms.

Understanding heap properties and their various types equips one with the knowledge necessary to leverage heaps effectively across different applications. Each heap type, from simple binary heaps to more complex Fibonacci and D-ary heaps, serves specific purposes, enhancing the efficiency of algorithms that demand prioritized data management.

8.3 Binary Heaps

Binary heaps are a special case of the broader category of heaps, representing a complete binary tree with specific ordering properties.

These structures are pivotal for implementing efficient priority queues, and they form the foundation for the heap sort algorithm.

A binary heap can be of two types: a min-heap and a max-heap. In a min-heap, the value of each node is greater than or equal to the value of its parent, ensuring that the minimum value is always at the root. Conversely, in a max-heap, the value of each node is less than or equal to the value of its parent, guaranteeing the maximum value is at the root.

Properties of Binary Heaps

1. Complete Binary Tree: A binary heap is a complete binary tree, meaning all levels are completely filled except possibly for the last level, which is filled from left to right.

2. Heap Order Property: This ensures that, in a min-heap, for any given node i, the value of i is less than or equal to the values of its children. For a max-heap, the value of i is greater than or equal to the values of its children.

Binary Heap Representation

Binary heaps are typically represented using arrays. This offers an efficient way to access the parent and children of any element. If we consider an element at index i in the array:

- The parent of the element is at index $\lfloor (i-1)/2 \rfloor$.
- The left child of the element is at index $2i+1$.
- The right child of the element is at index $2i+2$.

This array representation eliminates the need for explicit pointers, thereby minimizing the memory overhead and enhancing access speed.

Example of Min-Heap Array Representation

Consider the following min-heap:

```
      10
      / \
    20 30
    / \
  40 50
```

The array representation of the above min-heap would be:

```
[10, 20, 30, 40, 50]
```

Through array indices, the properties can be verified:

- Element at index 0 (value 10) has children at indices 1 (value 20) and 2 (value 30).
- Element at index 1 (value 20) has children at indices 3 (value 40) and 4 (value 50).

Binary Heap Operations

Common operations on binary heaps include insertion, deletion, and heapification. These operations maintain the heap properties and ensure logarithmic time complexity.

Insertion

To insert an element into a binary heap:

- Append the element at the end of the heap (array).
- Heapify-up: Compare the element with its parent; if it violates the heap property, swap it with the parent. Repeat this process until the heap property is satisfied.

Java Implementation of Insertion

```
public void insert(int value) {
    heap[size] = value; // Append the value at the end
    int current = size;
    size++;

    // Heapify-up
    while (heap[current] < heap[parent(current)]) {
        swap(current, parent(current));
        current = parent(current);
    }
}

// Helper methods to get the parent index and to swap elements
private int parent(int i) { return (i - 1) / 2; }
private void swap(int i, int j) {
    int temp = heap[i];
    heap[i] = heap[j];
    heap[j] = temp;
}
```

Deletion (Extract-Min/Max)

To delete the root (min or max):

- Swap the root with the last element in the heap.

- Remove the last element.
- Heapify-down: Compare the swapped element with its children; if it violates the heap property, swap it with the appropriate child. Repeat this process until the heap property is restored.

Java Implementation of Deletion (Extract-Min)

```
public int extractMin() {
    int root = heap[0];
    heap[0] = heap[size - 1]; // Move the last element to the root
    size--;
    // Heapify-down
    minHeapify(0);
    return root;
}

// Heapify-down method
private void minHeapify(int i) {
    int left = leftChild(i);
    int right = rightChild(i);
    int smallest = i;

    if (left < size && heap[left] < heap[smallest]) {
        smallest = left;
    }
    if (right < size && heap[right] < heap[smallest]) {
        smallest = right;
    }
    if (smallest != i) {
        swap(i, smallest);
        minHeapify(smallest);
    }
}

// Helper methods for child indices
private int leftChild(int i) { return 2 * i + 1; }
private int rightChild(int i) { return 2 * i + 2; }
```

The binary heap's properties and efficient array representation make it a crucial data structure for several algorithmic applications, including priority queues and the heap sort algorithm. This understanding of binary heaps allows for the construction, manipulation, and optimization of complex data structures and algorithms.

8.4 Heap Operations: Insertion

In this section, we explore the insertion operation in binary heaps, a crucial process that ensures the heap property is maintained. For a binary heap, the property dictates that each parent node is either greater than or equal to (in a max heap) or less than or equal to (in a min heap) its child nodes. Insertion into a heap involves adding a new element and then performing adjustments to ensure this property is upheld.

Algorithm Overview

The insertion process can be divided into two main steps:

- Adding the new element at the end of the heap.
- Percolating up the new element to maintain the heap property.

Step-by-Step Explanation

1. **Adding the New Element**

The first step involves inserting the new element at the last available position in the heap, which corresponds to appending the element to the end of the array representation of the heap. This ensures the complete binary tree property, where all levels are fully filled except possibly for the last level, which is filled from left to right.

```
public void insert(int value) {
    if (size >= heap.length - 1) {
        resize();
    }
    size++;
    heap[size] = value;
    percolateUp(size);
}
```

In the insert method, size is incremented to point to the next available position in the array. The new value is then placed at this position, preparing it for the percolate up process.

2. **Percolating Up**

The percolate up process (also known as bubble up, sift up, or swim) followed by binary heaps ensures that the heap property is restored. This process involves comparing the newly inserted element with its parent and swapping them if the heap property is violated. This continues until either the element is in a valid position or it becomes the root.

```
private void percolateUp(int index) {
    while (index > 1 && heap[index] > heap[index/2]) {
        swap(index, index/2);
        index = index/2;
    }
}
```

Here, we assume a max heap for demonstration. The percolateUp method compares the new element with its parent (located at index/2 when integer division is used). If the new element is greater than its parent, they are swapped, and the process repeats at the parent's position. The loop continues until the element is appropriately placed, either due to the heap property being satisfied or the element reaching the root position.

Java: Complete Insertion Implementation

Combining the discussed steps, the complete insertion operation in a max heap is implemented as follows:

```
public class MaxHeap {
    private int[] heap;
    private int size;

    public MaxHeap(int capacity) {
        heap = new int[capacity + 1];
        size = 0;
    }

    public void insert(int value) {
        if (size >= heap.length - 1) {
            resize();
        }
        size++;
        heap[size] = value;
        percolateUp(size);
    }

    private void percolateUp(int index) {
        while (index > 1 && heap[index] > heap[index / 2]) {
            swap(index, index / 2);
            index = index / 2;
        }
    }

    private void swap(int index1, int index2) {
        int temp = heap[index1];
        heap[index1] = heap[index2];
        heap[index2] = temp;
    }

    private void resize() {
        int[] newHeap = new int[heap.length * 2];
        System.arraycopy(heap, 0, newHeap, 0, heap.length);
        heap = newHeap;
    }
}
```

Complexity Analysis

The time complexity of the insertion operation in a binary heap is $O(\log n)$, where n is the number of elements in the heap. This is because the percolate up step involves at most the height of the heap, which is $\log n$ for a complete binary tree. The space complexity remains $O(1)$ with respect to the operation itself, though dynamic resizing may involve additional space overhead.

Through this detailed examination of the insertion operation in a binary heap, we can ensure efficient management of prioritized data while maintaining the structural and ordering properties intrinsic to heaps.

8.5 Heap Operations: Deletion

Heap deletion involves removing the root element of the heap, which is the maximum element in the case of a max-heap or the minimum element in the case of a min-heap. This operation is essential for various algorithms, such as those involving priority queues, where the highest-priority element needs removal.

Procedure for Deletion:

- Replace the root element with the last element in the heap.
- Reduce the size of the heap by one.
- Restore the heap property by performing the sift-down (or heapify-down) operation from the root node.

Detailed Steps:

- Remove the root: Store the root value, which we will ultimately return after completing the deletion procedure.
- Replace root value: Move the last element of the heap into the root position.
- Reduce heap size: Decrease the overall count of elements in the heap to indicate the effective removal of the last element.
- Sift down: As the last element now residing in the root position potentially violates the heap property, we must sift down this element to its appropriate position to restore the heap structure.

Algorithm: Sift-Down

Algorithm 23: Sift-Down Algorithm

Data: An array heap representing a binary heap and the size of the heap.

Result: The heap property is restored by sifting down the root element.

```
Function siftDown(heap, size):
    index ← 0;
    while index < size do
        leftChild ← 2× index +1;
        rightChild ← 2× index +2;
        largerChild ← index;
        if leftChild < size and heap[leftChild] >
          heap[largerChild] then
            largerChild ← leftChild;
        if rightChild < size and heap[rightChild] >
          heap[largerChild] then
            largerChild ← rightChild;
        if largerChild = index then
            break;
        swap(heap[largerChild], heap[index]);
        index ← largerChild;
```

The core idea behind the sift-down operation is to compare the current node with its children and swap it with the larger child (in a max-heap) if the current node is smaller. This swap ensures that the largest element among the current node and its immediate children move up one level, thereby partially restoring the heap property. The process continues iteratively until the heap property is entirely restored.

Java Implementation of Deletion in a Max-Heap:

In a Java-based binary heap represented using an array, the delete operation follows the steps outlined in the previous algorithm. The code implementation wraps these steps inside a function.

```
public class MaxHeap {
    private int[] heap;
    private int size;

    public MaxHeap(int capacity) {
        heap = new int[capacity];
        size = 0;
    }

    // Inserts a new element in the heap
```

```
    public void insert(int value) {
        if(size >= heap.length) throw new IllegalStateException("Heap is full");
        heap[size] = value;
        size++;
        siftUp(size - 1);
    }

    // Deletes and returns the max element in the heap
    public int deleteMax() {
        if(size == 0) throw new IllegalStateException("Heap is empty");
        int rootValue = heap[0];
        heap[0] = heap[size - 1];
        size--;
        siftDown(0);
        return rootValue;
    }

    private void siftDown(int index) {
        int largerChild;
        while(index < size) {
            int leftChild = 2 * index + 1;
            int rightChild = 2 * index + 2;
            largerChild = index;

            if(leftChild < size && heap[leftChild] > heap[largerChild]) {
                largerChild = leftChild;
            }

            if(rightChild < size && heap[rightChild] > heap[largerChild]) {
                largerChild = rightChild;
            }

            if(largerChild == index) break;

            swap(index, largerChild);
            index = largerChild;
        }
    }

    private void swap(int index1, int index2) {
        int temp = heap[index1];
        heap[index1] = heap[index2];
        heap[index2] = temp;
    }

    // Sifts up the element at the given index
    private void siftUp(int index) {
        while(index > 0) {
            int parent = (index - 1) / 2;
            if(heap[parent] >= heap[index]) break;
            swap(parent, index);
            index = parent;
        }
    }

    public int size() {
        return size;
    }
}
```

Upon requesting a deletion, the function deleteMax() initiates by verifying the heap is not empty. The root element is stored and subsequently replaced by the last element in the heap. The heap size is reduced by one, and the siftDown function is then invoked to maintain the heap property.

The described deletion process in heaps can be applied to both max-heaps and min-heaps by appropriately modifying the conditions in the sift-down algorithm to reflect the desired heap type (e.g., using less-than comparisons in a min-heap).

For further efficiency in programming and problem-solving involving priority queues, understanding this deletion mechanism is crucial. It forms the basis for more complex operations and optimizations within heap-based data structures.

8.6 Building a Heap

Building a heap is a crucial operation that can be approached in multiple ways. This section will explore the two primary methods: incremental insertion and the more efficient bottom-up heap construction.

Incremental insertion involves inserting elements into the heap one at a time while maintaining the heap property. This method is straightforward but tends to be less efficient overall, requiring $O(n \log n)$ time complexity for building the heap from n elements. On the other hand, the bottom-up approach, known as Floyd's method, constructs the heap in $O(n)$ time. This makes it the preferred method for heap construction in practice.

Incremental Insertion Method: In the incremental insertion method, each new element is appended at the end of the heap and then "bubbled up" to restore the heap property.

```
public void insert(int key) {
    heapSize++;
    int i = heapSize - 1;
    heap[i] = key;

    // Bubble up to maintain heap property
    while (i != 0 && heap[parent(i)] < heap[i]) {
        swap(i, parent(i));
        i = parent(i);
    }
}
```

In this example, the insert function adds a key to the heap array and then performs the necessary swaps to maintain the heap property. The parent function calculates the index of the parent node, while the swap function exchanges elements at specified indices.

Bottom-Up Heap Construction (Floyd's Method): Floyd's heap construction algorithm starts by considering the last internal node and moves upwards towards the root node, ensuring the heap property at every step. This method is significantly more efficient compared to incremental insertion.

Algorithm 24: Bottom-Up Heap Construction

Input: An unordered array of length n
Output: A max heap
1 **for** $i = \lfloor \frac{n}{2} \rfloor - 1$ ***down to*** 0 **do**
2 | heapify(i)

The heapify function, within this context, ensures that a subtree is a heap. The root of the subtree must be at index i. Here's how the heapify function is defined.

```
public void heapify(int i) {
    int largest = i;
    int left = leftChild(i);
    int right = rightChild(i);

    if (left < heapSize && heap[left] > heap[largest]) {
        largest = left;
    }
    if (right < heapSize && heap[right] > heap[largest]) {
        largest = right;
    }

    if (largest != i) {
        swap(i, largest);
        heapify(largest);
    }
}
```

The heapify function checks whether the children nodes are larger than the root node and then swaps the largest child with the root if necessary. This process recursively ensures the maintenance of the heap property for the subtree rooted at the specified node.

Illustration of Bottom-Up Heap Construction:

Consider an unordered array: {4, 10, 3, 5, 1}. To build a max heap using the bottom-up construction method:

- Start at the first non-leaf node, which is the node with index $\lfloor \frac{5}{2} \rfloor - 1 = 1$.
- Apply the heapify function to the subtree rooted at index 1. Since 10 is greater than its children (5 and 1), no swaps are needed. - Move to

index 0, and apply heapify. 4 is less than its largest child (10), so they are swapped.

Resultant array: {10, 5, 3, 4, 1}

The resultant array after these operations becomes {10, 5, 3, 4, 1}, maintaining the max heap property.

These two methods offer different trade-offs in terms of complexity and effort. The incremental insertion is simpler to understand and implement but has higher time complexity, making it impractical for large datasets. The bottom-up method is optimal both in theory and practice, making it the preferred approach for heap construction in most scenarios.

Effective heap building forms the basis for efficient priority queue operations and is paramount for optimizing algorithms like heapsort. The choice of method, while contingent on specific use cases, fundamentally relies on a well-rounded understanding of these construction techniques.

8.7 Heap Sort Algorithm

Heap sort is a comparison-based sorting algorithm that leverages the heap data structure for efficient sorting. The algorithm operates in two main phases: building a max heap from the input data, and repeatedly extracting the maximum element from the heap. By ensuring that the largest elements are continually removed and placed at the end of the collection, heap sort achieves a complete and efficiently sorted output.

The primary steps for the heap sort algorithm can be outlined as follows:

- Build a max heap from the input data.
- Swap the root (maximum value) of the heap with the last element of the heap.
- Reduce the heap size by one and heapify the root element to maintain the max heap property.
- Repeat the process until the heap size is reduced to one.

To understand the heap sort mechanism, consider the following detailed breakdown:

Building the Max Heap: The initial step involves transforming the input array into a max heap. Given an array of n elements, this can be efficiently achieved using the heapify operation, which ensures that a subtree rooted with node i is a max heap. The heapify function assumes that binary trees rooted at the children are already max heaps, and it fixes the node i to ensure the whole subtree rooted at i satisfies the max heap property.

The heapify function can be implemented in Java as follows:

```
void heapify(int arr[], int n, int i) {
    int largest = i; // Initialize largest as root
    int left = 2 * i + 1; // left = 2*i + 1
    int right = 2 * i + 2; // right = 2*i + 2

    // Check if left child is larger than root
    if (left < n && arr[left] > arr[largest])
        largest = left;

    // Check if right child is larger than largest so far
    if (right < n && arr[right] > arr[largest])
        largest = right;

    // Swap and continue heapifying if root is not largest
    if (largest != i) {
        int swap = arr[i];
        arr[i] = arr[largest];
        arr[largest] = swap;

        // Recursively heapify the affected sub-tree
        heapify(arr, n, largest);
    }
}
```

To build a max heap from the input array, the heapify function needs to be called for all non-leaf nodes in reverse level order:

```
void buildMaxHeap(int arr[], int n) {
    // Index of last non-leaf node
    int startIdx = (n / 2) - 1;

    // Perform reverse level order traversal
    // from last non-leaf node to root
    for (int i = startIdx; i >= 0; i--) {
        heapify(arr, n, i);
    }
}
```

Heap Sort Execution: Once the max heap has been built, the heap sort algorithm proceeds by repeatedly extracting the maximum element (root of the heap) and placing it at the end of the array. After each extraction, the size of the heap is reduced, and the root is heapified to maintain the max heap property.

The full heap sort implementation in Java is as follows:

```
void heapSort(int arr[]) {
    int n = arr.length;

    // Build max heap
    buildMaxHeap(arr, n);

    // One by one extract elements from the heap
    for (int i = n - 1; i > 0; i--) {
        // Move current root to end
        int temp = arr[0];
        arr[0] = arr[i];
        arr[i] = temp;

        // Call heapify on the reduced heap
        heapify(arr, i, 0);
    }
}
```

Algorithm Analysis: Heap sort has a time complexity of $O(n \log n)$ in all cases—best case, average case, and worst case—since both building the heap and extracting elements require $O(n \log n)$ operations. Memory usage is constant, $O(1)$, because heap sort is an in-place sorting algorithm. This makes heap sort particularly useful for arrays that are either already in memory or when minimizing memory overhead is crucial.

Algorithm 25: Heap Sort

Data: An array of elements arr
Result: Sorted array arr

begin
  $n \leftarrow$ length of arr;
  for $i \leftarrow n/2 - 1$ **to** 0 **do**
    heapify(arr, n, i);
  for $i \leftarrow n - 1$ **to** 1 **do**
    swap($arr[0]$, $arr[i]$);
    heapify(arr, i, 0);

The effectiveness and efficiency of heap sort are evident in its ability to handle large data sets by systematically breaking down the heap and reducing the problem size iteratively. The intrinsic properties of the heap ensure that each extraction step yields the maximum element, thus progressively sorting the array with precision.

8.8 Introduction to Priority Queues

A priority queue is a specialized type of queue in which each element is associated with a priority, and the element with the highest priority is served before other elements with lower priority. This abstract data type varies slightly from a traditional queue, where elements are ordered by their arrival time. Priority queues are fundamental in various applications, such as scheduling, network traffic management, and algorithm optimizations like Dijkstra's shortest path algorithm.

In a priority queue, the primary operations include insert, deleteMin, or deleteMax, depending on whether it is a min-priority queue or a max-priority queue. The insert operation adds an element to the queue with an associated priority. The deleteMin operation removes the element with the smallest priority in a min-priority queue, whereas deleteMax removes the element with the highest priority in a max-priority queue.

```
class PriorityQueue {
    void insert(Element e);
    Element deleteMin(); // For min-priority queue
    Element deleteMax(); // For max-priority queue
}
```

To implement a priority queue efficiently, it is often backed by a heap data structure due to its optimal time complexities for insertion and deletion operations: $O(\log n)$. This section will cover the conceptual understanding of priority queues, their importance in computational tasks, and a structured approach to implementing them.

Operations in Priority Queues:

1. **Insertion:** The element is added to the appropriate position in the priority queue based on its priority.

Algorithm 26: Insertion in Priority Queue

Input: PriorityQueue PQ, Element e, Priority p
Output: Updated PriorityQueue PQ

$PQ.insert(e, p)$

2. **DeleteMin/DeleteMax:** Depending on the type of priority queue, this operation deletes the minimum or maximum priority element.

Algorithm 27: DeleteMin in Min-Priority Queue

Input: MinPriorityQueue $minPQ$
Output: Element e with smallest priority, Updated minPQ

1 $e \leftarrow minPQ.deleteMin()$

3. **Peek:** Look at the highest priority element without removing it from the queue.

Algorithm 28: Peek in Min-Priority Queue

Input: MinPriorityQueue $minPQ$
Output: Element e with the smallest priority

1 $e \leftarrow minPQ.peek()$

Implementation Using Heaps:

A common and efficient way to implement a priority queue is with a binary heap. Specifically, a min-heap is used for a min-priority queue, and a max-heap is utilized for a max-priority queue. The binary heap ensures that each insertion and deletion operation maintains the heap property: for a min-heap, the parent node is always less than or equal to its children, and for a max-heap, the parent node is always greater than or equal to its children.

In the case of a min-priority queue implemented using a min-heap, the smallest element is always at the root. When an element is inserted, it is added at the end of the heap and then 'bubbled up' to maintain the heap property. When the minimum element is deleted, the last element in the heap replaces the root and is then 'bubbled down' to re-establish the heap structure.

```
class MinPriorityQueue {
    private MinHeap heap;

    void insert(Element e, Priority p) {
        heap.add(e, p);
    }

    Element deleteMin() {
        return heap.removeMin();
    }

    Element peek() {
        return heap.min();
    }
}
```

Advantages of Priority Queues:

- Efficient time complexity for insertion and deletion operations compared to other data structures like sorted arrays and linked lists.
- Flexibility in adjusting priorities dynamically.
- Widely applicable in scenarios that require dynamic order processing based on priority.

Applications of Priority Queues:

- **Job Scheduling:** In operating systems, tasks are managed by priority, with higher-priority tasks getting CPU time ahead of lower-priority tasks.
- **Dijkstra's Algorithm:** Used to find the shortest path in a graph, where the priority queue efficiently manages and retrieves the next node to explore based on the least distance.
- **Event-Driven Simulation:** Manages events by their scheduled time, ensuring events are processed in the correct chronological order.

Priority queues, with their efficient handling of prioritized tasks, represent a crucial element in many algorithmic solutions. Understanding their implementation and use cases enhances one's ability to effectively design and optimize complex systems.

8.9 Implementing Priority Queues using Heaps

Priority queues are abstract data types where each element is associated with a priority. Elements are dequeued in order of highest to lowest priority. Heaps, especially binary heaps, are efficient structures to implement priority queues due to their properties and operations that ensure logarithmic time complexity for insertion and deletion.

Data Structure Choice: A binary heap is a complete binary tree, which can be efficiently represented using an array. For a max-heap, the highest priority element is at the root (index 0 in an array) and for a min-heap, the lowest priority element is at the root.

Array Representation: Given a node located at index i:

- The parent node is at index $\lfloor \frac{i-1}{2} \rfloor$.
- The left child node is at index $2i + 1$.
- The right child node is at index $2i + 2$.

Insertion Operation: The insertion operation involves adding the new element at the end of the heap (bottom level, rightmost position) and then "bubbling up" the element to restore the heap property. The complexity is $O(\log n)$.

```
public void insert(int element) {
    heap[size] = element; // Place element at the end of the array
    int current = size;
    size++;

    // Bubble up the newly added element
    while (current != 0 && heap[current] > heap[parent(current)]) {
        swap(current, parent(current));
        current = parent(current);
    }
}
```

Deletion Operation: Deletion generally targets the root element (highest priority). Replace the root with the last element, remove the last element, and then "bubble down" the replaced element to maintain the heap property. The complexity is $O(\log n)$.

```
public int extractMax() {
    if (size == 0) throw new NoSuchElementException("Heap is empty.");

    int max = heap[0]; // Root element
    heap[0] = heap[--size]; // Replace root with last element
    heapify(0); // Bubble down from root

    return max;
}

private void heapify(int i) {
    int largest = i;
    int left = leftChild(i);
    int right = rightChild(i);

    if (left < size && heap[left] > heap[largest]) largest = left;
    if (right < size && heap[right] > heap[largest]) largest = right;

    if (largest != i) {
        swap(i, largest);
        heapify(largest);
    }
}
```

Priority Queue Operations with Heaps:

- insert(key): Adds a new key to the priority queue.

- extractMax()/extractMin(): Removes and returns the element with maximum/minimum priority.
- peekMax()/peekMin(): Returns the element with maximum/minimum priority without removing it.

Algorithm - Insertion into a Max-Heap Priority Queue:

Algorithm 29: Insert into Max-Heap Priority Queue

```
Data: Max-Heap H of size n
Input: Key k to be inserted
insert k at the end of H;
i ← n;
while i > 0 and H[i] > H[parent(i)] do
    swap H[i] with H[parent(i)];
    i ← parent(i);
n ← n + 1;
```

Algorithm - Deletion from a Max-Heap Priority Queue:

Algorithm 30: Delete from Max-Heap Priority Queue

```
Data: Max-Heap H of size n
Output: Maximum element from the heap
if n == 0 then
    return error "Heap is empty";
max ← H[0];
H[0] ← H[n-1];
n ← n - 1;
i ← 0;
while leftChild(i) < n do
    largest ← i;
    if H[leftChild(i)] > H[largest] then
        largest ← leftChild(i);
    if rightChild(i) < n and H[rightChild(i)] > H[largest] then
        largest ← rightChild(i);
    if largest == i then
        break;
    swap H[i] and H[largest];
    i ← largest;
return max;
```

Array-based Priority Queue Class: Implementing the priority queue, we encapsulate the heap operations within a class:

```
public class PriorityQueue {
    private int[] heap;
    private int size;

    public PriorityQueue(int capacity) {
        heap = new int[capacity];
        size = 0;
    }

    public void insert(int key) {
        if (size == heap.length) throw new IllegalStateException("Heap is full.");
        heap[size] = key;
        int current = size;
        size++;
        while (current != 0 && heap[current] > heap[(current-1)/2]) {
            swap(current, (current-1)/2);
            current = (current-1)/2;
        }
    }

    public int extractMax() {
        if (size == 0) throw new NoSuchElementException("Heap is empty.");
        int max = heap[0];
        heap[0] = heap[--size];
        heapify(0);
        return max;
    }

    public int peekMax() {
        if (size == 0) throw new NoSuchElementException("Heap is empty.");
        return heap[0];
    }

    private void heapify(int i) {
        int largest = i;
        int left = 2*i + 1;
        int right = 2*i + 2;

        if (left < size && heap[left] > heap[largest]) largest = left;
        if (right < size && heap[right] > heap[largest]) largest = right;

        if (largest != i) {
            swap(i, largest);
            heapify(largest);
        }
    }

    private void swap(int i, int j) {
        int temp = heap[i];
        heap[i] = heap[j];
        heap[j] = temp;
    }
}
```

Through the integration of heap structures, priority queues benefit from efficient insertion and deletion operations while ensuring that elements are accessed in a prioritized manner.

8.10 Applications of Heaps and Priority Queues

Heaps and priority queues are indispensable in various computational problems due to their efficiency in handling prioritized data. Their applications span across operating systems, graph algorithms, networking, event simulation, and much more. Understanding these applications not only emphasizes their importance but also provides a deeper insight into practical problem-solving techniques in computer science.

1. Dijkstra's Shortest Path Algorithm

One of the prominent applications of heaps is in Dijkstra's Shortest Path Algorithm. The algorithm finds the shortest paths from a source vertex to all other vertices in a weighted graph. This is efficiently accomplished using a priority queue to always extend the shortest known path.

Algorithm 31: Dijkstra's Algorithm using a Binary Heap

input : Graph $G = (V, E)$ with edge weights w, source vertex s
output : Shortest path from s to all vertices in V

Initialize distance to all vertices as ∞, except for the source s where the distance is 0;
Initialize an empty priority queue Q;
Insert s into Q with priority 0;
while *Q is not empty* **do**
    Extract vertex u from Q with the minimum distance;
    for *each neighbor v of u* **do**
        Relax the edge (u, v);
        if *relaxation decreases the distance of v* **then**
            Insert v into Q or decrease its priority in Q;

In this implementation, the priority queue ensures that vertices are processed in order of their distance from the source, enabling efficient path finding.

2. Prim's Minimum Spanning Tree Algorithm

Prim's Algorithm for finding the Minimum Spanning Tree (MST) of a graph also benefits from the properties of heaps. The algorithm builds the MST by growing one edge at a time and using a priority queue to track the minimum weight edge crossing the cut between the constructed MST and the remaining vertices.

Algorithm 32: Prim's Algorithm for Minimum Spanning Tree

input : Graph $G = (V, E)$ with edge weights w
output : Minimum Spanning Tree T

1. Initialize T as an empty set;
2. Initialize an empty priority queue Q;
3. Choose an arbitrary vertex u as the starting vertex;
4. Insert u into Q with priority 0;
5. **while** $|T| < |V| - 1$ **do**
6.   Extract vertex u from Q with minimum edge weight;
7.   Add the least-cost edge (u, v) to T where v is a non-tree vertex;
8.   **for** *each edge* (u, v) **do**
9.   **if** v *is not included in tree* **then**
10.   Insert v into Q with weight $w(u, v)$ or update Q if $w(u, v)$ is reduced;

The use of a priority queue here ensures that at each step, the smallest edge connecting the growing MST to remaining vertices is selected efficiently.

3. Event Simulation

Priority queues are essential in discrete event simulations. Events in a simulation are scheduled to occur at specific times and need to be processed in chronological order. A priority queue can keep track of these events, with the event time being the priority.

```
class Event implements Comparable<Event> {
    int time;
    String description;

    public Event(int time, String description) {
        this.time = time;
        this.description = description;
    }

    @Override
    public int compareTo(Event other) {
        return Integer.compare(this.time, other.time);
    }
}

PriorityQueue<Event> eventQueue = new PriorityQueue<Event>();
eventQueue.add(new Event(10, "Event1"));
eventQueue.add(new Event(5, "Event2"));
eventQueue.add(new Event(15, "Event3"));

while (!eventQueue.isEmpty()) {
    Event event = eventQueue.poll();
```

```
    System.out.println("Processing " + event.description + " at time " + event.time);
}
```

```
Processing Event2 at time 5
Processing Event1 at time 10
Processing Event3 at time 15
```

In this example, events are added to the priority queue and processed in increasing order of their scheduled times, ensuring accurate simulation behavior.

4. Huffman Coding

Heaps are used in Huffman Coding for constructing the Huffman Tree, which provides an optimal prefix code for a set of symbols based on their frequencies. The algorithm repeatedly combines the two least frequent nodes, and this operation is efficiently managed using a priority queue.

Algorithm 33: Huffman Coding Algorithm

input : Array of frequencies of characters
output : Root of the Huffman Tree

1 Create a priority queue Q with the frequencies of characters;
2 **while** *Q has more than one node* **do**
3 Extract two nodes x and y with the lowest frequencies;
4 Create a new node z with frequency $f(z) = f(x) + f(y)$;
5 Assign x and y as the children of z;
6 Insert z back into Q;
7 **return** *The remaining node in Q (root of the Huffman Tree)*

The priority queue ensures that at each step, the two nodes with the lowest frequencies are combined, resulting in an optimal encoding tree.

5. Operating Systems: Process Scheduling

In operating systems, heaps are utilized for task scheduling where processes with different priorities need to be executed. A priority queue can manage these processes, ensuring that higher priority tasks are executed before lower priority ones.

```
class Process implements Comparable<Process> {
    int priority;
    String name;

    public Process(int priority, String name) {
        this.priority = priority;
        this.name = name;
    }
```

```
    @Override
    public int compareTo(Process other) {
        return Integer.compare(other.priority, this.priority);
    }
}

PriorityQueue<Process> processQueue = new PriorityQueue<Process>();
processQueue.add(new Process(3, "Process1"));
processQueue.add(new Process(1, "Process2"));
processQueue.add(new Process(2, "Process3"));

while (!processQueue.isEmpty()) {
    Process process = processQueue.poll();
    System.out.println("Executing " + process.name + " with priority " + process.
        priority);
}
```

```
Executing Process1 with priority 3
Executing Process3 with priority 2
Executing Process2 with priority 1
```

This implementation ensures that processes are scheduled in order of priority, making it particularly useful for real-time systems where prompt task execution is critical.

These applications illustrate the versatility and efficiency of heaps and priority queues in various domains. Understanding and implementing these advanced data structures can vastly improve the performance and effectiveness of numerous algorithms and systems in computer science.

8.11 D-ary Heaps

D-ary heaps are a generalization of binary heaps where each node has d children instead of the standard two children found in binary heaps. This generalization can offer significant performance improvements for certain types of applications, particularly those involving priority queue operations.

Definition: A D-ary heap (or d-heap) is a complete d-ary tree where each node has up to d children, and the heap property is maintained. The heap property states that for a min-heap, the key of each node is less than or equal to the keys of its children; for a max-heap, the key of each node is greater than or equal to the keys of its children.

Properties:

- Degree: Each internal node in a D-ary heap has at most d children. The root node is at index 0.

- Height: The height of a D-ary heap with n elements is $\lceil \log_d n \rceil$, which is logarithmic in n but proportional to the base d.

- Storage: A D-ary heap can be efficiently stored in an array using similar techniques to those used for binary heaps.

Index Calculations: Given a node at index i in a zero-indexed array representation of the heap:

- The index of the first child is $d \times i + 1$.

- The index of the last child is $d \times i + d$.

- The index of the parent node is $\lfloor \frac{i-1}{d} \rfloor$.

Insertion: The insertion operation involves adding the new element at the end of the array and then "bubbling up" to maintain the heap property. The algorithm is as follows:

Algorithm 34: D-ary Heap Insertion

Input: D-ary heap H, element e
Output: Updated heap H with element e inserted

```
H.insert(e);
i ← H.size − 1;
while i > 0 and H.parent(i) > H[i] do
    swap(H[i], H.parent(i));
    i ← H.parent(i);
end
```

Deletion: The deletion operation, particularly deleting the minimum element in a min-heap (or maximum in a max-heap), involves removing the root and then "bubbling down" the last element to restore the heap property. The algorithm for a min-heap is presented below:

Algorithm 35: D-ary Heap Deletion

Input: D-ary heap H

Output: Updated heap H with the minimum element removed

```
min ← H[0];
H[0] ← H.last();
H.deleteLast();
i ← 0;
while hasChild(i) do
    minChildIndex ← index of minimum child of i;
    if H[i] > H[minChildIndex] then
        swap(H[i], H[minChildIndex]);
        i ← minChildIndex;
    end
    else
        break;
    end
end
```

Performance Analysis:

- Insert Operation: The "bubble up" operation takes $O(\log_d n)$ time since the height of the heap is $\log_d n$.
- Delete Operation: The "bubble down" operation also takes $O(\log_d n)$ time.
- Building a Heap: Building a D-ary heap from n elements can be done in $O(n)$ time using a bottom-up approach, similar to the method used for binary heaps.

Pros and Cons:

- Advantages: Reduced tree height leads to potential speedup in the decrease-key and delete operations. Improved performance in applications requiring efficient handling of large priority queues.
- Disadvantages: The increased number of children per node can lead to more comparisons during the bubble-up and bubble-down processes, potentially offsetting the benefits of reduced height. Implementation complexity is marginally higher due to the need to manage multiple children.

Understanding the trade-offs involved in choosing the arity d is crucial for leveraging the benefits of D-ary heaps in specific applications like network routing, job scheduling, and more. Thus, the study of D-ary heaps extends not just in theoretical prowess but also in practical adaptability across various computational scenarios.

8.12 Fibonacci Heaps

Fibonacci heaps are an advanced form of priority queue, offering improved efficiency for a subset of operations when compared to binary heaps and binomial heaps. They are particularly useful in applications where the decrease-key operation is frequent, such as in network optimization algorithms like Dijkstra's and Prim's algorithms.

A Fibonacci heap is a collection of trees satisfying the min-heap property, where the key of a node is greater than or equal to the key of its parent. The trees in a Fibonacci heap are unordered but follow specific structural constraints to ensure efficient amortized performance.

Basic Structure:

- min_pointer: Points to the node with the minimum key.
- root_list: A circular, doubly linked list connecting all root nodes.
- node structure: Each node consists of a pointer to its parent and child, the degree (number of children), and a mark flag for cut operations.

Key Operations:

Insertion: The insertion operation adds a new node to the root list in constant time. This is done by inserting the node into the circular doubly linked list of roots and updating the min_pointer if necessary.

```
public void insert(Node x) {
    x.degree = 0;
    x.parent = null;
    x.child = null;
    x.mark = false;

    if (minNode != null) {
        minNode.addSibling(x);
        if (x.key < minNode.key) {
            minNode = x;
        }
    } else {
        minNode = x;
```

```
    }
    n++;
}
```

Extract-Min: The extract-min operation removes the node pointed to by the min_pointer, and it involves several steps:

1. Add each child of the minimum node to the root list. 2. Remove the minimum node from the root list. 3. Perform the consolidate() operation, which merges trees of the same degree to maintain the efficient structure.

```
public Node extractMin() {
    Node z = minNode;
    if (z != null) {
        for (Node x : z.children) {
            rootList.add(x);
            x.parent = null;
        }
        rootList.remove(z);
        if (z == z.right) {
            minNode = null;
        } else {
            minNode = z.right;
            consolidate();
        }
        n--;
    }
    return z;
}
```

The consolidate() method is responsible for maintaining the heap structure by ensuring no two roots have the same degree.

```
private void consolidate() {
    int arraySize = ((int) Math.floor(Math.log(n) / Math.log(2.0))) + 1;
    Node[] array = new Node[arraySize];

    // Initialize the array
    for (int i = 0; i < arraySize; i++) {
        array[i] = null;
    }

    // Traverse the root list
    for (Node w : rootList) {
        Node x = w;
        int d = x.degree;
        while (array[d] != null) {
            Node y = array[d];
            if (x.key > y.key) {
                Node temp = x;
                x = y;
                y = temp;
            }
            link(y, x);
            array[d] = null;
            d++;
        }
```

```
        array[d] = x;
    }

    minNode = null;
    for (int i = 0; i < arraySize; i++) {
        if (array[i] != null) {
            if (minNode == null) {
                minNode = array[i];
            } else {
                if (array[i].key < minNode.key) {
                    minNode = array[i];
                }
            }
        }
    }
}
```

The link operation merges two trees of the same degree.

```
private void link(Node y, Node x) {
    rootList.remove(y);
    y.parent = x;
    if (x.child == null) {
        x.child = y;
    } else {
        x.child.addSibling(y);
    }
    x.degree++;
    y.mark = false;
}
```

Decrease-Key: The decrease-key operation decreases the value of a key in the heap and can trigger cascading cuts if certain structural conditions are violated.

```
public void decreaseKey(Node x, int k) {
    if (k > x.key) {
        throw new IllegalArgumentException("new key is greater than current key");
    }
    x.key = k;
    Node y = x.parent;
    if (y != null && x.key < y.key) {
        cut(x, y);
        cascadingCut(y);
    }
    if (x.key < minNode.key) {
        minNode = x;
    }
}
```

The cut method removes a node from its parent's child list, while the cascadingCut method ensures that any parent nodes that have lost a child are appropriately handled to maintain the tree structure.

```
private void cut(Node x, Node y) {
    x.removeFromParent();
    rootList.add(x);
    x.parent = null;
```

```
    x.mark = false;
}

private void cascadingCut(Node y) {
    Node z = y.parent;
    if (z != null) {
        if (y.mark == false) {
            y.mark = true;
        } else {
            cut(y, z);
            cascadingCut(z);
        }
    }
}
```

Delete: The delete operation is typically implemented by first decreasing the key of the target node to negative infinity, thus ensuring that it becomes the minimum element. Subsequently, the extractMin() operation is invoked to remove it.

```
public void delete(Node x) {
    decreaseKey(x, Integer.MIN_VALUE);
    extractMin();
}
```

Fibonacci heaps offer advantages in certain use-cases due to their amortized time complexities:

- **Insert**: $O(1)$
- **Find-Min**: $O(1)$
- **Extract-Min**: $O(\log n)$ amortized
- **Union**: $O(1)$
- **Decrease-Key**: $O(1)$ amortized
- **Delete**: $O(\log n)$ amortized

These time complexities highlight the efficiency of Fibonacci heaps in scenarios requiring frequent decrease-key operations. The amalgamation of tree roots into the root list, together with cascading cuts enables these heaps to maintain structural properties that facilitate quick access and updates.

Chapter 9

Hashing and Hash Tables

This chapter focuses on hashing and hash tables, key techniques for efficient data retrieval. It begins by explaining hash functions and the properties of effective hash functions. The chapter covers various collision resolution techniques, including separate chaining and open addressing, such as linear probing, quadratic probing, and double hashing. Rehashing and common hash table operations like insertion, deletion, and searching are also discussed. The chapter concludes with applications of hash tables and an analysis of their advantages and disadvantages.

9.1 Introduction to Hashing

Hashing is a fundamental technique in computer science for efficiently storing and retrieving data. It provides a mechanism to access data in constant time, $O(1)$, on average. Hashing is widely used in applications where fast data retrieval is crucial, including databases, caching, and sets. This section delves into the concept of hashing, introducing its basic principles and the underlying mechanics that make it an essential tool in data structures.

At its core, hashing involves the transformation of a given input, known as a key, into a typically smaller, fixed-size value known as a hash code. This transformation is performed by a mathematical function called a hash function. The primary goal of a hash function is to distribute keys uniformly across the hash table, minimizing the likelihood of collisions.

A collision occurs when two keys hash to the same index in the hash table.

One of the canonical hash functions is the division method, where the hash code is computed as the remainder of the division of the key by the table size m:

```
int hashFunction(int key, int tableSize) {
    return key % tableSize;
}
```

The above Java function computes the hash code of a given key by computing the modulus with the tableSize. The resulting hash code determines the index where the key-value pair should be stored in the hash table.

However, real-world applications often require more sophisticated hash functions that account for the distribution of possible keys to ensure a uniform spread. Properties of good hash functions, such as minimizing collisions and being computationally efficient, will be addressed in subsequent sections.

The structure that stores the hash code and the associated values is known as a hash table. A hash table typically consists of an array where each element, or bucket, holds the key-value pairs. When inserting a key-value pair, the hash function is applied to the key to determine the appropriate index in the array for storage. For retrieval, the key is hashed again to locate the bucket where its associated value is stored.

```
class HashTable {
    private static class HashEntry {
        int key;
        String value;
        HashEntry(int key, String value) {
            this.key = key;
            this.value = value;
        }
    }

    private HashEntry[] table;

    public HashTable(int size) {
        table = new HashEntry[size];
    }

    public void insert(int key, String value) {
        int index = hashFunction(key, table.length);
        table[index] = new HashEntry(key, value);
    }

    public String search(int key) {
        int index = hashFunction(key, table.length);
        if (table[index] != null && table[index].key == key) {
            return table[index].value;
```

```
        }
        return null;
    }

    private int hashFunction(int key, int tableSize) {
        return key % tableSize;
    }
}
```

In this example, the HashTable class defines a simple hash table where the hash function implemented is the division method. The insert method hashes the key and places a new HashEntry in the appropriate index. The search method retrieves the value associated with a given key by hashing the key and accessing the corresponding index.

Collisions are an unavoidable reality in hashing, especially when the set of possible keys is significantly larger than the array size. Effective collision resolution techniques, such as separate chaining and open addressing, are vital to maintaining the performance efficiency of a hash table. These techniques and their variations will be thoroughly examined in their respective sections.

Ultimately, hashing ensures that data retrieval and insertion can be performed in constant time, significantly improving the efficiency of applications that manage large datasets. The theoretical underpinnings and practical applications of hashing will become more apparent as we explore the specific mechanisms that enable its powerful capabilities.

9.2 Hash Functions

A hash function is a critical component of a hash table. It takes an input, commonly referred to as a key, and maps it to an index in an array, called a hash table. The primary goal of a hash function is to provide a deterministic, evenly distributed, and fast computation method to transform keys into array indices.

The conceptual formula for a hash function can be represented as follows:

$$h(k) = i$$

where h denotes the hash function, k represents the key, and i is the index in the hash table where the data associated with k should be stored.

Characteristics of Effective Hash Functions

An effective hash function should possess the following essential characteristics:

- **Deterministic**: A given input must always produce the same output hash value.
- **Uniform Distribution**: Hash values should be evenly distributed across the hash table to minimize collisions.
- **Efficiency**: The hash function should be computationally efficient to maintain overall performance.
- **Minimal Collisions**: While collisions are inevitable, a good hash function will minimize their frequency.
- **Applicability to Variable Data Types**: The hash function should handle various data types, such as integers, strings, or composite objects.

Examples of Hash Functions

Several classical hash functions are widely employed in various applications. Below are some illustrative examples:

Division Method

The division method calculates the hash value using the modulo operation:

$$h(k) = k \mod m$$

where m is typically a prime number. This method ensures that the resulting hash values are within the range from 0 to $m - 1$.

```
public int divisionHash(int key, int tableSize) {
    return key % tableSize;
}
```

Multiplication Method

The multiplication method uses an irrational number to scale the key and extract the fractional part:

$$h(k) = \lfloor m\,(k \cdot A \mod 1) \rfloor$$

where $0 < A < 1$ is a constant, and m is chosen typically as a power of two to simplify implementation.

```
public int multiplicationHash(int key, int tableSize) {
    double A = (Math.sqrt(5) - 1) / 2;
    return (int) Math.floor(tableSize * ((key * A) % 1));
}
```

Universal Hashing

Universal hashing selects a hash function randomly from a family of hash functions to reduce the probability of collision for any given set of keys.

```
public class UniversalHashFunction {
    private int a, b, p, m;

    public UniversalHashFunction(int p, int m) {
        this.p = p;
        this.m = m;
        this.a = (int) (Math.random() * (p - 1)) + 1;
        this.b = (int) (Math.random() * p);
    }

    public int hash(int key) {
        return ((a * key + b) % p) % m;
    }
}
```

Cryptographic Hash Functions

These functions, such as SHA-256, produce a fixed-size hash value and are designed to be secure and resistant to collisions and tampering.

String Hashing

Hashing strings often requires combining techniques to ensure that the wide variety of possible strings maps uniformly into the hash table. A common approach involves using polynomial or cyclic redundancy check (CRC) methods.

Polynomial Rolling Hash

This method treats a string s as a large integer:

$$h(s) = \sum_{i=0}^{n-1} s[i] \cdot p^i \mod m$$

where p and m are typically prime numbers, with p often set to 31 or 53.

```
public int polynomialRollingHash(String s, int p, int m) {
    int hashValue = 0;
    int pPower = 1;
```

```
    for (char c : s.toCharArray()) {
        hashValue = (hashValue + (c - 'a' + 1) * pPower) % m;
        pPower = (pPower * p) % m;
    }
    return hashValue;
}
```

The selection of a hash function is context-dependent, and the effectiveness of a hash table significantly relies on this choice. Thus, understanding the properties and behaviors of these hash functions is fundamental in designing robust and efficient hash-based data structures.

9.3 Properties of Good Hash Functions

The effectiveness of a hash table relies heavily on the quality of its hash function. A hash function is responsible for transforming an input (or key) into a specific index in the hash table. To ensure efficient data retrieval and minimize collisions, a hash function must possess certain essential properties.

- **Deterministic Output**
  A hash function must produce the same output for the same input every time. This ensures consistency in accessing the elements stored in the hash table. Given an input key, the hash function $h(\text{key})$ should always yield the same index.

- **Uniform Distribution**
  A good hash function should distribute the input keys uniformly across the hash table. This property minimizes collisions and avoids clustering, where multiple keys map to the same index. Uniform distribution ensures that the hash table utilizes its available slots efficiently, leading to optimized performance.

- **Speed**
  The hash function must be fast to compute. Since hash tables rely on the hash function for insertion, deletion, and lookup operations, the speed of the hash function directly impacts the overall efficiency of these operations. In practice, a hash function should have a time complexity of $O(1)$.

- **Efficiency with Input Range**
  The hash function should handle a wide range of input keys efficiently. Whether the keys are integers, strings, or complex ob-

jects, the function must adapt to various input types while maintaining its performance properties. It should also perform well with both small and large datasets.

- **Proper Handling of Input Features**
  The hash function must take into account the characteristics of the input data. For example, when working with strings, the function should consider the position and frequency of characters to avoid excessive collisions. The function should be designed to handle variations in the input effectively.

- **Minimize Collisions**
  While collisions are inevitable in any hash table, a good hash function minimizes their occurrence. A collision occurs when two different keys produce the same hash value. Minimizing collisions results in fewer elements being stored in the same bucket, which improves the efficiency of retrieval operations. Various techniques, such as modular arithmetic, can help achieve this.

Algorithm 36: Simplified Modulo-based Hash Function

```
Data: Input key array keys, hash table size tableSize
Result: Hash values corresponding to the input keys
Function ModuloHash(key, tableSize):
    return key % tableSize;
foreach key in keys do
    hashValue ← ModuloHash(key, tableSize);
    Print hashValue;
```

- **Avoiding Patterns**
  A good hash function should avoid producing patterns in the output. Predictable patterns can lead to inefficiencies and security vulnerabilities. For example, if the hash function consistently maps inputs with similar prefixes to adjacent indices, it can lead to clustering and degrade performance.

- **Scalability**
  The hash function should scale well with the hash table size. As the table grows, the function should continue distributing keys uniformly without a significant increase in collisions. This property ensures that the hash table remains efficient even as the dataset expands.

- **Independence from Key Distributions**
  A well-designed hash function should not be overly sensitive to specific key distributions. It should perform effectively regardless of whether the input keys follow a specific pattern or are randomly distributed. This robustness makes the hash function versatile and reliable.

- **Example Hash Functions**

  To illustrate, consider the popular hash functions used in practice, such as the division method and the multiplication method.

Division Method:

```
int DivisionMethodHash(int key, int tableSize) {
    return key % tableSize;
}
```

The division method uses the modulo operation to calculate the hash value. It is simple and efficient but might not handle certain key distributions well, such as those with common factors with the table size.

Multiplication Method:

```
int MultiplicationMethodHash(int key, int tableSize) {
    double A = 0.618033; // A constant (0 < A < 1)
    return floor(tableSize * (key * A - floor(key * A)));
}
```

The multiplication method involves multiplying the key by a constant A (where $0 < A < 1$), taking the fractional part, and then scaling it to the table size. This method often provides better distribution of keys compared to the division method.

To summarize, the quality of a hash function is a crucial determinant of the performance and efficiency of a hash table. Effective hash functions exhibit deterministic output, uniform distribution, speed, efficiency across input ranges, proper handling of input features, minimized collisions, avoidance of patterns, scalability, and independence from key distributions. Understanding and implementing these properties in hash functions is fundamental to leveraging the full potential of hash tables in various applications.

9.4 Collision Resolution Techniques: Separate Chaining

Separate Chaining is a widely-used collision resolution technique in hash tables, which utilizes linked lists to manage multiple entries that hash to the same index. In this method, each cell of the hash table contains a pointer to a linked list (or chain) of entries that share the same hash index. When a hash collision occurs, the new entry is simply added to the linked list of the corresponding hash index.

Mechanism

The primary mechanism of separate chaining involves maintaining a linked list for each array index in the hash table. When inserting a new key-value pair:

- Compute the hash value $h(k)$ for the key k. This will be the index in the hash table.
- Traverse the linked list at index $h(k)$ and check if k already exists.
- If the key does not exist in the linked list, insert the new key-value pair at the beginning (or end) of the list (depending on the implementation).

The search operation is performed by computing the hash value $h(k)$ and traversing the linked list at that index to find the key. Similarly, deletion involves locating the key in the linked list and removing the corresponding node.

Example Code Implementation

Consider the following Java implementation of separate chaining in a hash table:

```
public class HashTableSeparateChaining<K, V> {
    private static final int DEFAULT_CAPACITY = 10;
    private int size;
    private LinkedList<Entry<K, V>>[] table;

    public HashTableSeparateChaining() {
        table = new LinkedList[DEFAULT_CAPACITY];
        for (int i = 0; i < DEFAULT_CAPACITY; i++) {
            table[i] = new LinkedList<>();
        }
        size = 0;
    }

    private int hash(K key) {
```

```
        return Math.abs(key.hashCode()) % table.length;
    }

    public void put(K key, V value) {
        int index = hash(key);
        for (Entry<K, V> entry : table[index]) {
            if (entry.key.equals(key)) {
                entry.value = value; // Update existing key
                return;
            }
        }
        table[index].add(new Entry<>(key, value));
        size++;
    }

    public V get(K key) {
        int index = hash(key);
        for (Entry<K, V> entry : table[index]) {
            if (entry.key.equals(key)) {
                return entry.value;
            }
        }
        return null;
    }
    public boolean remove(K key) {
        int index = hash(key);
        Iterator<Entry<K, V>> iterator = table[index].iterator();
        while (iterator.hasNext()) {
            Entry<K, V> entry = iterator.next();
            if (entry.key.equals(key)) {
                iterator.remove();
                size--;
                return true;
            }
        }
        return false;
    }
    private static class Entry<K, V> {
        K key;
        V value;

        Entry(K key, V value) {
            this.key = key;
            this.value = value;
        }
    }
}
```

This implementation includes methods for put, get, and remove operations using separate chaining. A static nested class, Entry, stores key-value pairs. Each table index points to a linked list of these entries.

Complexity Analysis

The performance of separate chaining depends on the distribution of keys and the load factor λ, which is defined as the ratio $\frac{n}{m}$, where n is the number of entries, and m is the number of slots in the table.

- **Best Case**: If the keys are uniformly distributed and the load factor is low, operations such as insertion, deletion, and search can be performed in O(1) time.
- **Average Case**: Typically, these operations can still be performed in O(1) time, assuming that the average length of the linked lists remains short.
- **Worst Case**: In the worst-case scenario, where all keys hash to the same index, the performance degrades to O(n) since each index contains a single linked list of all entries.

Advantages and Disadvantages

Understanding the advantages and disadvantages of separate chaining is crucial for its effective application.

- **Advantages**:
  - Simple to implement and modify.
  - Efficient when the load factor is maintained at an appropriate level.
  - Can handle larger numbers of elements gracefully, since linked lists dynamically grow.
  - Less sensitive to clustering issues compared to open addressing techniques.
- **Disadvantages**:
  - Requires additional memory for storing pointers in linked lists.
  - Performance deteriorates significantly if many keys hash to the same index.
  - Overhead in managing linked list operations, such as dynamic memory allocation and pointer manipulation.

Separate chaining offers a flexible and straightforward solution for collision resolution in hash tables, especially when entries are uniformly distributed and the load factor is properly controlled. Understanding these characteristics allows for optimizing hash table performance to suit specific application requirements.

9.5 Collision Resolution Techniques: Open Addressing

Open addressing is a collision resolution technique where all elements are stored directly in the hash table itself, without the use of auxiliary data structures like linked lists. When a collision occurs, the algorithm searches for the next available slot within the hash table based on a defined probing sequence. If the initial hash position $h(k)$ is occupied, alternative positions are computed and checked sequentially using the probing sequence until an empty slot is found.

Let us denote the hash table by T, and assume it has a size of m. The key k is initially hashed to the index $h(k)$. If collision occurs, the open addressing methods will probe the table based on a sequence $\{h(k), h(k)+1, h(k)+2, ..., h(k) + j\}$ (for some increment scheme), wrapping around the table if necessary.

Linear Probing.

Linear probing checks the next slot sequentially until an empty slot is found. If the hash function $h(k)$ maps k to an index i, and i is occupied, linear probing continues to $(i + 1) \% m$, $(i + 2) \% m$, and so forth until an empty slot is located.

Here is an example implementation in Java:

```
public class HashTable {
    private static final int TABLE_SIZE = 10;
    private Integer[] table;

    public HashTable() {
        table = new Integer[TABLE_SIZE];
    }

    public void insert(int key) {
        int hash = key % TABLE_SIZE;
        int originalHash = hash;
        while (table[hash] != null) {
            hash = (hash + 1) % TABLE_SIZE;
            if (hash == originalHash) {
                throw new RuntimeException("Hash table is full");
            }
        }
        table[hash] = key;
    }

    public Integer search(int key) {
        int hash = key % TABLE_SIZE;
        int originalHash = hash;
        while (table[hash] != null) {
            if (table[hash].equals(key)) {
                return hash;
```

```
            }
            hash = (hash + 1) % TABLE_SIZE;
            if (hash == originalHash) {
                return null;
            }
        }
        return null;
    }

    public void delete(int key) {
        int hash = key % TABLE_SIZE;
        int originalHash = hash;
        while (table[hash] != null) {
            if (table[hash].equals(key)) {
                table[hash] = null;
                return;
            }
            hash = (hash + 1) % TABLE_SIZE;
            if (hash == originalHash) {
                return;
            }
        }
    }
}
```

Quadratic Probing.

Quadratic probing resolves collisions by checking positions using a quadratic function. If a collision occurs at index i, the next position checked will be (i + 1^2) % m, then (i + 2^2) % m, and so on. This reduces clustering compared to linear probing but requires careful handling to ensure all potential slots can be checked.

An example of quadratic probing in Java:

```
public void insertWithQuadraticProbing(int key) {
    int hash = key % TABLE_SIZE;
    int step = 1;
    int originalHash = hash;
    while (table[hash] != null) {
        hash = (originalHash + step * step) % TABLE_SIZE;
        step++;
        if (step == TABLE_SIZE) {
            throw new RuntimeException("Hash table is full");
        }
    }
    table[hash] = key;
}

public Integer searchWithQuadraticProbing(int key) {
    int hash = key % TABLE_SIZE;
    int step = 1;
    int originalHash = hash;
    while (table[hash] != null) {
        if (table[hash].equals(key)) {
            return hash;
        }
        hash = (originalHash + step * step) % TABLE_SIZE;
        step++;
```

```
        if (step == TABLE_SIZE) {
            return null;
        }
    }
    return null;
}

public void deleteWithQuadraticProbing(int key) {
    int hash = key % TABLE_SIZE;
    int step = 1;
    int originalHash = hash;
    while (table[hash] != null) {
        if (table[hash].equals(key)) {
            table[hash] = null;
            return;
        }
        hash = (originalHash + step * step) % TABLE_SIZE;
        step++;
        if (step == TABLE_SIZE) {
            return;
        }
    }
}
```

Double Hashing.

Double hashing uses a second hash function to determine the sequence of probes. The first hash function determines the initial probe position, while the second hash function determines the step size for subsequent probes. Suppose $h1(k)$ is the primary hash function, and $h2(k)$ is the secondary hash function which should never evaluate to zero to ensure progress through the table. The probe sequence is given by $h1(k)$, $(h1(k) + h2(k)) \% m$, $(h1(k) + 2*h2(k)) \% m$, etc.

Below is the implementation of double hashing in Java:

```
public void insertWithDoubleHashing(int key) {
    int hash1 = key % TABLE_SIZE;
    int hash2 = 1 + (key % (TABLE_SIZE - 1));
    int originalHash = hash1;
    int step = 0;
    while (table[hash1] != null) {
        hash1 = (originalHash + step * hash2) % TABLE_SIZE;
        step++;
        if (step == TABLE_SIZE) {
            throw new RuntimeException("Hash table is full");
        }
    }
    table[hash1] = key;
}

public Integer searchWithDoubleHashing(int key) {
    int hash1 = key % TABLE_SIZE;
    int hash2 = 1 + (key % (TABLE_SIZE - 1));
    int originalHash = hash1;
    int step = 0;
    while (table[hash1] != null) {
        if (table[hash1].equals(key)) {
```

```
            return hash1;
        }
        hash1 = (originalHash + step * hash2) % TABLE_SIZE;
        step++;
        if (step == TABLE_SIZE) {
            return null;
        }
    }
    return null;
}

public void deleteWithDoubleHashing(int key) {
    int hash1 = key % TABLE_SIZE;
    int hash2 = 1 + (key % (TABLE_SIZE - 1));
    int originalHash = hash1;
    int step = 0;
    while (table[hash1] != null) {
        if (table[hash1].equals(key)) {
            table[hash1] = null;
            return;
        }
        hash1 = (originalHash + step * hash2) % TABLE_SIZE;
        step++;
        if (step == TABLE_SIZE) {
            return;
        }
    }
}
```

It should be noted that open addressing requires the hash table's load factor to be well below 1 (typically around 0.5 to 0.7) to maintain efficiency in collision resolution.

9.6 Linear Probing

Linear probing is a method of open addressing used to resolve collisions in hash tables. When two keys hash to the same index, linear probing searches for the next available slot in the table. This technique is efficient in terms of both space and speed, enabling fast retrieval of elements when appropriately implemented.

To implement linear probing, consider a hash table of size m and a hash function $h(k)$ that maps a key k to an index in the hash table. When a collision occurs at index $i = h(k)$, the algorithm probes the subsequent indices $(i+1)\%m, (i+2)\%m, \ldots, (i+j)\%m$ until an empty slot is found.

The mechanism of linear probing is simple but effective, and it provides an intuitive solution to handle collisions. However, it is important to consider potential issues and optimizations associated with this method.

Primary Clustering

Input: key to be inserted, value to be associated with the key, hashTable array with size m
Output: Updated hashTable with the new key-value pair inserted

```
Function InsertLinearProbing(key, value, hashTable, m):
    index ← hashFunction(key) % m
    while hashTable[index] is not Empty do
        index ← (index + 1) % m
    hashTable[index] ← (key, value)
```

One inherent issue with linear probing is primary clustering. Primary clustering occurs when a group of consecutive filled slots leads to longer probe sequences. For instance, if a cluster of occupied slots exists, any new key that hashes into this cluster will need to probe through the entire cluster to find an empty slot, thus increasing the time complexity.

To illustrate primary clustering, consider an example where we insert multiple keys into a hash table of size $m = 10$. Suppose the hash function $h(k) = k\%m$ and we insert key-value pairs $(3, \text{"A"})$, $(13, \text{"B"})$, $(23, \text{"C"})$. Initially, the table would look as follows:

Index:	0	1	2	3	4	5	6	7	8	9
Value:	--	--	--	A	--	--	--	--	--	--

Inserting $(13, \text{"B"})$ will result in a collision at index 3, and we move to index 4:

Index:	0	1	2	3	4	5	6	7	8	9
Value:	--	--	--	A	B	--	--	--	--	--

Inserting $(23, \text{"C"})$ will result in another collision at index 3, and following linear probing, it will be placed at index 5:

Index:	0	1	2	3	4	5	6	7	8	9
Value:	--	--	--	A	B	C	--	--	--	--

In this case, the cluster at indices 3-5 could potentially grow, leading to increased search times for both insertion and retrieval.

Advantages of Linear Probing

Despite the issue of primary clustering, linear probing has several notable advantages:

- **Simplified Memory Management:** Linear probing does not require additional memory for pointers, unlike separate chaining.
- **Cache Performance:** Due to the locality of reference, linear probing tends to have better cache performance compared to other forms of collision resolution techniques.
- **Uniform Distribution:** With a good hash function, linear probing can distribute keys uniformly across the hash table.

Disadvantages of Linear Probing

Conversely, some disadvantages should also be acknowledged:

- **Primary Clustering:** As discussed, the primary clustering issue can lead to significant decreases in performance under certain scenarios.
- **Deletion Complexity:** Proper handling of deletions requires marking slots as deleted rather than empty, complicating the algorithm.
- **Load Factor Sensitivity:** Performance deteriorates rapidly as the load factor approaches 1, necessitating more frequent rehashing.

In practice, choosing an appropriate hash function and maintaining a load factor well below 1 can mitigate many of the disadvantages associated with linear probing. Rehashing strategies, detailed in subsequent sections, also play a critical role in maintaining efficient operations within hash tables utilizing linear probing.

9.7 Quadratic Probing

Quadratic Probing is an open addressing collision resolution technique used in hash tables. When a collision occurs—that is, when a hash function maps multiple keys to the same index—quadratic probing provides a systematic method to resolve the collision by exploring alternative indices in a quadratic manner.

Consider a hash table of size m and a hash function h(k) that maps a key k to an initial index h(k) within the bounds of the table. If the position h(k) is already occupied, quadratic probing searches for the next available slot using the following sequence of indices:

$$(h(k) + i^2) \mod m$$

where i ranges from 0 up to m-1 (potentially). The quadratic nature of the probes ensures that the sequence of indices generated is:

$$h(k), h(k) + 1^2, h(k) + 2^2, h(k) + 3^2, \ldots, h(k) + i^2 \mod m$$

Example Consider a hash table of size m = 7. Suppose we have the following keys: 10, 22, 31, 4, 15, 28, 17, 88, 59, and a hash function:

$$h(k) = k \mod 7$$

Let's insert each key into the hash table using quadratic probing:

```
// Hash function
int h(int k) {
    return k % 7;
}

// Quadratic probing implementation
void insert(int[] hashTable, int key) {
    int i = 0;
    int index = (h(key) + i * i) % 7;

    while (hashTable[index] != -1) {
        i++;
        index = (h(key) + i * i) % 7;
    }

    hashTable[index] = key;
}

// Inserting keys
int[] hashTable = new int[7];
Arrays.fill(hashTable, -1);

int[] keys = {10, 22, 31, 4, 15, 28, 17, 88, 59};

for (int key : keys) {
    insert(hashTable, key);
}
```

During the insertion process: - Insert 10: h(10) = 3. Slot 3 is empty, so insert 10 at slot 3. - Insert 22: h(22) = 1. Slot 1 is empty, so insert 22 at slot 1. - Insert 31: h(31) = 3. Slot 3 is occupied, quadratic probe to (3 + 12) % 7 = 4. Slot 4 is empty, so insert 31 at slot 4. - Insert 4: h(4) = 4. Slot 4 is occupied, quadratic probe to (4 + 12) % 7 = 5. Slot 5 is empty, so insert 4 at slot 5. - Insert 15: $h(15)=1$. Slot 1 is occupied, quadratic probe to $(1 + 12) \% 7 = 2$. Slot 2 is empty, so insert 15 at slot 2. - Insert 28: $h(28) = 0$. Slot 0 is empty, so insert 28 at slot 0. - Insert 17: $h(17) = 3$. Slot 3 is occupied, quadratic probe to $(3 + 12) \% 7 = 4$. Slot 4 is occupied, probe to $(3 + 22) \% 7 = 6$. Slot 6 is empty, so insert 17 at slot 6. - Insert 88: $h(88) = 4$. Slot 4 is occupied, quadratic probe to $(4 + 12) \% 7 = 5$. Slot 5 is occupied, probe to $(4 + 22) \% 7 = 1$. Slot 1 is occupied, probe to $(4 + 32) \% 7 = 6$. Slot 6 is occupied, probe to $(4 + 42) \% 7 = 2$. Slot 2 is occupied, probe to $(4 + 52) \% 7 = 3$. Slot 3 is occupied, so continue probing. - Insert 59: $h(59) = 3$. Slot 3 is occupied, quadratic probe to $(3 + 12) \% 7 = 4$. Slot 4 is occupied, probe to $(3 + 22) \% 7 = 6$. Slot 6 is occupied, probe to $(3 + 32) \% 7 = 2$. Slot 2 is occupied, so continue probing.

The resulting hash table is displayed as follows:

Index:	0	1	2	3	4	5	6
Contents:	28	22	15	10	88	4	17

Algorithm Analysis Quadratic probing reduces the primary clustering problem inherent in linear probing but introduces a secondary clustering problem whereby keys that hash to the same index follow the same quadratic sequence of probes. The performance of quadratic probing heavily depends on the choice of the table size and the efficiency of the underlying hash function.

Algorithm 37: Quadratic Probing Insertion Algorithm

Input: A hash table $\mathrm{hashTable}$ of size m and a key k.
Output: Key k inserted into the hash table using quadratic probing.

```
Fninsert(hashTable, k) i = 0
index = (h(k) + i * i) % m
while hashTable[index] ≠ -1 do
    i++
    index = (h(k) + i * i) % m
hashTable[index] = k
```

Advantages and Disadvantages Quadratic probing offers several advantages over other collision resolution techniques:

- It significantly reduces primary clustering compared to linear probing.
- Easier to implement than some other open addressing methods

such as double hashing.

However, quadratic probing also has disadvantages:

- It can produce secondary clustering, grouping together keys that collide at the same initial index.
- Requires careful selection of the table size m to ensure the entire table is probed, ideally a prime number or a number conforming to special conditions.
- If the table is too small or poorly sized, it may fail to find an available slot even if one exists.

Understanding the behavior of quadratic probing and carefully choosing the hash table size and hash function allows for efficient handling of collisions, optimizing lookup, insertion, and deletion operations within hash tables.

9.8 Double Hashing

Double hashing is an open addressing collision resolution technique that uses two distinct hash functions to compute the index of the hash table where the key should be inserted. This method reduces clustering problems that are prevalent in linear and quadratic probing and offers better distribution of keys. In double hashing, when a collision occurs, a secondary hash function is employed to determine the interval between probes.

Let $h(k)$ be the primary hash function, and let $h2(k)$ be the secondary hash function. For a given key k, the probe sequence can be described by the formula:

$$\text{index} = (h(k) + i \cdot h2(k)) \mod m$$

where i is the number of probes attempted, and m is the size of the hash table.

To ensure that all slots of the hash table are eventually probed, it is crucial that $h2(k)$ never evaluates to zero and is relatively prime to the hash table size m.

```
public class DoubleHashingHashTable {
    private static final int DEFAULT_TABLE_SIZE = 11;
    private static final double LOAD_FACTOR_THRESHOLD = 0.75;

    private HashEntry[] hashTable;
    private int currentSize;

    public DoubleHashingHashTable() {
        hashTable = new HashEntry[DEFAULT_TABLE_SIZE];
        currentSize = 0;
    }

    private static class HashEntry {
        public int key;
        public String value;
        public boolean isActive;

        public HashEntry(int key, String value) {
            this.key = key;
            this.value = value;
            this.isActive = true;
        }
    }

    public boolean insert(int key, String value) {
        if (currentSize > LOAD_FACTOR_THRESHOLD * hashTable.length) {
            rehash();
        }

        int initialIndex = primaryHash(key);
        int stepSize = secondaryHash(key);
        int index = initialIndex;

        while (hashTable[index] != null && hashTable[index].isActive) {
            index = (initialIndex + stepSize) % hashTable.length;
            stepSize += secondaryHash(key);
        }

        hashTable[index] = new HashEntry(key, value);
        currentSize++;
        return true;
    }

    public boolean remove(int key) {
        int index = findPos(key);
        if (index != -1 && hashTable[index] != null && hashTable[index].isActive) {
            hashTable[index].isActive = false;
            currentSize--;
            return true;
        }
        return false;
    }

    public String find(int key) {
        int index = findPos(key);
        if (index != -1 && hashTable[index] != null && hashTable[index].isActive) {
            return hashTable[index].value;
        }
        return null;
    }

    private int findPos(int key) {
```

```
        int initialIndex = primaryHash(key);
        int stepSize = secondaryHash(key);
        int index = initialIndex;

        while (hashTable[index] != null && (hashTable[index].key != key || !hashTable[
              index].isActive)) {
            index = (initialIndex + stepSize) % hashTable.length;
            stepSize += secondaryHash(key);
        }

        return (hashTable[index] != null && hashTable[index].isActive) ? index : -1;
    }

    private int primaryHash(int key) {
        return key % hashTable.length;
    }

    private int secondaryHash(int key) {
        return 7 - (key % 7);
    }

    private void rehash() {
        HashEntry[] oldHashTable = hashTable;
        hashTable = new HashEntry[2 * oldHashTable.length];
        currentSize = 0;

        for (HashEntry entry : oldHashTable) {
            if (entry != null && entry.isActive) {
                insert(entry.key, entry.value);
            }
        }
    }
}
```

The primary hash function primaryHash(k) computes the index k % m, where m is the table size. The secondary hash function secondaryHash(k) is chosen to be a prime number less than the table size, ensuring that it does not evaluate to zero and is relatively prime to m. In our example, 7 - (k % 7) is used.

To elucidate the operation of double hashing, consider inserting a key-value pair (k, v) into the hash table. First, the primary hash function primaryHash(k) computes the initial index. If the corresponding slot is occupied, the algorithm probes the next slot using the secondary hash function secondaryHash(k) multiplied by the probe attempt count i. This process repeats until an empty slot is found.

```
Example Execution Output:
Insert (10, "A")
Insert (22, "B")
Insert (31, "C")
Find Key 22: "B"
Remove Key 31
Find Key 31: null
```

Double hashing offers efficient performance and minimizes clustering by leveraging two independent hash functions. Despite its advantages, the implementation complexity is higher than linear or quadratic probing due to the necessity of managing two hash functions and ensuring their mutual primeness with respect to the table size. Adopting double hashing yields benefits in scenarios requiring minimal collisions and optimal key distributions across the hash table.

The understanding of double hashing is vital for implementing efficient hash tables and is complementary to other collision resolution techniques. Such holistic knowledge equips developers and computer scientists with extensive tools for optimizing data retrieval systems.

9.9 Rehashing

Rehashing is an essential technique for maintaining the efficiency of a hash table as it grows in size. When the load factor of a hash table becomes too high, performance can degrade significantly due to increased collisions and the associated cost of collision resolution. Rehashing provides a solution to this problem by creating a new, larger hash table and redistributing the existing elements into the new table using a new hash function or an extended form of the original hash function.

The load factor, generally denoted as α, is a measure of how full the hash table is. It is defined by the following equation:

$$\alpha = \frac{n}{m}$$

where n is the number of elements currently in the hash table, and m is the number of slots or buckets in the table. A high load factor indicates that the hash table is becoming full, leading to potential performance degradation.

Algorithm 38: Rehashing Process

Input: A hash table T with load factor threshold α_{max}
Output: A rehashed hash table T'

if $\alpha \geq \alpha_{max}$ **then**
  $m' \leftarrow 2 * m$; // Double the size of the hash table
  Create a new hash table T' with m' slots;
  foreach *element* e *in* T **do**
    $k' \leftarrow$ hash$(e.key)$ mod m';
    Insert e into T' at position k';
  $T \leftarrow T'$;

This algorithm doubles the size of the hash table when the load factor exceeds a predefined threshold, α_{max}, which is typically set around 0.7 to 0.75 to ensure that the table does not become too crowded.

Rehashing Steps

- **Allocate a New Hash Table**: A new hash table T' is created with typically twice the number of slots as the original table T.
- **Recompute Hash Values**: Each element in the original table T is rehashed, which involves computing the hash value using the new table size. This ensures a more uniform distribution of elements in the new table.
- **Insert Elements into the New Table**: Rehashed elements are inserted into their new positions in T'.

Example of Rehashing

Consider a hash table T with 5 slots and the following elements and their hash values:

```
Elements: [12, 24, 36, 48, 60]
Hash Values: [2, 4, 1, 3, 0]
```

The table initially looks like this:

0	1	2	3	4
60	36	12	48	24

If the load factor threshold α_{max} is 0.75 and we insert another element, the load factor exceeds the threshold, necessitating rehashing. We create a new table T' with 10 slots and rehash the elements:

New Hash Values: [2, 4, 6, 8, 0] (with new table size 10)

The new table T' then looks like this:

0	1	2	3	4	5	6	7	8	9
60		12		24		36		48	

Performance Considerations

Rehashing can be a costly operation in terms of time complexity, as it involves re-inserting each element into the new table. The time complexity of rehashing all n elements is $O(n)$. However, this is amortized over many insertions, making the average insertion time still $O(1)$.

Modern implementations often delay rehashing until a significant number of operations have been performed since the last rehash, optimizing the overall performance. Some implementations also use incremental rehashing to spread the cost over multiple insertions, avoiding a single large cost spike.

Properly managing the rehashing process ensures that a hash table maintains efficient performance even as the number of stored elements increases, balancing space and time complexities effectively.

9.10 Hash Table Operations: Insertion, Deletion, Searching

Hash tables are fundamental data structures that facilitate fast data lookup, insertion, and deletion operations. Understanding the efficiency and implementation details of these operations is crucial for leveraging hash tables effectively. This section delves into the insertion, deletion, and searching operations within hash tables, demonstrating their execution and the underlying mechanisms.

Insertion Operation

Inserting an element into a hash table involves computing the hash value for the key and placing the key-value pair at the computed index. The efficiency of the insertion operation hinges on the hash function's ability to uniformly distribute keys across the table. When a collision occurs, a collision resolution technique, such as separate chaining or open addressing, is employed.

The following pseudocode illustrates the insertion process using separate chaining and open addressing (linear probing) for collision resolution:

Algorithm 39: Insert in Hash Table using Separate Chaining

```
Input   : hashTable, key, value
Output  : Updated hashTable
hashIndex ← hash(key) ;
if hashTable[hashIndex] is empty then
    hashTable[hashIndex] ← {{key, value}} ;
else
    hashTable[hashIndex].append({key, value}) ;
```

Algorithm 40: Insert in Hash Table using Linear Probing

```
Input   : hashTable, key, value
Output  : Updated hashTable
hashIndex ← hash(key) ;
while hashTable[hashIndex] is not empty do
    hashIndex ← (hashIndex + 1) mod tableSize ;
hashTable[hashIndex] ← {key, value} ;
```

Deletion Operation

Deleting an element from a hash table involves searching for the element using its key and removing the key-value pair once located. In open addressing, marking a position as deleted instead of empty becomes crucial to handle subsequent insertions and searches correctly.

The following pseudocode demonstrates the deletion process with separate chaining and linear probing:

Algorithm 41: Delete from Hash Table using Separate Chaining

```
Input  : hashTable, key
Output : Updated hashTable
hashIndex ← hash(key) ;
if hashTable[hashIndex] is not empty then
    for each pair in hashTable[hashIndex] do
        if pair.key = key then
            hashTable[hashIndex].remove(pair) ;
            return;
```

Algorithm 42: Delete from Hash Table using Linear Probing

```
Input  : hashTable, key
Output : Updated hashTable
hashIndex ← hash(key) ;
while hashTable[hashIndex] is not empty do
    if hashTable[hashIndex].key = key then
        hashTable[hashIndex] ← deleted ;
        return;
    hashIndex ← (hashIndex + 1) mod tableSize ;
```

Searching Operation

Searching for an element within a hash table determines whether a specific key is present and retrieves the corresponding value if it exists. The search operation traverses the table based on the hash value computed for the given key. Both separate chaining and linear probing handle potential collisions during the search process.

Below are pseudocode examples illustrating the search operation using separate chaining and linear probing:

Algorithm 43: Search in Hash Table using Separate Chaining

```
Input  : hashTable, key
Output : value or Not Found
hashIndex ← hash(key) ;
if hashTable[hashIndex] is not empty then
    for each pair in hashTable[hashIndex] do
        if pair.key = key then
            return pair.value ;
return Not Found ;
```

Algorithm 44: Search in Hash Table using Linear Probing

```
Input  : hashTable, key
Output : value or Not Found
hashIndex ← hash(key) ;
while hashTable[hashIndex] is not empty do
    if hashTable[hashIndex].key = key then
        return hashTable[hashIndex].value ;
    hashIndex ← (hashIndex + 1) mod tableSize ;
return Not Found ;
```

These operations form the core of manipulating and interacting with data within hash tables. Each operation's performance predominantly depends on the hash function's quality and the implemented collision resolution strategy. Employing efficient hash functions and appropriate collision resolution techniques ensures that hash table operations maintain their average-case time complexity of $O(1)$, promoting rapid data storage and retrieval.

9.11 Applications of Hash Tables

Hash tables are versatile data structures that offer efficient data retrieval in constant average time complexity, making them suitable for a multitude of real-world applications. Their utility spans various domains, including databases, compilers, network services, and more. This section delves into some prominent applications of hash tables, illustrating their critical role in contemporary computing.

Symbol Tables in Compilers

Compilers use symbol tables extensively to manage information about identifiers (such as variable names, function names, etc.) during the compilation process. These identifiers must be retrieved and updated efficiently as the source code is parsed and compiled, and hash tables provide the ideal mechanism for these operations. The symbol table holds information such as the scope of identifiers, data type, and memory location.

Consider the scenario where a compiler must track variable declarations and usages:

```
import java.util.Hashtable;

public class SymbolTable {
    private Hashtable<String, Symbol> table;

    public SymbolTable() {
        table = new Hashtable<>();
    }

    public void addSymbol(String identifier, Symbol symbol) {
        table.put(identifier, symbol);
    }

    public Symbol getSymbol(String identifier) {
        return table.get(identifier);
    }
}
```

Database Indexing

Hash tables are often employed in database indexing to improve the speed of data retrieval operations. An index can be thought of as a table that maps values of a specific column (or set of columns) to the corresponding rows in the database. When a hash table is used as an index, it can provide rapid access to the data rows corresponding to a given index key.

```
import java.util.Hashtable;

public class DatabaseIndex {
    private Hashtable<String, Row> index;

    public DatabaseIndex() {
        index = new Hashtable<>();
    }

    public void addToIndex(String key, Row row) {
        index.put(key, row);
    }

    public Row getFromIndex(String key) {
        return index.get(key);
    }
}
```

Caching

Caching is a technique to store interim results of computations or frequently accessed data to reduce the time taken to retrieve this data in future operations. Hash tables serve as efficient structures for implementing caches because of their constant average time complexity for insertion and search operations. Common implementations include LRU (Least Recently Used) and LFU (Least Frequently Used) caches.

```
import java.util.Hashtable;

class CacheEntry {
    String key;
    Object value;
    CacheEntry next;
    CacheEntry prev;
}

class LRUCache {
    private final int capacity;
    private Hashtable<String, CacheEntry> cache;
    private CacheEntry head;
    private CacheEntry tail;

    public LRUCache(int capacity) {
        this.capacity = capacity;
        this.cache = new Hashtable<>(capacity);
    }

    public void put(String key, Object value) {
        if (cache.containsKey(key)) {
            CacheEntry entry = cache.get(key);
            remove(entry);
        } else if (cache.size() >= capacity) {
            cache.remove(tail.key);
            remove(tail);
        }
        CacheEntry newEntry = new CacheEntry();
        newEntry.key = key;
        newEntry.value = value;
        addToHead(newEntry);
        cache.put(key, newEntry);
    }

    public Object get(String key) {
        if (cache.containsKey(key)) {
            CacheEntry entry = cache.get(key);
            remove(entry);
            addToHead(entry);
            return entry.value;
        }
        return null;
    }

    private void remove(CacheEntry entry) {
        if (entry.prev != null) {
            entry.prev.next = entry.next;
        } else {
            head = entry.next;
        }
```

```
        if (entry.next != null) {
            entry.next.prev = entry.prev;
        } else {
            tail = entry.prev;
        }
    }

    private void addToHead(CacheEntry entry) {
        entry.next = head;
        entry.prev = null;
        if (head != null) {
            head.prev = entry;
        }
        head = entry;
        if (tail == null) {
            tail = entry;
        }
    }
}
```

Implementing Associative Arrays

Associative arrays, also known as maps or dictionaries, are collections of key-value pairs and are utilized in various programming languages for quick data lookup based on keys. Hash tables are the backbone of associative arrays, leveraging efficient key-value mappings.

```
import java.util.Hashtable;

public class AssociativeArray {
    private Hashtable<String, Object> hashMap;

    public AssociativeArray() {
        hashMap = new Hashtable<>();
    }

    public void put(String key, Object value) {
        hashMap.put(key, value);
    }

    public Object get(String key) {
        return hashMap.get(key);
    }

    public boolean containsKey(String key) {
        return hashMap.containsKey(key);
    }
}
```

Routing and Load Balancing

In network routing and load balancing, hash tables can be utilized to direct requests to the appropriate server or route quickly. They help maintain state information regarding active connections and distribute requests based on hashed keys representing client requests.

```
import java.util.Hashtable;
```

```
public class LoadBalancer {
    private Hashtable<String, Server> routingTable;

    public LoadBalancer() {
        routingTable = new Hashtable<>();
    }

    public void addServer(String clientKey, Server server) {
        routingTable.put(clientKey, server);
    }

    public Server getServer(String clientKey) {
        return routingTable.get(clientKey);
    }
}
```

Each application exemplifies the versatility and efficiency of hash tables in managing data through rapid insertion, deletion, and access operations. Their adaptability to differing requirements underlines their integral role in modern computing.

9.12 Advantages and Disadvantages of Hashing

Hashing, as a technique, presents numerous advantages and some disadvantages that must be carefully considered when choosing it as a data retrieval method. This section explores these facets to provide a balanced understanding of hashing's implications in real-world applications.

One of the primary advantages of hashing is its efficiency in search operations. Hash tables provide constant time complexity, $O(1)$, for average-case insertions, deletions, and lookups, assuming a good hash function and low load factor. This is significantly more efficient compared to other data structures, such as binary search trees, which have a time complexity of $O(\log n)$. The following code snippet demonstrates the average case $O(1)$ complexity of performing insertions in a hash table:

```
public void insert(String key, Integer value) {
    int hashValue = hashFunction(key);
    hashTable[hashValue] = value;
}
```

The main drawback of hashing arises from collisions. Although good hash functions minimize collision occurrences, they cannot be entirely eliminated. Collision handling strategies, such as separate chaining and open addressing, mitigate this problem, but they can introduce additional complexity and performance overhead. Consider the following example of a separate chaining collision resolution implemented in Java:

```
public class HashTable {
    private LinkedList<Entry>[] buckets;

    public void insert(String key, Integer value) {
        int bucketIndex = hashFunction(key);
        LinkedList<Entry> bucket = buckets[bucketIndex];
        for (Entry entry : bucket) {
            if (entry.key.equals(key)) {
                entry.value = value;
                return;
            }
        }
        bucket.add(new Entry(key, value));
    }
}
```

In this scenario, although the insertion remains relatively efficient, the presence of linked lists to handle collisions can degrade performance if the length of the chains increases. This issue is particularly acute in high load factor situations where such chains become long, making operations proportionally slower and potentially degrading to a linear time complexity, $O(n)$, in the worst case.

Hash tables are also simple to implement and use, requiring relatively straightforward coding and minimal lines of code to achieve significant performance benefits, such as illustrated in the above insert method. This simplicity can make hash tables an attractive option for numerous applications, such as symbol tables in compilers, caching mechanisms, and databases.

However, hash tables suffer from an additional disadvantage in the context of memory usage. Generally, hash tables require pre-allocation of an array larger than the number of elements they are intended to store to maintain efficiency and avoid high load factors. This over-allocation can lead to wasted memory. Consider the following schematic representation of the underlying array in a hash table:

```
[--][key1:val1][--][--][key2:val2][--][--][key3:val3]
```

The gaps between keys illustrate the 'wasted' slots necessary to maintain low collision rates. Furthermore, dynamic resizing and rehashing — necessary for maintaining efficiency — can be time-intensive and resource-heavy operations. The resizing typically involves re-allocating the array with a larger size and reinserting all keys, as demonstrated in the following method:

```
private void resize() {
    LinkedList<Entry>[] newBuckets = new LinkedList[buckets.length * 2];
    for (LinkedList<Entry> bucket : buckets) {
        for (Entry entry : bucket) {
            int newBucketIndex = hashFunction(entry.key) % newBuckets.length;
            newBuckets[newBucketIndex].add(entry);
        }
    }
    buckets = newBuckets;
}
```

An important consideration is the complexity of implementing optimal hash functions. An effective hash function needs to be consistent, distribute keys uniformly, and minimize the likelihood of collisions. Designing such a function can be non-trivial, requiring a good balance between simplicity and randomness while avoiding clustering, a phenomenon where many keys hash to the same slot.

Additionally, hash tables are inefficient for operations requiring ordered data. Unlike balanced binary search trees or linked lists, hash tables do not maintain any meaningful order of elements. This inherent lack of order makes operations such as finding the smallest or largest key, or iterating over elements in a sorted manner, less efficient or impractical without additional data structures, as shown below:

```
public List<KeyValue> getSortedKeyValuePairs() {
    List<KeyValue> list = new ArrayList<>();
    for (LinkedList<Entry> bucket : buckets) {
        for (Entry entry : bucket) {
            list.add(entry);
        }
    }
    list.sort(Comparator.comparing(Entry::getKey));
    return list;
}
```

Hash tables also have security considerations. Poorly designed hash functions can be vulnerable to collision attacks, where an adversary systematically creates keys that hash to the same bucket, leading to performance degradation. This type of attack can drastically reduce the hash table's efficiency, as illustrated by the Denial of Service (DoS) vulnerabilities. Secure hash functions, such as cryptographic hashes, can mitigate these risks but usually come with higher computational costs.

Advantages of hashing include efficient average-case performance for insertions, deletions, and lookups, simplicity of implementation, and broad applicability in various domains. Disadvantages encompass the potential for collisions, memory overhead due to over-allocation, inefficiency in ordered data operations, complexity in designing optimal hash functions, and security vulnerabilities in poorly implemented hash functions. Understanding these factors is critical for effectively leveraging hashing in different scenarios.

Chapter 10

Graphs and Graph Algorithms

This chapter introduces graphs and essential graph algorithms, fundamental for solving complex computational problems. It covers graph terminology and representations, including adjacency matrices and lists. Key graph traversal algorithms such as Depth-First Search (DFS) and Breadth-First Search (BFS) are explained. The chapter further explores algorithms for finding the shortest path, such as Dijkstra's and Bellman-Ford, and algorithms for constructing minimum spanning trees, like Prim's and Kruskal's. Additional topics include topological sorting, graph coloring, and practical applications of graph algorithms.

10.1 Introduction to Graphs

Graphs are a critical representation in computer science and discrete mathematics, used to model pairwise relations between objects. Formally, a graph G consists of a set of vertices V and a set of edges E that connect pairs of vertices. This means that a graph G can be represented as $G(V, E)$, where $V = \{v_1, v_2, \ldots, v_n\}$ is a set of vertices, and $E \subseteq V \times V$ is a set of edges, each defined as a pair of vertices.

Types of Graphs

Graphs can be categorized into several types based on their characteristics:

- **Undirected Graphs:** In an undirected graph, edges have no direction. Hence, if there is an edge between v_i and v_j, it can be traversed from v_i to v_j and from v_j to v_i with equal ease.
- **Directed Graphs (Digraphs):** In a directed graph, edges have a direction associated with them, represented as ordered pairs. Thus, an edge from v_i to v_j is not the same as an edge from v_j to v_i.
- **Weighted Graphs:** A weighted graph is a graph in which each edge has an associated numerical value (weight). These weights could represent costs, distances, or other quantities, depending on the problem context.
- **Unweighted Graphs:** These are graphs with unweighted edges, where each edge simply represents a connection between vertices.

Graph Representation

To efficiently work with graphs in computational tasks, it is crucial to represent them appropriately in memory. The two primary methods for graph representation are:

Adjacency Matrix: This is a 2D array of size $V \times V$, where each cell $adj[i][j]$ is set to 1 (or the weight, in case of weighted graphs) if there is an edge between vertices v_i and v_j. Otherwise, it is set to 0.

```
int[][] adjMatrix = new int[V][V];

// Initializing the adjacency matrix
for(int i = 0; i < V; i++) {
    for(int j = 0; j < V; j++) {
        adjMatrix[i][j] = 0;
    }
}

// Adding edges
adjMatrix[0][1] = 1;
adjMatrix[1][2] = 1;
// ... Add all necessary edges
```

Advantages:

- Simple and easy to implement.
- Efficient for densely connected graphs.

Disadvantages:

- Requires $O(V^2)$ space irrespective of the number of edges.
- Inefficient for sparse graphs.

Adjacency List: This consists of an array of lists. The array size is V. Each element of the array $adj[i]$ is a list that contains all vertices connected to vertex v_i.

```
class Graph {
    private int V;
    private LinkedList<Integer> adjListArray[];

    Graph(int V) {
        this.V = V;
        adjListArray = new LinkedList[V];

        // Initialize adjacency list for each vertex
        for (int i = 0; i < V; i++) {
            adjListArray[i] = new LinkedList<>();
        }
    }

    // Function to add an edge to the graph
    void addEdge(int src, int dest) {
        adjListArray[src].add(dest);
        adjListArray[dest].add(src); // For undirected graph, add dest -> src as well.
    }
}
```

Advantages:

- Requires $O(V + E)$ space, which is efficient for sparse graphs.
- Easy to traverse the adjacency list.

Disadvantages:

- Less efficient for certain types of operations, such as checking for the presence of a specific edge, compared to adjacency matrices.

Fundamental Operations

Understanding and working with graphs requires familiarity with the basic operations used to manipulate graph structures:

- AddVertex(V): Adds a vertex to the graph.
- AddEdge(u, v): Adds an edge between vertices u and v.

- RemoveVertex(V): Removes a vertex and all edges associated with it.
- RemoveEdge(u, v): Removes the edge between vertices u and v.
- GetAdjacentVertices(V): Returns a list of vertices adjacent to vertex V.
- CheckEdge(u, v): Checks whether an edge exists between vertices u and v.

```
void addVertex(int v) {
    // Implementation
}

void addEdge(int u, int v) {
    adjListArray[u].add(v);
    adjListArray[v].add(u);
}

void removeVertex(int v) {
    // Implementation
}

void removeEdge(int u, int v) {
    adjListArray[u].remove((Integer)v);
    adjListArray[v].remove((Integer)u);
}

List<Integer> getAdjacentVertices(int v) {
    return adjListArray[v];
}

boolean checkEdge(int u, int v) {
    return adjListArray[u].contains(v);
}
```

Further exploration of graphs includes various algorithms and techniques for traversing, searching, and analyzing these structures. This requires a deep understanding of both the aforementioned representations and operations, as well as the theoretical foundations that govern graph theory.

10.2 Graph Terminology

A graph G is a fundamental data structure that represents a set of objects where some pairs of the objects are connected by links. These objects are called nodes (or vertices), and the links are called edges (or arcs). Graph theory is a branch of combinatorial mathematics that studies the properties and applications of graphs. Understanding the terminology associated with graphs is crucial for grasping more advanced concepts and algorithms. Below, we will discuss the fundamental terminology used in graph theory.

Vertex (Node): A vertex (denoted as v or V) is a fundamental unit by which graphs are formed. Each vertex may possess a variable number of properties such as a label or value.

Edge (Arc): An edge (denoted as e or E) is a connection between two vertices. An edge e is defined as a pair (u, v), where u and v are vertices in the graph. Edges can be undirected or directed.

Directed Graph (Digraph): In a directed graph, each edge has a direction, going from one vertex to another. An edge in a directed graph is represented as an ordered pair (u, v), indicating that the edge is directed from vertex u to vertex v.

Undirected Graph: In an undirected graph, edges do not have a direction. An edge is an unordered pair $\{u, v\}$, implying a bi-directional relationship between the vertices u and v.

Weighted Graph: A graph in which a numerical value (weight) is associated with each edge. The weight might represent cost, distance, or any other quantifiable factor. A weighted edge between vertices u and v is denoted as (u, v, w) where w is the weight.

Path: A path in a graph is a sequence of edges that connects a sequence of vertices. A path is often represented as $v_1, v_2, ..., v_k$ where each pair (v_i, v_{i+1}) is an edge in the graph.

Cycle: A cycle is a path that starts and ends at the same vertex and includes at least one edge. In a cycle, all vertices are distinct except for the initial and terminal vertices.

Connected Graph: An undirected graph is connected if there is a path between any pair of vertices. In other words, every vertex is reachable from any other vertex.

Strongly Connected Graph: A directed graph is strongly connected if there is a directed path from any vertex to every other vertex.

Degree: The degree of a vertex is the number of edges incident to it. In directed graphs, we distinguish between in-degree (number of incoming edges) and out-degree (number of outgoing edges).

Subgraph: A subgraph is a subset of a graph's vertices and edges. For a graph G, G' is a subgraph if all edges in G' are also in G and all vertices in G' are connected by these edges.

Isomorphic Graphs: Two graphs G and H are isomorphic if there is a one-to-one correspondence between their vertex sets and their edge sets, preserving the incidence relationships.

Complete Graph (Clique): A complete graph is one in which there is a unique edge between every pair of distinct vertices. A complete graph with n vertices is denoted K_n.

Acyclic Graph: A graph that contains no cycles. If a graph is both acyclic and directed, it is called a directed acyclic graph (DAG).

Bipartite Graph: A bipartite graph is a graph whose vertices can be divided into two disjoint and independent sets U and V such that every edge connects a vertex in U to one in V.

Planar Graph: A graph is planar if it can be drawn on a plane without any edges crossing each other.

Multigraph: A multigraph is a graph which is permitted to have multiple edges (also called parallel edges), i.e., edges that have the same end nodes.

This terminology lays the groundwork for understanding more advanced graph algorithms and their applications. It is essential to grasp these definitions to effectively describe, analyze, and implement graph-related solutions in computer science.

10.3 Graph Representations: Adjacency Matrix and Adjacency List

A graph G is defined as a set of vertices V and a set of edges E connecting these vertices. The representation of graphs is crucial for implementing graph algorithms efficiently. Two common representations are the adjacency matrix and the adjacency list.

Adjacency Matrix

An adjacency matrix is a two-dimensional array Adj of size $|V| \times |V|$, where $|V|$ is the number of vertices in the graph. In this matrix, an element $\mathrm{Adj}[i][j]$ is non-zero if there is an edge between vertex i and vertex j, otherwise it is zero.

```
public class Graph {
    private int[][] adjacencyMatrix;
    private int numberOfVertices;

    public Graph(int numberOfVertices) {
```

```
        this.numberOfVertices = numberOfVertices;
        adjacencyMatrix = new int[numberOfVertices][numberOfVertices];
    }

    public void addEdge(int i, int j) {
        adjacencyMatrix[i][j] = 1;
    }

    public void removeEdge(int i, int j) {
        adjacencyMatrix[i][j] = 0;
    }

    public boolean isEdge(int i, int j) {
        return adjacencyMatrix[i][j] != 0;
    }

    public void printGraph() {
        for (int i = 0; i < numberOfVertices; i++) {
            for (int j = 0; j < numberOfVertices; j++) {
                System.out.print(adjacencyMatrix[i][j] + " ");
            }
            System.out.println();
        }
    }
}
```

The adjacency matrix representation is straightforward and allows $O(1)$ time complexity to check if there is an edge between two vertices. However, this representation can be memory-intensive as it requires $O(|V|^2)$ space, which is inefficient for sparse graphs.

Consider a graph G with the following edges: (0,1), (0,2), (1,2), and (2,0).

```
Graph g = new Graph(3);
g.addEdge(0, 1);
g.addEdge(0, 2);
g.addEdge(1, 2);
g.addEdge(2, 0);
g.printGraph();
```

The above code will produce the following adjacency matrix for the graph:

```
0 1 1
0 0 1
1 0 0
```

Adjacency List

An adjacency list is a collection of lists or arrays, one for each vertex in the graph. Each list $\text{Adj}[v]$ contains all the vertices adjacent to vertex v. This representation is more space-efficient for sparse graphs, requiring $O(|V| + |E|)$ space.

```
import java.util.LinkedList;

public class Graph {
```

```
    private LinkedList<Integer>[] adjacencyList;
    private int numberOfVertices;

    public Graph(int numberOfVertices) {
        this.numberOfVertices = numberOfVertices;
        adjacencyList = new LinkedList[numberOfVertices];
        for (int i = 0; i < numberOfVertices; i++) {
            adjacencyList[i] = new LinkedList<>();
        }
    }

    public void addEdge(int i, int j) {
        adjacencyList[i].add(j);
    }

    public void removeEdge(int i, int j) {
        adjacencyList[i].remove((Integer) j);
    }

    public boolean isEdge(int i, int j) {
        return adjacencyList[i].contains(j);
    }

    public void printGraph() {
        for (int i = 0; i < numberOfVertices; i++) {
            System.out.print(i + " -> ");
            for (Integer node : adjacencyList[i]) {
                System.out.print(node + " ");
            }
            System.out.println();
        }
    }
}
```

For the same graph G with edges: (0,1), (0,2), (1,2), and (2,0), using the adjacency list representation allows for efficient iteration of adjacent nodes.

```
Graph g = new Graph(3);
g.addEdge(0, 1);
g.addEdge(0, 2);
g.addEdge(1, 2);
g.addEdge(2, 0);
g.printGraph();
```

The code above will produce the following adjacency list for the graph:

```
0 -> 1 2
1 -> 2
2 -> 0
```

The adjacency list offers efficient space utilization for graphs where most vertices have a relatively small number of edges. The time complexity to check if there is an edge between two vertices is $O(K)$, where K is the number of adjacent vertices.

When choosing between these two representations, consider the specific requirements of the graph and the operations to be performed. The adjacency matrix allows for quick edge queries but is less space-efficient, especially for sparse graphs. The adjacency list is more memory-efficient for sparse graphs, though edge queries are slower. Proper representation ensures optimal performance in graph algorithms applied to the given dataset.

10.4 Graph Traversal Algorithms: Depth-First Search (DFS)

Depth-First Search (DFS) is a fundamental algorithm for traversing or searching tree or graph data structures. The DFS algorithm starts at the root node (for trees) or an arbitrary node (for graphs) and explores as far as possible along each branch before backtracking. This process utilizes a stack data structure, either implicitly through recursion or explicitly with a stack.

Algorithm Description: The pseudocode for DFS is as follows:

```
Input: Graph G = (V, E), starting vertex v
Output: All vertices reachable from v in G
Function DFSRecursive(vertex v, set visited):
    mark v as visited;
    for each neighbor u of v do
        if u is not in visited then
            DFSRecursive(u, visited);
        end
    end
initialize visited as an empty set;
DFSRecursive(v, visited)
```

Steps in the DFS algorithm:

- DFSRecursive is called with the starting vertex v and an initially empty set visited.
- The starting vertex v is marked as visited.
- From the current vertex v, iterate through each of its neighbors.
- If a neighbor u has not been visited, recursively call DFSRecursive with u and the updated visited set.

- This process repeats until all vertices reachable from the starting vertex v have been visited.

Graph Representation: DFS can be implemented using either an adjacency list or an adjacency matrix. We will demonstrate DFS using an adjacency list for its efficiency in terms of space complexity when dealing with sparse graphs.

```
import java.util.*;

public class Graph {
    private Map<Integer, List<Integer>> adjacencyList;

    public Graph() {
        adjacencyList = new HashMap<>();
    }

    public void addEdge(int v, int w) {
        adjacencyList.computeIfAbsent(v, k -> new LinkedList<>()).add(w);
    }

    public void DFS(int start) {
        Set<Integer> visited = new HashSet<>();
        DFSRecursive(start, visited);
    }

    private void DFSRecursive(int v, Set<Integer> visited) {
        visited.add(v);
        System.out.print(v + " ");

        for (int neighbor : adjacencyList.getOrDefault(v, new LinkedList<>())) {
            if (!visited.contains(neighbor)) {
                DFSRecursive(neighbor, visited);
            }
        }
    }

    public static void main(String[] args) {
        Graph g = new Graph();
        g.addEdge(0, 1);
        g.addEdge(0, 2);
        g.addEdge(1, 2);
        g.addEdge(2, 0);
        g.addEdge(2, 3);
        g.addEdge(3, 3);

        System.out.println("Depth First Traversal starting from vertex 2:");
        g.DFS(2);
    }
}
```

When the above program is executed, the DFS starting from vertex 2 will be as follows:

```
Depth First Traversal starting from vertex 2:
2 0 1 3
```

Complexity Analysis:

- **Time Complexity:** The time complexity is $O(V + E)$ for an adjacency list representation, where V is the number of vertices and E is the number of edges. This is because every vertex and edge is explored once.
- **Space Complexity:** The space complexity is $O(V)$ due to the space required to store the visited set and the recursive function call stack.

DFS is particularly useful in scenarios where the entire graph needs to be traversed, such as in topological sorting, strongly connected components detection, and solving puzzles like mazes. The choice of using recursion or an explicit stack depends on the programming language and the specific constraints of the problem at hand.

Edge Cases and Considerations: When implementing DFS, attention should be given to potential stack overflow issues in languages that have a limit on the depth of recursive calls, such as Java or Python. In these cases, using an explicit stack to simulate the recursion can be a more robust solution. Additionally, handling graphs with cycles requires careful marking of visited nodes to avoid infinite loops.

Iterative Approach: For completeness, let us consider an iterative approach using an explicit stack. This method can be particularly advantageous in languages where recursion depth is a concern.

```
public void DFSIterative(int start) {
    Set<Integer> visited = new HashSet<>();
    Stack<Integer> stack = new Stack<>();
    stack.push(start);

    while (!stack.isEmpty()) {
        int v = stack.pop();

        if (!visited.contains(v)) {
            visited.add(v);
            System.out.print(v + " ");
        }

        for (int neighbor : adjacencyList.getOrDefault(v, new LinkedList<>())) {
            if (!visited.contains(neighbor)) {
                stack.push(neighbor);
            }
        }
    }
}
```

This iterative implementation uses a stack to manage the traversal, providing an alternative to recursion and offering better control over the stack depth.

Overall, DFS is a versatile and fundamental graph traversal technique that underpins many advanced graph algorithms. Understanding its mechanics, implementation strategies, and limitations is crucial for leveraging its capabilities in computational problems.

10.5 Graph Traversal Algorithms: Breadth-First Search (BFS)

Breadth-First Search (BFS) is an algorithm used for traversing or searching tree or graph data structures. It starts at a given node (often referred to as the "source" node) and explores all its neighbors at the present depth prior to moving on to nodes at the next depth level. BFS is a cornerstone in graph theory applications and is fundamental for solving problems such as finding the shortest path in an unweighted graph.

Algorithm Description:

1. Initialize a queue Q and enqueue the source node. 2. Mark the source node as visited. 3. While Q is not empty: - Dequeue the front node u from Q. - For each neighbor v of u: - If v has not been visited: - Enqueue v to Q. - Mark v as visited.

The BFS algorithm can be described more formally in pseudocode using the algorithm2e package:

Algorithm 45: Breadth-First Search (BFS)

```
Data: Graph G(V, E), Source node s
Result: Visited nodes and the order of traversal
Initialize all nodes as unvisited;
Create a queue Q;
Enqueue s to Q;
Mark s as visited;
while Q is not empty do
    u ← Dequeue Q;
    for each neighbor v of u do
        if v is not visited then
            Enqueue v to Q;
            Mark v as visited;
```

Implementation:

To implement BFS in Java, we use a queue data structure to facilitate level-order traversal. Key concepts include marking nodes as visited and exploring neighbor nodes methodically. Below is a practical Java implementation of BFS:

```
import java.util.*;

class Graph {
    private int V; // Number of vertices
    private LinkedList<Integer> adj[]; // Adjacency List representation

    // Constructor
    Graph(int v) {
        V = v;
        adj = new LinkedList[v];
        for (int i = 0; i < v; ++i)
            adj[i] = new LinkedList();
    }

    // Function to add an edge into the graph
    void addEdge(int v, int w) {
        adj[v].add(w);
    }

    // BFS traversal from the given source node
    void BFS(int s) {
        boolean visited[] = new boolean[V];
        LinkedList<Integer> queue = new LinkedList<Integer>();

        visited[s] = true;
        queue.add(s);

        while (queue.size() != 0) {
            s = queue.poll();
            System.out.print(s + " ");

            Iterator<Integer> i = adj[s].listIterator();
            while (i.hasNext()) {
                int n = i.next();
                if (!visited[n]) {
                    visited[n] = true;
                    queue.add(n);
                }
            }
        }
    }
}
```

Example Execution:

Consider the following graph:

```
0 - 1
|   |
2 - 3
```

Adding edges and performing BFS starting from node 2:

```
// Driver method to demonstrate BFS
public static void main(String args[]) {
    Graph g = new Graph(4);

    g.addEdge(0, 1);
    g.addEdge(0, 2);
    g.addEdge(1, 2);
    g.addEdge(2, 0);
    g.addEdge(2, 3);
    g.addEdge(3, 3);

    System.out.println("Breadth First Traversal starting from node 2:");
    g.BFS(2);
}
```

```
Breadth First Traversal starting from node 2:
2 0 3 1
```

Analysis and Complexity:

BFS has a time complexity of $O(V + E)$, where V is the number of vertices and E is the number of edges in the graph. This is because each vertex and each edge is processed exactly once. The space complexity of BFS is $O(V)$ due to the additional queue used for traversal and the visited list.

BFS is particularly useful for finding the shortest path in unweighted graphs, detecting connected components, and in algorithms that require a full traversal of the graph's nodes at each depth level. It is an indispensable tool in graph theory and network analysis, finding applications in numerous domains, such as social network analysis, web crawling, and artificial intelligence. The efficacy and simplicity of BFS make it a fundamental algorithm for computer science practitioners and researchers alike.

10.6 Shortest Path Algorithms: Dijkstra's Algorithm

Dijkstra's Algorithm, named after the Dutch computer scientist Edsger W. Dijkstra, is a classical algorithm for finding the shortest paths between nodes in a graph. It operates on graphs with non-negative edge weights and can be used for both directed and undirected graphs.

The fundamental principle behind Dijkstra's Algorithm is to repeatedly select the vertex with the smallest known distance from the starting point and to perform a relaxation process on all its neighboring vertices. The relaxation process updates the cost of reaching neighboring vertices by comparing the newly computed path with the previously known shortest path and choosing the smaller one.

The formal definition of Dijkstra's Algorithm is detailed below and involves several steps, including initialization, updating distances through relaxation, and extraction of the vertex with the minimum known distance.

```
import java.util.*;

class Dijkstra {

    static class Edge {
        int target;
        int weight;

        Edge(int target, int weight) {
            this.target = target;
            this.weight = weight;
        }
    }

    static class Node implements Comparable<Node> {
        int vertex;
        int distance;

        Node(int vertex, int distance) {
            this.vertex = vertex;
            this.distance = distance;
        }

        public int compareTo(Node other) {
            return Integer.compare(this.distance, other.distance);
        }
    }

    public static int[] dijkstraAlgorithm(List<List<Edge>> adjList, int start) {
        int n = adjList.size();
        int[] distances = new int[n];
        Arrays.fill(distances, Integer.MAX_VALUE);
        distances[start] = 0;

        PriorityQueue<Node> priorityQueue = new PriorityQueue<>();
        priorityQueue.offer(new Node(start, 0));

        while (!priorityQueue.isEmpty()) {
            Node currentNode = priorityQueue.poll();
            int currentVertex = currentNode.vertex;

            for (Edge edge : adjList.get(currentVertex)) {
                int neighbor = edge.target;
                int newDist = distances[currentVertex] + edge.weight;

                if (newDist < distances[neighbor]) {
                    distances[neighbor] = newDist;
                    priorityQueue.offer(new Node(neighbor, newDist));
                }
            }
        }
        return distances;
```

```
    }
}
```

Dijkstra's Algorithm relies on several key components, which are elaborated below:

- **Graph Representation:** The graph is represented using an adjacency list where each vertex has a list of edges. Each edge is defined by its target vertex and the weight of the edge.

- **Distance Array:** An array distances is maintained to store the shortest distance from the starting vertex to each vertex in the graph. Initially, all distances are set to infinity (Integer.MAX_VALUE), except for the starting vertex, which is set to 0.

- **Priority Queue:** To efficiently retrieve the vertex with the smallest known distance, a priority queue is utilized. The priority queue stores nodes comprising the vertex and its current shortest distance.

- **Relaxation Process:** The relaxation process updates the distance to a neighboring vertex if a shorter path is found via the current vertex. If the update occurs, the neighboring vertex is added to the priority queue with its new distance.

The algorithm follows these steps in detail:

1. **Initialization:**

- Initialize the distances array with Integer.MAX_VALUE.

- Set the distance of the start vertex to 0.

- Insert the start vertex into the priority queue with a distance of 0.

2. **While Loop:** The core of the algorithm is a while loop that continues until the priority queue is empty:

- Extract the vertex currentVertex with the minimum distance from the priority queue.

- For each neighboring vertex, calculate the potential new distance by adding the edge weight to the distance of the currentVertex.

- If this computed distance is less than the currently known distance to the neighboring vertex, update the distance and add the neighboring vertex to the priority queue.

3. **Result Extraction:** Once the priority queue is empty, the distances array contains the shortest path distances from the start vertex to all other vertices.

```
Example execution:

Graph:
0 -- 1 (weight: 4)
0 -- 2 (weight: 1)
2 -- 1 (weight: 2)
1 -- 3 (weight: 1)
2 -- 3 (weight: 5)

Adjacency List:
[[Edge(1, 4), Edge(2, 1)],
 [Edge(3, 1)],
 [Edge(1, 2), Edge(3, 5)],
 []]

Execution with start vertex 0:

Steps:
1. Initialize distances = [0, ∞, ∞, ∞]
2. Insert vertex 0 in priority queue with distance 0.
3. Pop vertex 0, update neighbors:
    distances = [0, 4, 1, ∞]
    insert vertices 1 and 2 in priority queue.
4. Pop vertex 2, update neighbors:
    distances = [0, 3, 1, ∞]
    insert vertex 1 again with distance 3.
5. Pop vertex 1 with distance 3, update neighbors:
    distances = [0, 3, 1, 4]
    insert vertex 3 with distance 4.
6. Pop vertex 1 with distance 4, no updates.
7. Pop vertex 3, no updates.

Resulting shortest paths: [0, 3, 1, 4]
```

The correctness of Dijkstra's Algorithm hinges on the invariant that when a vertex is extracted from the priority queue, its shortest distance is finalized. This is ensured due to the non-decreasing order in which vertices are processed.

Finally, it is important to note the time complexity of Dijkstra's Algorithm. When implemented with a priority queue (binary heap), the overall time complexity is $O((V + E) \log V)$, where V and E are the number of vertices and edges, respectively. With a Fibonacci heap, this complexity can be reduced further, but the binary heap implementation provides a practical balance of efficiency and simplicity suitable for most applications.

10.7 Shortest Path Algorithms: Bellman-Ford Algorithm

The Bellman-Ford algorithm is a robust method for finding the shortest paths from a single source vertex to all other vertices in a weighted graph. It is capable of handling graphs with negative weight edges, distinguishing itself from Dijkstra's algorithm. This characteristic is essential for many real-world problems where edges can represent costs, losses, or other metrics that could be negative.

Algorithm Definition: The Bellman-Ford algorithm iteratively relaxes the edges of the graph, improving the estimates of the shortest path between the source vertex and other vertices. The process is repeated for $|V| - 1$ times, where $|V|$ is the number of vertices. If the $|V|$-th iteration detects any further relaxation, it identifies the presence of a negative weight cycle.

Algorithm 46: Bellman-Ford Algorithm

Data: Graph $G = (V, E)$ with weight function $w : E \to \mathbb{R}$, source vertex s

Result: Shortest path distances from s to all vertices $v \in V$

```
for each vertex v ∈ V do
    dist[v] := ∞;
    parent[v] := NIL;
dist[s] := 0;
for i := 1 to |V| − 1 do
    for each edge (u, v) ∈ E do
        if dist[u] + w(u, v) < dist[v] then
            dist[v] := dist[u] + w(u, v);
            parent[v] := u;
for each edge (u, v) ∈ E do
    if dist[u] + w(u, v) < dist[v] then
        report a negative-weight cycle;
```

Initialization: The algorithm starts by initializing the distance to the source vertex s as 0 and all other distances $\mathrm{dist}[v]$ to infinity (∞). The parent of each vertex $\mathrm{parent}[v]$ is initially set to NIL.

```
for each vertex v in V:
    dist[v] := ∞
    parent[v] := NIL
```

```
dist[s] := 0
```

Relaxation: The core of the Bellman-Ford algorithm is the edge relaxation process. For each edge (u, v), if the distance to vertex v through u is shorter than the known distance to v, the distance is updated:

```
for i := 1 to |V| - 1:
    for each edge (u, v) in E:
        if dist[u] + w(u, v) < dist[v]:
            dist[v] := dist[u] + w(u, v)
            parent[v] := u
```

This edge relaxation is performed for $|V|-1$ iterations to ensure that the shortest paths are correctly computed, accounting for the worst-case scenario in which a shortest path can have $|V|-1$ edges.

Checking for Negative-Weight Cycles: After completing the $|V|-1$ iterations, a final pass through the edges is performed to detect any negative weight cycles. If any shorter path is found during this iteration, it indicates the presence of a negative weight cycle.

```
for each edge (u, v) in E:
    if dist[u] + w(u, v) < dist[v]:
        report a negative-weight cycle
```

Time Complexity: The time complexity of the Bellman-Ford algorithm is $O(|V||E|)$. This is because each of the $|V|-1$ passes examines all $|E|$ edges, and in the worst case, the algorithm performs this examination $|V|-1$ times plus one additional time for cycle detection.

Space Complexity: The space complexity is $O(|V|)$ since it requires maintaining the distance and parent arrays for each vertex.

Practical Applications: The Bellman-Ford algorithm is particularly useful in applications dealing with negative edge weights, such as in financial models, routing protocols like the Distance Vector Routing, and certain network flow problems.

The Bellman-Ford algorithm provides a systematic approach to finding the shortest paths in graphs with possibly negative edge weights. Its ability to detect negative weight cycles further enhances its applicability in a wide range of computational problems.

10.8 Minimum Spanning Tree Algorithms: Prim's Algorithm

Prim's Algorithm is an essential algorithm used to find the Minimum Spanning Tree (MST) of a weighted undirected graph. An MST of a graph is a subgraph that connects all the vertices together, without any cycles, and with the minimum possible total edge weight. Prim's algorithm operates by building this tree one vertex at a time, from an arbitrary starting vertex, by always adding the cheapest possible connection from the tree to another vertex.

Prim's algorithm starts with a single node and explores all the edges connecting this node to the other nodes, greedily selecting the edge with the smallest weight. This process extends to include new vertices and continues until all vertices are included in the MST.

To effectively implement Prim's algorithm, we often use a priority queue (or a min-heap) to keep track of the edges with the smallest weight that extend the growing tree.

The pseudocode for Prim's algorithm is as follows:

Data: Graph $G = (V, E)$ with V vertices and E edges, and a starting vertex $s \in V$

Result: Set of edges T that forms the Minimum Spanning Tree

Initialize $T \leftarrow \emptyset$;
Initialize Q to be a priority queue containing all vertices in V with key value ∞ ;
Set the key value of vertex s to 0 in Q ;
while *Q is not empty* **do**
    Extract vertex u from Q with the smallest key value ;
    foreach *vertex v adjacent to u* **do**
        if $v \in Q$ and *weight(u, v) < key value of v* **then**
            set key value of v to weight(u, v) in Q ;
            Update the parent of v to u ;
foreach *vertex v in V* except for s **do**
    Add edge $(parent(v), v)$ to T
return T

Here is a Java implementation of Prim's Algorithm using an adjacency list representation and a priority queue.

```
import java.util.*;

class PrimMST {
    static class Edge {
        int target, weight;
        Edge(int target, int weight) {
            this.target = target;
            this.weight = weight;
        }
    }

    public static void primMST(ArrayList<ArrayList<Edge>> graph) {
        int V = graph.size();
        boolean[] inMST = new boolean[V];
        int[] key = new int[V];
        int[] parent = new int[V];

        PriorityQueue<Edge> pq = new PriorityQueue<>(V, Comparator.
            comparingInt(e -> e.weight));
        Arrays.fill(key, Integer.MAX_VALUE);
        Arrays.fill(parent, -1);
        key[0] = 0;
        pq.add(new Edge(0, key[0]));

        while (!pq.isEmpty()) {
            int u = pq.poll().target;

            if (inMST[u]) continue;

            inMST[u] = true;
            for (Edge edge : graph.get(u)) {
                int v = edge.target;
                int weight = edge.weight;

                if (!inMST[v] && weight < key[v]) {
                    key[v] = weight;
                    parent[v] = u;
                    pq.add(new Edge(v, key[v]));
                }
            }
        }

        // Print the constructed MST
        for (int i = 1; i < V; i++) {
            System.out.println("(" + parent[i] + " - " + i + ")");
        }
    }

    public static void main(String[] args) {
        // Create a graph
        int V = 5;
        ArrayList<ArrayList<Edge>> graph = new ArrayList<>();
        for (int i = 0; i < V; i++) {
            graph.add(new ArrayList<>());
        }

        // Add edges
        graph.get(0).add(new Edge(1, 2));
        graph.get(0).add(new Edge(3, 6));
        graph.get(1).add(new Edge(0, 2));
        graph.get(1).add(new Edge(2, 3));
```

```
        graph.get(1).add(new Edge(3, 8));
        graph.get(1).add(new Edge(4, 5));
        graph.get(2).add(new Edge(1, 3));
        graph.get(2).add(new Edge(4, 7));
        graph.get(3).add(new Edge(0, 6));
        graph.get(3).add(new Edge(1, 8));
        graph.get(4).add(new Edge(1, 5));
        graph.get(4).add(new Edge(2, 7));

        PrimMST.primMST(graph);
    }
}
```

The above program starts by initializing the key values of all vertices to infinity and the in-MST set to false. It initializes the priority queue and starts the loop to extract the smallest key vertex. For each vertex, it checks the weight to the adjacent vertices, updates the key values, and adds the edge to T with the smallest weight. The resulting MST is then printed.

The output of the example execution would be:

```
(0 - 1)
(1 - 2)
(1 - 4)
(0 - 3)
```

This output represents the edges in the MST. The numbers in the parentheses show the connection between nodes in the resulting MST, representing the lowest total weight connection that spans all vertices.

Prim's Algorithm is efficient and well-suited for dense graphs due to its use of the priority queue to manage the edges being considered. With a time complexity of $O(E \log V)$ for graphs represented by adjacency lists (where E is the number of edges and V is the number of vertices), Prim's Algorithm is highly effective for practical applications like designing network cables or circuits where the goal is to minimize the total connection cost without any cycles.

10.9 Minimum Spanning Tree Algorithms: Kruskal's Algorithm

Kruskal's algorithm is a classic algorithm used to find the Minimum Spanning Tree (MST) of a connected, undirected graph. It belongs to a class of algorithms known as greedy algorithms, which make a series of choices, each of which looks best at the moment, with the hope of finding a global optimum. Kruskal's algorithm specifically focuses on edge selection to construct the MST.

Kruskal's algorithm begins by sorting all the edges in the graph by their weights in non-decreasing order. It then selects the shortest edge and adds it to the growing spanning tree, ensuring that no cycles are formed. This process continues until exactly $V - 1$ edges have been included, where V is the number of vertices in the graph.

To ensure that adding an edge does not create a cycle, the algorithm employs a data structure known as Union-Find (or Disjoint Set). This structure supports efficient union and find operations to keep track of the connected components of the growing MST.

```
import java.util.*;

// Edge class to represent an edge in the graph
class Edge implements Comparable<Edge> {
    int src, dest, weight;

    // Comparator for sorting edges based on weight
    public int compareTo(Edge compareEdge) {
        return this.weight - compareEdge.weight;
    }
};

// Subset class for Union-Find
class Subset {
    int parent, rank;
};

public class KruskalAlgorithm {
    int V, E; // Number of vertices and edges
    Edge edge[]; // Collection of all edges

    KruskalAlgorithm(int v, int e) {
        V = v;
        E = e;
        edge = new Edge[E];
        for (int i = 0; i < e; ++i)
            edge[i] = new Edge();
    }

    // A utility function to find set of an element i using path compression
    int find(Subset subsets[], int i) {
        if (subsets[i].parent != i)
            subsets[i].parent = find(subsets, subsets[i].parent);
        return subsets[i].parent;
    }

    // A function that does union of two sets of x and y using union by rank
    void union(Subset subsets[], int x, int y) {
        int xroot = find(subsets, x);
        int yroot = find(subsets, y);

        if (subsets[xroot].rank < subsets[yroot].rank) {
            subsets[xroot].parent = yroot;
        } else if (subsets[xroot].rank > subsets[yroot].rank) {
```

```
            subsets[yroot].parent = xroot;
        } else {
            subsets[yroot].parent = xroot;
            subsets[xroot].rank++;
        }
    }

    // Kruskal's algorithm to construct the MST
    void kruskalMST() {
        Edge result[] = new Edge[V];
        int e = 0; // Index variable for result[]
        int i = 0; // Index variable for sorted edges
        for (i = 0; i < V; ++i)
            result[i] = new Edge();

        // Step 1: Sort all the edges in non-decreasing order of their weight
        Arrays.sort(edge);

        // Allocate memory for creating V subsets
        Subset subsets[] = new Subset[V];
        for (i = 0; i < V; ++i)
            subsets[i] = new Subset();

        // Create V subsets with single elements
        for (int v = 0; v < V; ++v) {
            subsets[v].parent = v;
            subsets[v].rank = 0;
        }

        i = 0; // Index used to pick next edge

        // Number of edges to be taken is equal to V-1
        while (e < V - 1) {
            // Step 2: Pick the smallest edge. Check if it forms a cycle with the
                spanning tree formed so far. If not, include it in the result
            Edge nextEdge = new Edge();
            nextEdge = edge[i++];

            int x = find(subsets, nextEdge.src);
            int y = find(subsets, nextEdge.dest);

            if (x != y) {
                result[e++] = nextEdge;
                union(subsets, x, y);
            }
        }

        // Print the contents of the MST
        System.out.println("Following are the edges in the constructed MST:");
        for (i = 0; i < e; ++i)
            System.out.println(result[i].src + " -- " + result[i].dest + " == " + result[i].
                weight);
    }

    // Driver Code
    public static void main(String[] args) {
        int V = 4; // Number of vertices in the graph
        int E = 5; // Number of edges in the graph
        KruskalAlgorithm graph = new KruskalAlgorithm(V, E);

        // adding edge 0-1
        graph.edge[0].src = 0;
```

```
        graph.edge[0].dest = 1;
        graph.edge[0].weight = 10;

        // adding edge 0-2
        graph.edge[1].src = 0;
        graph.edge[1].dest = 2;
        graph.edge[1].weight = 6;

        // adding edge 0-3
        graph.edge[2].src = 0;
        graph.edge[2].dest = 3;
        graph.edge[2].weight = 5;

        // adding edge 1-3
        graph.edge[3].src = 1;
        graph.edge[3].dest = 3;
        graph.edge[3].weight = 15;

        // adding edge 2-3
        graph.edge[4].src = 2;
        graph.edge[4].dest = 3;
        graph.edge[4].weight = 4;

        graph.kruskalMST();
    }
}
```

The algorithm follows these steps:

- Initially, each vertex is in its own subset. The find function uses path compression to find the representative of the subset, effectively keeping the tree flat.

- The union function combines two subsets into a single subset by attaching the tree of the subset with the smaller rank to the tree of the subset with the larger rank.

- Kruskal's algorithm sorts the edges and iterates through them, using find to check if the current edge connects two different subsets. If it does, the edge is included in the result, and union is used to merge the subsets.

This approach ensures that the graph remains acyclic while progressively building up to the Minimum Spanning Tree. The complexity of the algorithm is primarily dominated by the sorting step, which is $O(E \log E)$, where E is the number of edges.

The following Java program demonstrates the implementation of Kruskal's algorithm. Upon execution, it outputs the edges that constitute the Minimum Spanning Tree for the given graph:

```
Following are the edges in the constructed MST:
2 -- 3 == 4
0 -- 3 == 5
0 -- 1 == 10
```

The Union-Find data structure is critical to the efficiency of the algorithm, ensuring that both the find and union operations run in nearly constant time due to path compression and union by rank. This makes Kruskal's algorithm suitable for dense graphs where the number of edges E is significantly larger than the number of vertices V.

10.10 Topological Sorting

Topological sorting of a Directed Acyclic Graph (DAG) is a linear ordering of its vertices such that for every directed edge uv, vertex u comes before v in the ordering. This concept is fundamental in scenarios where a precise sequence of operations is necessary. Some common applications include task scheduling, resolving symbol dependencies in linkers, and building course prerequisite chains in curriculum planning.

To create a topological sort of a DAG, we leverage the fact that these graphs have no cycles, ensuring that a valid linear ordering of vertices is always possible. We'll delve into a commonly used algorithm based on Depth-First Search (DFS).

Algorithm 47: Topological Sort using DFS

Input: A Directed Acyclic Graph $G = (V, E)$

Output: A list of vertices in topologically sorted order

```
Mark all the vertices as not visited;
Create an empty stack to store the topological order;
for each vertex v ∈ V do
    if v is not visited then
        topologicalSortUtil(v, visited, stack);
Print the contents of the stack;
Function topologicalSortUtil(v, visited, stack):
    Mark v as visited;
    for each vertex i adjacent to v do
        if i is not visited then
            topologicalSortUtil(i, visited, stack);
    Push v to stack;
```

In the above algorithm, we first mark all vertices as not visited. We then create an empty stack to store the topologically sorted vertices. For each vertex v in the graph, if it has not been visited, we call the recursive utility function topologicalSortUtil. This function performs a DFS from the vertex v, marking it as visited and recursively visiting all its adjacent vertices. After all adjacent vertices are visited, v is pushed onto the stack, ensuring that it appears after all its dependencies.

The contents of the stack are then printed, providing the vertices in topologically sorted order. Below, we provide the Java implementation of the aforementioned algorithm within the TopologicalSort class.

```
import java.util.*;

public class TopologicalSort {
    private int V; // No. of vertices
    private LinkedList<Integer> adjacencyList[]; // Adjacency List

    // Constructor
    TopologicalSort(int v) {
        V = v;
        adjacencyList = new LinkedList[v];
        for (int i = 0; i < v; ++i)
            adjacencyList[i] = new LinkedList();
    }

    // Function to add an edge into the graph
    void addEdge(int v, int w) {
        adjacencyList[v].add(w);
    }

    // A recursive function used by topologicalSort
    void topologicalSortUtil(int v, boolean visited[], Stack<Integer> stack) {
        // Mark the current node as visited.
        visited[v] = true;
        Integer i;

        // Recur for all the vertices adjacent to this vertex
        for (Integer neighbor : adjacencyList[v]) {
            if (!visited[neighbor])
                topologicalSortUtil(neighbor, visited, stack);
        }

        // Push current vertex to stack which stores result
        stack.push(v);
    }

    // The function to perform Topological Sort. It uses recursive topologicalSortUtil()
    void topologicalSort() {
        Stack<Integer> stack = new Stack<>();

        // Mark all the vertices as not visited
        boolean visited[] = new boolean[V];
        for (int i = 0; i < V; i++)
            visited[i] = false;

        // Call the recursive helper function to store Topological Sort starting from all
                vertices one by one
```

```
        for (int i = 0; i < V; i++) {
            if (!visited[i])
                topologicalSortUtil(i, visited, stack);
        }

        // Print contents of stack
        while (!stack.empty())
            System.out.print(stack.pop() + " ");
    }

    // Driver code
    public static void main(String args[]) {
        TopologicalSort g = new TopologicalSort(6);

        g.addEdge(5, 2);
        g.addEdge(5, 0);
        g.addEdge(4, 0);
        g.addEdge(4, 1);
        g.addEdge(2, 3);
        g.addEdge(3, 1);

        System.out.println("Topological sort of the given graph:");
        g.topologicalSort();
    }
}
```

The above Java program defines a TopologicalSort class for performing the topological sort. The addEdge method is used to add an edge to the adjacency list. The main logic resides in the topologicalSortUtil method, which performs the DFS and stores the vertices in a stack once all their neighbors are processed. The vertices are then printed from the stack, producing the desired topological order.

When the above code is executed, it yields the following output:

```
Topological sort of the given graph:
5 4 2 3 1 0
```

In this example, one can observe that each vertex appears before all vertices to which it has edges, respecting the dependencies.

Topological sorting's utility in various domains solidifies its essential standing in the realm of graph algorithms. Proper understanding and implementation enable efficient problem-solving in complex dependency-driven contexts.

10.11 Graph Coloring

Graph coloring is a method of assigning colors to the vertices of a graph such that no two adjacent vertices share the same color. This problem is significant in various applications, including scheduling, register allocation in compilers, and frequency assignment in mobile networks.

Formally, given a graph $G = (V, E)$, the objective of graph coloring is to assign a color $c(v)$ to each vertex $v \in V$ such that $c(u) \neq c(v)$ for every edge $(u, v) \in E$. The minimum number of colors needed to color a graph G is called the graph's chromatic number, denoted as $\chi(G)$.

We will now explore some algorithms for graph coloring, focusing on both exact and heuristic approaches.

Algorithm 48: Greedy Coloring Algorithm

Data: Graph $G = (V, E)$
Result: A coloring of graph G

```
Function GreedyColoring(G):
    foreach vertex v in V do
        Let L_v be the list of colors assigned to v's neighbors
        color_v ← smallest non-negative integer not in L_v
    return the color assignment for each vertex
```

The GreedyColoring algorithm, while not guaranteeing the use of the minimum number of colors, is simple and fast, often employed in real-world scenarios. It colors each vertex one by one, ensuring that no two adjacent vertices share the same color.

Consider the following example graph:

```
class Graph {
    private int numVertices;
    private LinkedList<Integer> adjList[];

    Graph(int vertices) {
        numVertices = vertices;
        adjList = new LinkedList[vertices];
        for (int i = 0; i < vertices; ++i)
            adjList[i] = new LinkedList();
    }

    void addEdge(int v, int w) {
        adjList[v].add(w);
        adjList[w].add(v);
    }

    void greedyColoring() {
        int result[] = new int[numVertices];
        Arrays.fill(result, -1);
        result[0] = 0;

        boolean available[] = new boolean[numVertices];
        Arrays.fill(available, true);

        for (int u = 1; u < numVertices; u++) {
            Iterator<Integer> it = adjList[u].iterator();
```

```
            while (it.hasNext()) {
                int i = it.next();
                if (result[i] != -1)
                    available[result[i]] = false;
            }

            int cr;
            for (cr = 0; cr < numVertices; cr++) {
                if (available[cr])
                    break;
            }

            result[u] = cr;
            Arrays.fill(available, true);
        }

        for (int u = 0; u < numVertices; u++)
            System.out.println("Vertex " + u + " ---> Color " + result[u]);
    }
}
```

Running the above greedyColoring function on a graph will produce an output where each vertex is assigned a color.

```
Vertex 0 ---> Color 0
Vertex 1 ---> Color 1
Vertex 2 ---> Color 0
Vertex 3 ---> Color 1
Vertex 4 ---> Color 2
```

The algorithm operates in $O(V + E)$ time complexity, which makes it efficient for large graphs.

To shed light on more complex cases, exact algorithms such as backtracking are useful but computationally expensive.

Algorithm 49: Backtracking Algorithm for Coloring

```
Data: Graph G = (V, E), Number of colors m
Result: A coloring of graph G
Function Coloring(G, m):
    if G is empty then
        return solution found
    Choose a vertex v
    foreach color c in 1 to m do
        if No adjacent vertex of v is colored c then
            Assign color c to vertex v
            if Coloring the rest of the graph with V − v and m
              then
                return true
            Remove color c from v
    return false
```

This Coloring function recursively attempts to color the graph with m colors. If a solution is feasible, it returns true; otherwise, it backtracks and tries a different coloring.

While backtracking guarantees finding a valid coloring if one exists, it operates in exponential time complexity $O(m^V)$, making it impractical for graphs with a large number of vertices.

Understanding the complexity and nuances of graph coloring enables the selection of appropriate algorithms tailored to specific applications, balancing between efficiency and optimality.

10.12 Applications of Graph Algorithms

Graph algorithms are integral tools for solving various real-world problems across multiple domains. These applications span from computer networking to bioinformatics, from geographical information systems to social network analysis. Understanding the practical applications of graph algorithms allows for a comprehensive grasp of their significance. Here, we will discuss several notable applications.

1. Computer and Communication Networks

Graphs naturally model computer and communication networks. Nodes represent computers or switches, and edges represent links between them. Graph algorithms play crucial roles in network design, routing, and managing these networks. Algorithms such as Dijkstra's and Bellman-Ford are employed for routing purposes, finding the shortest path from a source to a destination. Consider the following example where Dijkstra's algorithm determines the shortest paths from a source node:

```
import java.util.*;

class Graph {
    private final int vertices;
    private final List<List<Node>> adjList;

    static class Node implements Comparable<Node> {
        int node;
        int cost;

        Node(int node, int cost) {
            this.node = node;
            this.cost = cost;
        }

        @Override
        public int compareTo(Node other) {
            return Integer.compare(this.cost, other.cost);
        }
    }

    public Graph(int vertices) {
        this.vertices = vertices;
        adjList = new ArrayList<>(vertices);
        for (int i = 0; i < vertices; i++) {
            adjList.add(new ArrayList<>());
        }
    }

    public void addEdge(int src, int dest, int cost) {
        adjList.get(src).add(new Node(dest, cost));
        adjList.get(dest).add(new Node(src, cost)); // For undirected graph
    }

    public void dijkstra(int src) {
        PriorityQueue<Node> pq = new PriorityQueue<>();
        int[] dist = new int[vertices];
        Arrays.fill(dist, Integer.MAX_VALUE);
        pq.add(new Node(src, 0));
        dist[src] = 0;

        while (!pq.isEmpty()) {
            Node currentNode = pq.poll();
            for (Node neighbor : adjList.get(currentNode.node)) {
                if (dist[currentNode.node] + neighbor.cost < dist[neighbor.node]) {
                    dist[neighbor.node] = dist[currentNode.node] + neighbor.cost;
                    pq.add(new Node(neighbor.node, dist[neighbor.node]));
                }
            }
        }

        System.out.println("Shortest paths from node " + src + ":");
        for (int i = 0; i < vertices; i++) {
```

```
            System.out.println("To node " + i + ": " + dist[i]);
        }
    }
}
```

Output:
Shortest paths from node 0:
To node 0: 0
To node 1: 4
To node 2: 2
To node 3: 7
...

2. Social Network Analysis

Social networks can be represented as graphs where nodes denote individuals and edges represent relationships between them. Algorithms such as Breadth-First Search (BFS) and Depth-First Search (DFS) can analyze properties like connected components, shortest paths, and centrality measures. For instance, the BFS algorithm can be utilized to find the degree of separation between two individuals:

```
import java.util.*;

class SocialNetwork {
    private final int vertices;
    private final LinkedList<Integer>[] adjList;

    public SocialNetwork(int vertices) {
        this.vertices = vertices;
        adjList = new LinkedList[vertices];
        for (int i = 0; i < vertices; i++) {
            adjList[i] = new LinkedList<>();
        }
    }

    public void addEdge(int src, int dest) {
        adjList[src].add(dest);
        adjList[dest].add(src);
    }

    public int bfs(int start, int end) {
        boolean[] visited = new boolean[vertices];
        int[] distance = new int[vertices];
        Queue<Integer> queue = new LinkedList<>();

        visited[start] = true;
        queue.add(start);

        while (!queue.isEmpty()) {
            int node = queue.poll();
            for (int neighbor : adjList[node]) {
                if (!visited[neighbor]) {
                    visited[neighbor] = true;
                    distance[neighbor] = distance[node] + 1;
                    queue.add(neighbor);
                    if (neighbor == end) {
```

```
                    return distance[neighbor];
                }
            }
        }
    }
    return -1; // If no path exists
  }
}
```

Output:
Degree of separation from 0 to 5: 3
Degree of separation from 0 to 2: 1
...

3. Urban Planning and Transportation

In urban planning and transportation, graphs represent road networks, where nodes are intersections, and edges are roads connecting these intersections. Algorithms like Dijkstra's and Floyd-Warshall are used to find the shortest routes for navigation systems. In public transportation networks, graphs help optimize schedules and routes.

4. Biology and Bioinformatics

Graphs are extensively used in bioinformatics for modeling molecular structures, protein-protein interactions, and genetics. For instance, sequence alignment can be modeled using graphs where vertices represent sequences, and edges represent matches between sequences. Algorithms like the Hamiltonian path and cycle detect pathways in genetic networks.

5. Web Search Engines

Search engines use graph algorithms to rank web pages. The PageRank algorithm models the web as a directed graph where pages are nodes, and hyperlinks are edges. This algorithm determines the importance of web pages based on their structure by iterating through the graph's adjacency matrix:

```
import java.util.*;

class PageRank {
    private final int vertices;
    private final double[][] adjMatrix;
    private double[] rank;
    private static final double DAMPING_FACTOR = 0.85;
    private static final double EPSILON = 1e-6;

    public PageRank(int vertices) {
        this.vertices = vertices;
        adjMatrix = new double[vertices][vertices];
        rank = new double[vertices];
        Arrays.fill(rank, 1.0 / vertices);
```

```
    }

    public void addEdge(int src, int dest) {
        adjMatrix[src][dest] = 1.0;
    }

    public void calculatePageRank(int iterations) {
        for (int k = 0; k < iterations; k++) {
            double[] newRank = new double[vertices];
            for (int i = 0; i < vertices; i++) {
                newRank[i] = (1 - DAMPING_FACTOR) / vertices;
                for (int j = 0; j < vertices; j++) {
                    if (adjMatrix[j][i] == 1.0) {
                        newRank[i] += DAMPING_FACTOR * rank[j] / getOutDegree(j)
                            ;
                    }
                }
            }
            rank = newRank;
            if (hasConverged(rank, newRank)) {
                break;
            }
        }
    }

    private int getOutDegree(int node) {
        int outDegree = 0;
        for (int i = 0; i < vertices; i++) {
            if (adjMatrix[node][i] == 1.0) {
                outDegree++;
            }
        }
        return outDegree;
    }

    private boolean hasConverged(double[] oldRank, double[] newRank) {
        for (int i = 0; i < vertices; i++) {
            if (Math.abs(oldRank[i] - newRank[i]) > EPSILON) {
                return false;
            }
        }
        return true;
    }

    public void printRanks() {
        System.out.println("PageRank values:");
        for (int i = 0; i < vertices; i++) {
            System.out.println("Node " + i + ": " + rank[i]);
        }
    }
}
```

```
Output:
PageRank values:
Node 0: 0.15
Node 1: 0.65
Node 2: 0.20
...
```

6. Game Development

In game development, graphs enable pathfinding and navigation. Algorithms like A* search are commonly used for determining the shortest path in game environments. Nodes represent different positions or states within the game, and edges represent possible moves or transitions between states.

7. Geographic Information Systems (GIS)

GIS applications use graphs to represent and analyze spatial networks such as roads, rivers, and utility networks. Algorithms like Prim's and Kruskal's help in constructing minimum spanning trees to design efficient networking within a geographical area. This can optimize resources and improve connectivity.

The ability to apply graph algorithms effectively across these varied domains underscores their versatility and utility in solving complex problems. Each algorithm provides a structured way to model, process, and analyze data, leading to efficient and optimized solutions.

Made in United States
Orlando, FL
04 November 2026

90207065R00207